THE
LAST
PSYCHOANALYST

by

Stuart Schneiderman

Prologue

FREUD CALLED IT "the talking cure," but psychoanalysis has always been more talk than cure.

Freud did not coin the phrase. He borrowed it from a young hysteric named Bertha Pappenheim, aka Anna O. She was the ur-patient, the first to undergo what would later become psychoanalysis.

As it happened, he did not hear about "the talking cure" directly from Anna O. either. She told it to her physician, Freud's colleague, Josef Breuer, who reported it to him.

Eventually, the case of Anna O. became the first chapter in Breuer and Freud's *Studies on Hysteria*. There, Breuer claimed that Anna O.'s symptoms vanished in June, 1882 after she recalled a repressed memory.

In Breuer's words:

> *She was moreover free from the innumerable disturbances which she had previously exhibited.*

When he wrote about the case, Breuer qualified his conclusion. He declared that it had taken some time for Anna O. to recover completely, but that she was enjoying "complete health."

When Freud referred to the case himself, he confidently asserted that Anna O.'s talking cure was "a great therapeutic success."

These claims may not descend to the level of an outright lie, but both Breuer and Freud were peddling a rank distortion.

Freud described the real outcome in a letter to his fiancée Martha Bernays, written on August 5, 1883:

> *Bertha is once again in the sanatorium in Gross-Enzensdorf,*
> *I believe [Inzersdorf, in fact]. Breuer is constantly talking*
> *about her, says he wishes she were dead so that the poor*
> *woman could be free of her suffering. He says she will never*
> *be well again, that she is completely shattered.*

(For a full account of the case, see Mikkel Borch-Jacobsen's *Remembering Anna O.: A Century of Mystification.*)

Both men were physicians and both wanted their patients to get well. Being physicians, they believed that they were offering a medical treatment. Surely, they did not see themselves as faith healers.

And, it made a perverse sense for them to pretend that their new therapy was effective. They were not going to attract more patients by saying that their new discovery had failed.

I imagine that Breuer, and especially Freud believed fervently in the promise of a talking cure. They could not allow a few failures to deter them. Bad clinical results did not shake their conviction.

For his part, Freud might have ignored the clinical results because he was convinced that he was a genius. If reality did not prove him right, reality must have been wrong.

Freud often presented psychoanalysis as a medical practice based on scientific fact. It was a ruse. Freud knew it was a ruse.

When he was a young man, he told his friend Wilhelm Fliess that he himself was really not a scientist. In truth, Freud saw himself a culture warrior:

> *I am actually not at all a man of science, not an observer, not*
> *an experimenter, not a thinker. I am by temperament nothing*
> *but a conquistador.*

Nevertheless, Freud continued to call himself a scientist. He insisted that empirical evidence had validated his theories. Boastfully, he placed himself in the company of Copernicus and Darwin.

Unfortunately for him, saying doesn't make it so. Persuading a lot of people that you are a scientist does not make you a scientist, either.

By wrapping his theories in the mantle of science Freud gave them an authority that they would otherwise have lacked. Freud needed science more than science needed Freud.

He needed it because his audience of disaffected intellectuals, having ceased to believe in God, worshipped scientific genius.

By now, Freud's ruse has been exposed. Few serious thinkers believe that psychoanalysis is science. Fewer still see it as a therapy. As a clinical practice, it is mostly moribund.

Despite it all, Freud's name still commands respect. Many people count him as one of the great modern thinkers.

He may have been wrong about human psychology, but in today's Western world many people live Freudian lives.

It's a dubious achievement, but it is an achievement.

How did he do it? Freud used a rhetorical ploy that had been perfected by demagogues and cult leaders. He made grandiose claims and acted as though he was completely convinced of their truth.

In a 1898 letter he wrote:

> ...we shall in the end conquer every resistance by emphasizing the unshakeable nature of our conviction.

No scientist gathers adherents by advertising the depth of his conviction. Demagogues do it. Cult leaders do it. Scientists do not do it.

Freud believed that his theories could solve the great psychological conundrums. He thought they could explain why we do as we do, feel as we feel and desire as we desire. He added that his ideas could put us on the road to treating, if not curing, mental illness and human anguish.

Eventually, he admitted the truth. In *The Question of Lay Analysis* he declared that a psychoanalyst resembled a "secular pastoral worker." He added that his method could do what religion had done, but without "receiving [people] into the catholic, protestant or socialist community."

It took more than Freud's words to convince his followers that they were not practicing a medical subspecialty based on a scientific psychology.

Even today, many psychoanalysts do not understand that Freud's theories derived more from philosophy and theology than from medical or psychological science.

True scientists respect nature's laws. Humble to a fault, they abandon their hypotheses when reality does not confirm them.

Freud was different. Throughout his career he clung desperately to his theories, regardless of the evidence. He was not trying to learn about reality; he did not want to negotiate with reality; he wanted to make it fulfill his wishes.

Freud barely tried to prove his theories empirically, but many others have. Edward Erwin examined these efforts thoroughly in his book: *A Final Accounting*. He concluded:

> More than 1500 Freudian experiments have been done dur-
> ing this period [of more than sixty years], many reflecting
> great ingenuity and immense labor. Yet, the amount of
> confirmation of distinctly Freudian hypotheses is close to
> zero.

Erwin continued:

> ...the evidence supports the following verdicts. Has the
> effectiveness of Freudian therapy been established? No. How
> much of his theory has been confirmed? Virtually none of it.
> These verdicts are likely to be final.

Some psychoanalysts dream that cognitive neuroscience will be their salvation. They have not noticed that the new science of human psychology owes nothing to Freud.

In the end Freud was a gifted storyteller who created a cult by duping a lot of people into believing that his opinions were science.

The great Freudian mystery has nothing to do with how much you lust after your mother or why you get off on sucking your thumb. It concerns how a pseudo-scientist made himself into a demi-god. Or better, how a pseudo-science became a pseudo-religion.

Nobel Prize-winning physicist Richard Feynman explained the difference between science and pseudo-science. In *Surely You're Joking, Mr. Feynman,* he began with the obvious. True science proves or disproves hypotheses experimentally. Feynman wrote:

> During the Middle Ages there were all kinds of crazy ideas,
> such as that a piece of rhinoceros horn would increase
> potency. Then a method was discovered for separating the
> ideas—which was to try one to see if it worked, and if it
> didn't, to eliminate it. This method became organized, of
> course into science.

Credit for the shift belongs to Galileo.

In an essay in the *BBC News Magazine* Adam Gopnik wrote that Galileo set the course of modern science by devising experiments that could test the ideas in Aristotle's *Physics*:

> *When he [Galileo] wanted to find out if Aristotle was wrong to say that a small body would fall at a different speed from a large body, he didn't look the answer up in an old book about falling objects. Instead, he threw cannonballs of two different sizes off the Tower of Pisa, and, checking to make sure that no-one was down there, watched what happened. They hit the ground at the same time.*

At the time, Church teachers did not value experiments. They based their understanding of physics on the theories of a pagan philosopher.

After Galileo, Gopnik wrote:

> *Truth no longer depended on the prestige, or the intelligence or even the integrity of any one person.*

Or better, it didn't until Freud arrived on the scene.

Psychoanalysis calls itself science, but its "truth" has mostly depended on the prestige and brilliance of Sigmund Freud.

There is another reason why Freud was not a scientist.

Feynman argued that true scientists, unlike shamans, storytellers and psychoanalysts, report information that might invalidate their theories.

He wrote:

> *If you make a theory, for example, and advertise it, or put it out, you must put down all the facts that disagree with it, as well as all those that agree with it.*

In his 1974 Caltech commencement address Feynman elaborated the point:

> *In summary, the idea is to try to give all the information to help others judge the value of your contribution; not just the information that leads to judgment in one particular direction or another.*

By providing the most complete information a scientist allows others to judge his work freely. If he only reports the evidence that makes him appear to be right he will be trying to manipulate the minds of his fellow scientists. At root, science respects an individual's free will.

It should go without saying, but true scientists do not lie about their results.

Since scientists live in doubt, they do not try to produce a culture where everyone holds the same beliefs. Scientific fact should never be taken as dogmatic truth.

Shamans and sorcerers, however, would not be able to function if their patients doubted them.

They were Freudians before the fact.

More shaman than scientist, more aspiring god than experimenter, Freud did not believe, for example, that any piece of evidence could disprove his theory of dream interpretation. If a patient had a dream that did not appear to fulfill a wish, Freud declared that it was fulfilling an unconscious wish to prove him wrong.

When Freud's patients did not get well, he did not accept that their cases had discredited his theories. When a patient he called Dora abruptly left treatment, Freud concluded that she was too neurotic to accept the truth.

Among physicians, Freud was unique. Have you ever heard a physician assert that treatment failed because his patient was insufficiently credulous? Such an explanation belongs to the world of faith healers.

In *Structural Anthropology*, Claude Lévi-Strauss showed that, to the extent that they heal, shamans do so by telling stories. A shaman will make sense of his patient's suffering by rendering it in a narrative about mythic beings.

The story does not offer a scientific explanation. In an example that Lévi-Strauss offered, when a shaman described a woman's labor pains in terms of a dramatic struggle, he was rendering them meaningful.

Lévi-Strauss added, tellingly, that when a physician offers a scientific explanation of his patient's suffering, the words do not produce a therapeutic benefit.

Of course, given a choice between a primitive incantation and an epidural most women, I suspect, would choose the latter.

Obviously, a shaman's story only works for believers. Patients who receive such ministrations must also, Lévi-Strauss emphasized, belong to a community where no one has ever doubted its myths.

Beyond its ability to render unintelligible pain meaningful, the shaman's ritual reaffirms the afflicted woman's membership in her group. If her pains make her feel separate and apart, the shaman returns her to her community.

When he offered his analysis Lévi-Strauss argued that psychoanalysis had more in common with shamanism than with science.

If so, psychoanalysis was destined to become a pseudo-religion.

To sustain itself as treatment, psychoanalysis has had to replicate the conditions that produced shamanistic cures. It has had to produce a subculture where people believed that it was an effective treatment. Eventually, it founded a cult of true believers, a community separate and apart from the doubt-ridden science-laden modern world.

Freud did not limit his ambitions to individual patients. He also dreamt of using psychoanalysis to cure the larger community. He knew that he, like Moses, would never reach the Promised Land, but he wanted to show others the way.

In *Civilization and Its Discontents*, he wrote:

> *I would not say that an attempt to carry psychoanalysis over to the cultural community was absurd or doomed to fruitlessness.... In spite of all the difficulties, we may expect that one day someone will venture to embark on a pathology of cultural communities.*

If you want to cure a community of its "pathology," you can begin by establishing a "healthy" subgroup in its midst. The subgroup will have different values, different customs and a different set of ethical (or unethical) precepts.

This cult will then militate to have the surrounding community respect its choices. If it convinces people to accept its behavior and its values, it will influence the customs, mores and values of the larger community. Then, its leaders will feel like true conquistadors.

Most psychoanalysts downplay Freud's colonialist yearnings. Believing themselves to be children of the Enlightenment, they pretend to be champions of rational ideas. They do not merely aim at curing human beings of their emotional problems; they want to rid the culture of superstition and illusion.

For his part Freud also insisted that psychoanalysis was the antidote to human arrogance. Placing himself in the company of Copernicus and Darwin, he claimed that psychoanalytic science could disembarrass people of their naïve belief that the ego is the master of its house.

In Freud's words:

> *Humanity has in the course of time had to endure from the hands of science two great outrages upon its naive self-love. The first was when it realized that our earth was not the center of the universe, but only a tiny speck in a world-system of a magnitude hardly conceivable; this is associated in our minds with the name of Copernicus, although Alexandrian doctrines taught something very similar. The second was when biological research robbed man of his peculiar privilege of having been specially created, and relegated him to a descent from the animal world, implying an ineradicable animal nature in him: this transvaluation has been accomplished in our own time upon the instigation of Charles Darwin, Wallace, and their predecessors, and not without the most violent opposition from their contemporaries. But man's craving for grandiosity is now suffering the third and most bitter blow from present-day psychological research which is endeavoring to prove to the ego of each one of us that he is not even master in his own house, but that he must remain content with the veriest scraps of information about what is going on unconsciously in his own mind. We psycho-analysts were neither the first nor the only ones to propose to mankind that they should look inward; but it appears to be our lot to advocate it most insistently and to support it by empirical evidence which touches every man closely.*

His protestations notwithstanding, Freud was hardly the first to say that some human behaviors were directed by forces beyond the ego's control. It would be more difficult to find philosophers who have believed that the ego was master of its own house.

Blaise Pascal, for example, famously said: "*Le coeur a ses raisons que la raison ne connaît point.*" It means: "The heart has its reasons which reason knows nothing about."

Pascal was saying that we are not conscious of the reasoning that directs the seemingly irrational human heart. His idea may not render Freud's theory precisely, but it belongs in the same theoretical neighborhood.

What did Freud mean when he declared that psychoanalysis had provided "empirical evidence" to buttress its claim? Unfortunately, he was referring to the material his patients presented when called on to convince him that his interpretations were correct.

When Pascal spoke of the human "heart," he was probably referring to human sentiment. He might also have been alluding to an even more mysterious and more Freudian muscle, the male erectile organ.

If Pascal had said that the phallus has its reasons but that consciousness knows nothing about them he would have been offering a "high concept" version of Freudian theory.

As you know, Freud was too preoccupied with sex to pay very much attention to the human heart. His theory is a waltz of organs and orifices, with one organ, in particular standing out.

His grandiose claims to originality notwithstanding, Freud was following a path laid down by one of the most eminent Christian theologians, Augustine of Hippo.

In *The City of God*, Augustine remarked that the phallus has a unique characteristic. It does not function autonomously, as the heart muscle does, and it is not controlled by the will, as our thumbs are.

The erectile function of the phallus is a mystery. If a man's mind does not control it, what mind does?

To the Bishop of Hippo the problem was not so much that the ego is not master of its own house, but that the ego does not control the *pudenda*.

Augustine also took up the question in *A Treatise on the Merits and Forgiveness of Sins*:

> *Now, these members are on this account, in every man of chastity, rightly called "pudenda," because they excite themselves, just as they like, in opposition to the mind which is their master, as if they were their own masters; and the sole*

*authority which the bridle of virtue possesses over them is to
check them from approaching impure and unlawful pollutions.*

Freud might have had difficulty accepting that his theories were so intimately connected to theology, but he certainly approached problems philosophically. After all, he did once admit that nothing about medical training would prepare a person to study psychoanalysis.

In Freud's theory, the phallus stands as an It that escapes the I's mastery. Of course, you know these psychic agencies in their Latin translations, as the id and the ego. Using the English pronouns renders Freud's concept more intelligible. After all, Freud used German, not Latin pronouns.

Freud defined neurosis as the I's repudiation of the It's intentions and motives. He believed that the I feared what it would look like if it accepted the It's criminal intentions as its own.

If the It is riddled with insalubrious intentions, what should I do about them? Should I embrace them and behave accordingly or should I sublimate them into writing poetry and throwing pots.

Many psychoanalysts have been horrified at the implications of Freud's moral imperative: *Wo Es war, soll Ich werden.* It translates roughly: Where It was, there I ought to become.

Freud's more temperate followers believed that their master was telling them to let the I control the It's impulses. Yet, Jacques Lacan was more correct to say that Freud wanted the I to embrace the It's impulses as its own.

Freud did not uncover all of that repressed depravity in order to send it back into hiding. In some cases he prescribed sublimation, but, it makes good sense for people to conclude that they can best show how well they have overcome sexual repression by debauching themselves.

The Freudian view of sexuality has much in common with that of Augustine. Surely, it does not look or feel like science.

Curiously, for someone who declared himself to be a physician and a man of science, Freud was not trying to make people more normal. After all, he believed that what we consider normal is merely a way to repress our libido.

So, Freud was offering an alternative to normality. Philosophers and poets had dreamt of such a thing, but Freud took it a step further by offering it to the general public. He was smart enough to offer it to those whose mental anguish made them most susceptible to his charms.

In Freud's dreams psychoanalysis would eventually transform Western civilization itself. For someone who believed that he had helped human beings to overcome their arrogance, he seems to have been suffering from a terminal case of hubris.

But, isn't that what it means to have an Oedipus complex?

1

EVERYONE KNOWS THAT Freud's name sounds like the German word *Freude*. Everyone knows it, but no one pays it much mind.

Freude is one of the more cheerful words in the German language. It means "joy." Beethoven wrote an uplifting ode to it: *Ode an die Freude*.

Clearly, Freud was not inspired by Beethoven. He was on much better terms with *Schadenfreude*.

It is hard to imagine that Freud's German-speaking patients ignored the fact that they were consulting with Dr. Joy. Why would they not have believed, unconsciously, that a doctor named Freud would be handing out *Freude*?

As the founding father of negative psychology, Freud rarely, if ever, allowed any joy to enter his theories. For all we know, he might have been trying to live down the meaning his name would have had if it had been a word.

Today, Freud's name is not associated with joy; it has become synonymous with sex. Yet, Freud did not write *The Joy of Sex*. He could not have.

Freud did not see sex as a very joyful experience. By his theories the human sex drive was infected with perverse criminal intentions.

He added that this thwarted and perverted drive could never really achieve full satisfaction. Obviously, Freud was bringing bad news.

Freud suggested that we are all condemned to strive toward an impossible goal: the free and open expression of our sexuality. Since we can never attain that blissful transcendence, we yearn for nothing but. So much so that we make all forms of human happiness variants of sexual gratification.

Having noticed that sexual climax produced an intense satisfaction, Freud took it as the model for human happiness.

In his words:

> What we call happiness in the strictest sense comes from the (preferably sudden) satisfaction of needs which have been dammed up to a high degree, and it is from its nature only possible as an episodic phenomenon.

He followed with a rationale for decadence:

> ...man's discovery that sexual (genital) love afforded the strongest experience of satisfaction, and in fact provided him with the prototype of all happiness must have suggested to him that he should continue to seek the satisfaction of happiness in his life along the path of sexual relations and that he should make genital eroticism the central point of his life.

Immediately after making this statement, Freud advised people not to seek happiness through sexual gratification. Anyone who does, he said, will become dependent on inconstant and unreliable lovers.

He might have added that decadence is not the most efficient use of your energy and intelligence. If you want to excel at decadence you should make it a way of life. But, you can only do so if you have a source of income that does not require very much work. And you will need to find someone who will protect you against anyone who might be tempted to exploit your weakness.

All told, decadence looks like childishness, with an emphasis on its polymorphous perversity.

For most human beings, adulthood brings other satisfactions. They may or may not be stronger than what are now called mind-blowing orgasms, but they are often more meaningful.

Freud ignored them. He could not easily account for the satisfaction people gain through achievement, either their own or that of their children.

After all, the happiness you gain from worldly success has little to do with releasing dammed-up impulses.

Sad to say, having an orgasm does not count as a great accomplishment. Any idiot can have an orgasm.

When Jacques Lacan arrived on the scene, he added some joy to Freud's theory of sexuality. By giving a special place to what he called *jouissance*, or enjoyment, Lacan redeemed Freudian sexuality. The French word *jouissance* has a decidedly positive connotation. Its lilting cadence even sounds joyous.

It's easier to sell enjoyment than to peddle Freud's stoically tragic vision.

Good Freudian that he was Lacan also had to insist that *jouissance* was ultimately destructive. To his mind it was more like the thrill an addict gets from a fix than the feeling you have playing Bach, winning a race or hearing that your son has been accepted into college.

For all their talk about sexual satisfaction, neither Freud nor Lacan gave their patients any practical advice about how to enhance it. They were not handing out sex toys or copies of *Venus in Furs*. Living in a mind-over-body world they believed, as an article of faith, that people who overcame their inhibitions and repressions would have more, better sex.

Unfortunately, all the talk about sexual enjoyment is something of a ruse. Freud cared less about sexual experience than about the cultural cost of covering up the *pudenda*. Psychologically speaking, he was declaring war on shame.

That is, he wanted to lead a crusade against decorum, propriety and civility. Practicing those virtues defines a sense of shame.

All human beings have an innate sense of shame. They are predisposed to keep their pants on and to hide their most intimate secrets. Those who do not respect this rule are often ostracized from their communities.

Freud believed that people were sexually repressed because civilization had taught them shame. It had taught them to cover up sexuality, to refuse to talk about it openly and to censor obscene fantasies. Coupled with the practice of civility these mental defects had inhibited the expression of instinct and had caused sexual deprivation.

Since Freud did not, by his own admission, indulge in the sexual liberation his theory was promising, we must conclude that he was using sex as a lure to attract people into his cult.

He was intimating that those who followed him would have more, better orgasms. All they needed to do was to lose their sense of shame. It's a lot more appealing and a lot easier to achieve than something as imprecise as mental health.

Luckily for psychoanalysis, Freud did not quite put it in these terms. If he had, people would quickly have discovered that there were cheaper ways to attain orgasmic ecstasy.

Naively, Freud believed that people who overcame their sense of shame would get in closer touch with their inner libertines.

In particular, and tellingly, he began his clinical practice insisting that his female patients speak openly and explicitly about sex. In many ways, his "dangerous method" was, at the onset, a full frontal attack on feminine modesty. It did not cross Freud's mind that modesty might enhance sexual desire, and not vice versa.

Many of his followers have found Freud's obsessive interest in sex embarrassing. If he had been a biomedical researcher, his focus would have been acceptable, but as long as he was treating mental illnesses, his interest seemed prurient. His acolytes have often felt obliged to cover his shame.

Some did so by placing a greater emphasis on earlier, pre-Oedipal stages of childhood development. Some theorized about the ego and about object relations. Others argued for the importance of Self.

Whatever you think of these theoretical excursions, they obscured the raw, sexual side of Freudian theory. They also masked Freud's war on shame.

Freud's translators also tried to fog over Freud's fixation on the genitalia. When his English language translators rendered Freud's famous *Lustprinzip* as the "pleasure principle," they obscured the fact that the German word *Lust* evokes a special kind of pleasure called "lust."

Most of us think we know something about sex. We have been learning about it since elementary school. Most of us have some practical experience with it.

It will come as unwelcome news, especially to those who still identify as Freudians, but Freud was not talking about the sexuality that they know and occasionally enjoy.

Most of us understand that sex is a biological process designed for a procreative function. We also understand that sexual attraction is intrinsic to our biological nature.

Freud saw sex differently. He accepted that sex might involve procreation, but he saw it arising from a desire to commit incest.

Strangely, Freud was implying that the future of the human species depends on a mistake. By his theory, when two people couple, the man does not really want the woman and the woman does not really want the man. If they produce a child, they are not fulfilling their heart's desire. Conception is an accidental byproduct that might occur when they are enacting their repressed Oedipal longings.

If, on the other hand, sex is a biological function, human beings can moderate and even manage it. Most people know better than to consume themselves seeking out extreme forms of sexual gratification.

In reality, most humans balance their search for orgasmic release with a duty to do their jobs and to raise their children. Once children enter the equation, the decadent pursuit of lubricious pleasures becomes too costly, for the individual, for the family and for the community.

Abrogating responsibilities in the interest of having better orgasms will not put you on the road to happiness.

When Lacan took up Freud's theory he shocked the bourgeoisie by being more Freudian than Freud.

First, he insisted that the sexes were not naturally attracted to each other. For good measure, he added that human beings do not possess an instinct that shows them how to copulate. In distinction to all other organisms, humans need to be taught how to have sex. Speak of a design flaw!

One would like to believe that Lacan was offering those gems of pseudo-wisdom in order to test his students' gullibility.

Alas, he was not. For one of the few times in his career, he said what he meant and meant what he said.

In so doing, Lacan wrote the human species out of the animal kingdom. He consigned us all to the world of spirits. More precisely, he recreated us as fictional beings.

Following Freud, Lacan theorized that sexual desire is always produced by a prohibition. Some might think that we want what we do not have. Lacan thought that we only want what we are forbidden to have. We are especially inclined, Freudian theory told him, to lust after the first and primary forbidden sexual object: Mother.

Obviously, this theory is driven by the Oedipal narrative. It has little to do with the reality of human experience.

A more rational view should begin with the observation that sexual attraction is a natural function that serves a reproductive purpose.

Shame, through its handmaiden modesty, can enhance and direct desire. Normally, sexual attraction is provoked, sustained and oriented by the interplay of exposure and concealment, especially as practiced by the female of the human species.

Too much exposure, like too much concealment stifles desire. When it comes to sex, showing too much is no better than showing too little.

Freud rejected the experience-based—dare I call it scientific—theory of human sexuality. His narrative-driven theory claims that humans hide their genitalia because they want to cover up their criminal intentions. They refuse to accept that their desire to commit incest is haunting their choices of sexual partners.

Freud cut sexual desire off from its biological purpose and folded it into a narrative involving the incest taboo. He then added that real or imaginary transgressions would provoke castration anxiety, an anti-cipation of punishment. He recommended that human beings allay their anxiety by doing a form of penance that he called symbolic castration.

Significantly, Freud's narrative was all about guilt. It left no place for shame.

Where Augustine believed that humans concealed their sexual organs because they were embarrassed at their inability to master them, Freud declared that humans turned away from the phallus because they could not accept its criminal intentions as their own.

He was less preoccupied with the possibility for exposure than with the horrific crimes the It would commit if left to its own devices. To Freud, Augustinian pollutions were the least of the male sexual organ's problems.

Surely, Freud noticed that the phallus, however much it refuses the will's commands, sometimes responds to feminine desire. Unfortunately, he was so caught up in the mental conflict between the I and the It that he forgot all about You.

When Lacan arrived on the scene, he solved the problem by redefining Oedipal desire. He analyzed it into two components: a child's lust for his mother and a mother's incestuous longings for her child. It is clearer in French than in English, but the genitive in the phrase—the desire of the mother—can be either subjective or objective.

Obviously, a very young child is functionally incapable of copulating with his mother. But Freud believed—and Lacan seconded him—that even at a young age, a child must learn that he will never be allowed to have carnal relations with her. Well before the information is relevant, a child should hear from his father that incest is strictly forbidden.

Freud and Lacan imagined that children experience this momentous, desire-producing event when they are around four or five years of age.

According to Freud's theory, no child takes this prohibition lying down. He redirects his drives toward compensatory satisfactions.

If he cannot act on his desire for his mother, a child can still dream. That is, he can fantasize about what has been forbidden. In fact, the theory assumes that taboos provoke fantasies in which a child sees himself enjoying the forbidden object of desire.

Also, a child will compensate for not having carnal knowledge of his mother by settling for parts of her body. He might fetishize the breast that provided him his first experience of satisfaction.

When a child grows up, he might use his favorite fetish objects to provoke fantasies that can help to instigate sexual desire. Supposedly, these fantasies will do for the phallus what willpower or even the will to power cannot do.

No fantasy can provoke tumescence at will, but in the best of Freudian cases, it can help out as need be.

By all appearances, Freud was not merely selling the promise of better orgasms. He was trafficking in the illusion that a man might command and control his phallic appendage.

Psychoanalysts like to say that they want their patients to have a rich fantasy life. In so saying, they are allowing their patients to believe that they can gain some measure of control over their unruly sexual organs by entertaining all manner of depraved sexual fantasies.

Put that way, it doesn't sound like such a bad deal.

It can only happen if a patient accepts that his degenerate fantasies, especially the ones he had been repressing, constitute his desire. Psychoanalysis can help out by showing him how to own them.

Through psychoanalysis a patient should recover his ugliest fantasies from his memory bank. He can take possession of them by integrating them in a shiny, new life story.

In that story, he will recreate himself as a new character, a new dramatic persona.

Many psychoanalysts have rejected this apparent call to decadence. They have pretended that their patients can learn to overcome their appalling Oedipus impulses.

Freud saw it differently. He wrote:

> *A man should not strive to eliminate his complexes but to get into accord with them: they are legitimately what direct his conduct in the world.*

If a psychoanalytic patient believes that his new persona is his true persona, he cannot just keep it to himself. He will need to show it to the world.

A good Freudian patient does not cover up his salacious desires because he fears opprobrium. What purpose would treatment have served if he ended up hiding who he really was in order to conform to civilization's strictures?

Besides, if your mental life is filled with sordid fantasies and your outward appearance is modest and humble, you will never know which is the real you.

It isn't that difficult to make your public persona accord with your sordid and depraved complexes. You need but become rude, lewd, crude and screwed. You might even throw in some emotional incontinence and moral exhibitionism, to taste. After a while you will no longer recognize yourself. No one else will, either.

With any luck you won't care. You will have shown to the world that you have been liberated from decorum, decency and especially shame.

It may not cure what ails you, but the process will certainly transform you. Better yet, it will show the world that you have become a new You.

Your change might not be as radical as the one that befell Gregor Samsa, but if you live your new narrative you will fulfill the rarely stated goal of psychoanalysis: you will become someone else.

When Peter Kramer famously declared that Prozac could change you into someone else, he was subtly suggesting that Prozac could deliver what psychoanalysis had promised.

If psychoanalysis makes you into someone else, how do you know that the new You is the real You? Why would it not be a more convenient fake?

Happily for you, your psychoanalyst will know which is which.

If the new You exists in a story that reads like a Greek tragedy, your analyst will pronounce it to be true. If your new story makes you look good, your Freudian analyst will call it a self-serving lie.

Once you have persuaded your analyst that you have been transformed, you will need to convince your entourage that the new You is the real You. What if they believe that you have changed for the worse?

If you are living a new story, your friends and family will find themselves with new roles. Your job, should you choose to accept it, will be to seduce them into embracing those roles and living in your new script.

To do so you will need to control other people's minds. To be blunt, you will need to practice a new avocation, that of "wild" psychoanalyst.

A properly conducted psychoanalysis should teach you how to persuade, manipulate, convince, cajole, browbeat and terrorize other people into accepting your new incarnation.

If that doesn't work, you can induce friends and family to undergo psychoanalysis themselves. Anyone who rejects the new shameless You must be suffering from unresolved psychosexual issues.

If your friends and family balk, and if your entourage refuses to accept the new well-analyzed You, fear not. Psychoanalysis will provide you with a coterie of like-minded people who have dedicated their lives to the Freudian cause.

Some will call it a cult. Others will see it as a pseudo-religion. In the best case, you will feel like you belong to a vanguard leading a cultural revolution.

You and your comrades will tell yourselves that you are living a higher truth. It will not be a happy day when you discover that you have been living a lesser truth, one that was probably not even true.

2

PSYCHIATRISTS WILL TELL you that people who hear voices, who suffer auditory hallucinations, are likely to be psychotic. All rules have exceptions, and Joan of Arc was an exception to this one. So was Ray Kinsella.

Joan of Arc's voices sent her to the battlefield where she fought alongside Gilles de Rais at the siege of Orleans. Her leadership turned the tide in the Hundred Years War. A champion of French nationalism, she helped restore the French monarchy through the person of King Charles VII.

Ray Kinsella's voices told him to transform his corn field into a baseball field.

Joan of Arc was a martyr and a saint. She fought for the glory of France. The British burned her at the stake because they thought she was a witch.

Ray Kinsella was a farmer. He was the central character in the 1989 film, *Field of Dreams*.

One day, when Kinsella was walking through his Iowa cornfield, he heard a voice. It told him: "If you build it, he will come." The "it" was a baseball field; the "he" was a baseball player, or better a team.

Kinsella was faced with a dilemma: should he plow under his ethanol crop and build a baseball field on spec or should he ignore the voice?

Joan of Arc had no such problem. When God calls, you do not weigh your options.

Eventually, Kinsella built his baseball field. Lo and behold, Shoeless Joe Jackson—of the Black Sox Scandal—appeared. Not in the flesh, but in spirit. Eventually, real teams arrived and his investment paid off.

It was a movie; what did you expect? Kinsella seemed to be following his dream, but, in truth, he was making a risky investment.

Like Ray Kinsella, Sigmund Freud built a field of dreams. He constructed psychoanalysis on dream interpretation.

When he built it, people came. They came to be analyzed by Freud and his followers.

If they thought that the field of dreams was an arena where they could learn how to play the game of life, Freud wanted to disabuse them of their naive notion.

If they believed that psychoanalysis would mitigate their anguish and help them to overcome their issues, they would learn that they were wrong about that too.

The Freudian field of dreams is not like a playing field. It is more like a stage on which patients can turn their lives into drama.

The course of a game, be it baseball or cricket or even solitaire is never predetermined. Knowing the rules and knowing how to play does not mean that you know the course of the game or its outcome. You might win, but you might also lose. By how much or how little, no one can know until the game is over.

In the theatre, the script dictates how the drama will unfold. Actors and directors interpret the script, but they cannot change the play's course or its ending. Cordelia always dies in her father's arms.

Scientific experiments, of course, are more like games than like theatre. They follow a game plan, not a script. Your experiment might work out, but, then again, it might not. The results might be clear, but they might be inconclusive.

Scientific experiments produce practical results. Theatrical dramas produce aesthetic satisfaction.

Despite it all, psychoanalysts, beginning with Freud, have pretended to be men and women of science.

When you strip away that pretense, psychoanalysis bears an uncanny resemblance to the living theatre that Richard Feynman called a cargo cult.

After World War II indigenous inhabitants of the Pacific Islands constructed these cults. During the war, when American troops were stationed on their islands, these people watched in awe as cargo planes landed, bringing an untold bounty. They had never imagined such a thing, even in their dreams.

When the war ended the troops left and the cargo planes stopped coming. Some of the local inhabitants could not accept that there would be no more deliveries, so they built an imitation landing strip, manned it with imitation controllers and waited for the planes to land.

Thus, they created a cargo cult. Feynman saw it as a perfect rendering of pseudo-science. Here he described how the Pacific islanders did it:

> So they've arranged to make things like runways, to put fires along the sides of the runways, to make a wooden hut for a man to sit in, with two wooden pieces on his head like headphones and bars of bamboo sticking out like antennas— he's the controller—and they wait for the planes to land. They're doing everything right. The form is perfect. It looks exactly the way it looked before. But it doesn't work. No airplanes land. So I call these things cargo cult science because they follow all the apparent precepts and forms of scientific investigation, but they're missing something essential, because the planes don't land.

Psychoanalysis is like a cargo cult. It goes through the motions but doesn't deliver the goods.

If the planes don't land, why do people continue to participate in the cult's rituals? Are they, like Ray Kinsella, waiting for their investment to pay off?

Cargo cultists invest their labor in building an ersatz landing field. It's not a real landing field, but they have incurred a real expense, of time and material. It makes sense that they are expecting a return on their investment.

We are tempted to deride their illusion, but they are not completely irrational. Were you to ask them why they persevere in the face of failure, they might tell you that no one knows for certain what will happen tomorrow. Thus, no one can prove scientifically that the planes will never land.

They know for a fact that at one time the planes did land. Nothing says that it cannot happen again. Besides, if there is no landing strip, the planes will definitely not land.

In the meantime, cult members are gaining a psycho-social benefit. By manning the *faux* landing field they affirm their membership in an organized subgroup. They might even believe that they are superior to those who are provisioning themselves the old fashioned way.

If they feel any shame for failing to bring home the goods, it is mitigated, even numbed, by their membership in a privileged group of hopers and dreamers.

Cargo cults, like other cults, use logical arguments to obscure the fact that reality is making them look like fools. The same applies to psychoanalysis.

After a time, some cultists might rationalize their activities by redefining the context. Their landing strip is not really a landing strip. It is an open air theatre. If no plane lands, that just means that theirs is the theatre of the absurd.

It's difficult to know when Freud and any of his followers recognized that psychoanalysis was cargo cult science. I cannot pinpoint the moment when psychoanalysts grasped, not just that their technique did not work, but that it could never work.

Obviously, they did not trumpet the bad news. If people wanted to believe that psychoanalysis could cure, practitioners were happy to use this belief to produce placebo cures. It was better than nothing.

By now, most psychoanalysts understand that in his struggle with reality, Freud lost.

He lost because reality was not obliged to fulfill Freud's wishes. It doesn't have to fulfill yours either.

True believing Freudians did not give up without a fight. Slightly more sophisticated than native Pacific Islanders, they argued that their theories should be judged on aesthetic grounds. Freud's grand system was beautiful, and beauty does not admit to empirical verification, *n'est-ce pas?*

Some psychoanalysts took it a step further and acted as though Freud had given them access to the sacred or the spiritual. They insisted passionately that no one has the right to discredit sacred texts for failing to represent reality.

Here, Freud set the standard. He proclaimed that: "the Secret of Dreams was Revealed" to him on July 24, 1895.

I suspect that he was not hearing voices. I do not think that he was seeing things, either. Yet, he doesn't answer the basic question: revealed by whom?

Be that as it may, a revealed secret seems more like an epiphany than like science. More so because Freud insisted that nothing could disprove his revelation.

Freud's epiphany differed significantly from the messages sent to Joan of Arc and Ray Kinsella.

The spiritual being who revealed the secret of dreams to Freud did not direct him toward a future action or goal. It induced him to look to his past in order to recall forgotten childhood memories.

In contrast, the voices that Joan of Arc and Ray Kinsella heard pointed them toward the future.

What secret was revealed to Freud in 1895? Dreams, he concluded, always fulfilled wishes. Your dreams, he said, are trying to show you what you really, really want.

Next, Freud folded his theory of dreams into a larger theory of mind. He posited a dramatic conflict between an unconscious part of the mind that is trying to show you what you want and a conscious part that doesn't want to know.

As Freud saw it, your mind is divided against itself. Your unconscious mind knows your desire; your conscious mind refuses to have anything to do with it. Your I insists that whatever It wants is not what I want.

Freud believed that consciousness was a shadow mind, a pale imitation of your true, unconscious mind. To guard its dominion and to sustain its illusion of control, consciousness represses the truth that the unconscious mind wants to express.

Ultimately, consciousness will fail. Like it or not, your unconscious mind will make itself heard. In Freudian theory, the unconscious cannot be denied.

At best, you should allow your unconscious mind to express itself, preferably through language. Whatever your dreams are telling you in the privacy of your sleep, your language should be expressing to a larger public. It is better to tell others than to talk to yourself.

If you refuse to allow your unconscious mind to trumpet its truths, it will punish you by carving out non-verbal channels of communication.

Freud was not saying that you can choose whether or not you want your unconscious mind to express itself. He was saying that in one way or another, your unconscious mind will have its way.

If you block your unconscious mind's access to language, it will express itself through tics, twitches, numbness and paresthesia. Freud believed that he had seen the process at work in hysterical conversion symptoms.

Having spun out this theoretical narrative Freud drew the logical conclusion: since people fall mentally ill when they silence the unconscious, cure must involve letting it have its say.

It made for a good story, but it wasn't science. It provided a plausible narrative explanation for hysteria, but it did not produce very many cures.

Freud was not alone in believing that hysteria could only be understood by introducing metaphysics. Many of his contemporaries also concluded that if a hysterical conversion symptom had no discernible physical cause, it must have a mental cause.

If medicine could not explain why a woman's arm had gone numb, Freud concluded that an unconscious idea was expressing itself through her symptom. Since she refused to think a certain thought, no less to speak it, it was having its say through her body.

Theorizing that hysterics were suffering from repressed memories, that is, from repressed ideas, Freud imagined that if they could verbalize them, the ideas would no longer need to express themselves through conversion symptoms.

Why had women found it so difficult to express these thoughts? Freud believed that hysterics were closing their minds to sexual thoughts because social custom had taught them to be modest.

Late-Victorian ladies did not allow their minds to be filled with sordid fantasies. Aspiring to be proper and demure they refused to think or to talk about sexual traumas. They did not spend their time in reveries about lurid scenarios. If they did, they certainly did not share their fantasies.

Perhaps they took it a bit too far, but their sense of shame dictated that sex remain discretely covered. They might have believed that if they allowed themselves to think dirty thoughts, the thoughts might pop into their conversation. Who knows what would happen next?

Strangely, Freud was implying that hysterics could not process sexual traumas because they were behaving ethically. Their good character was making them sick.

He set out to cure of them of their modesty by trying to open their minds to obscenity. Unsurprisingly, they resisted. Freud was not sure whether they were resisting the truth or his charms.

To convince them that resistance was futile, he invented a technique that was a cross between X-ray vision and mind reading. If his hysterics believed that they could hide their more intimate thoughts, Freud declared that psychoanalysis could see through the veils.

He did not grant these women the freedom to choose whether to cover or expose their sexuality. If they opted for the former, he would strip away their modesty and force them to face their truth.

Once they embraced it, he implied, they would be cured of what ailed them. Better yet, their minds would instruct their bodies to open themselves to better sexual experience.

The theory makes good narrative sense. Unfortunately, that is the only sense it makes. When Freud put it to work on his hysterics, the results were unsatisfactory.

As a naïve young neurologist, Freud believed that he had shown hysterics how to recover memories of sexual traumas. He co-authored a book, *Studies on Hysteria* where he and Josef Breuer asserted that they had cured a bevy of hysterics.

Recent scholars, especially Mikkel Borch-Jacobsen (in *The Freud Files* among other writings) have shown that Freud was not being entirely truthful. Whether he was lying to himself or to the world, his miracle cures were more wish fulfillment than reality.

Besides, Borch-Jacobsen discovered, many of his patients' memories of sexual abuse had been suggested by Freud himself.

At some point, Freud recognized that treatment based on recovered memories was ineffective. So he shifted his focus to dreams and recovered fantasies. It no longer mattered whether the trauma had happened. Freud wanted to know why his patients had wanted it to happen.

Most of his followers believe that when Freud turned away from real traumas and toward desire he founded psychoanalysis.

When the new approach did not produce better clinical results, Freud stopped writing about hysterics. They were, he seems to have concluded, unworthy of his genius.

Freud published his last study of hysteria in 1905. In it, he admitted that he had failed to help an adolescent he named Dora. From that time until his death in 1939 he did not write up another case of hysteria.

Yet, he never saw failure as failure. He merely redefined the goal of treatment. Unable to provide mental health, he decided that it would be better to give access to self-knowledge.

Thus psychoanalysis redefined, and not for the last time, the goal of treatment. It replaced mental health with insight, awareness and self-consciousness. Eventually, it dispensed with self-consciousness, because the term reeks of inhibition.

Psychoanalysis would help people to know their own minds. It would teach them why they had been doing what they had been doing and why they had not been doing what they had not been doing.

The message has often been garbled, so it needs to be stated. Psychoanalysis tells people not to worry if they do not feel better. It tells them that they should not be concerned about their inability to manage their lives. It pretends to offer something that is even better: personal enlightenment.

On that score, psychoanalysis has also not delivered the goods. When called upon to explain human motives and intentions Freud merely trotted out a couple of recycled pagan myths. The first and most important was the myth of Oedipus.

For those of his followers who were uncomfortable with the criminal sexuality of Oedipus, Freud brought out the story of Narcissus. They took it as a godsend.

Even though the story of Narcissus did not end well, it was less frightening than what happened to Oedipus. Falling in love with your beautiful reflection is less horrifying than murdering your father and marrying your mother.

Obviously, it's not science. Had psychoanalysis been held to the standards that affirm or disprove scientific theories, it would never have survived.

Therein lies a mystery. Even though it has failed in clinical practice psychoanalysis has had an outsized cultural influence. Few people still undergo Freudian psychoanalysis, but many people live according to precepts, principles and values that Freud concocted.

It's as though large numbers of people have decided to take up residence in Freud's field of dreams.

It happened because psychoanalysis provided a religious experience for unbelievers. People who no longer believed in God could believe in Freud. People who stopped going to confession could bare their souls to their therapists, Freudian or not. People who rejected classical ethics found in Freud, not a new ethic, but an aesthetic way of life.

There is another, more complicated reason why people found solace in Freud.

While pretending to offer a cure for illness, Freud was exploiting a real problem: the psycho-social disruptions caused by the Industrial Revolution.

Beginning in the eighteenth century the Industrial Revolution transformed the world, often for better, sometimes for worse. It brought people great material advantages, but it broke up human communities and undermined social cohesion.

Nations that adopted mechanized agriculture, new forms of trans-portation and communication, factory production, corporate structures and free trade became economic dynamos and military powers. Their citizens gained economic opportunity and increased pride, but at the cost of community.

Social mobility was a mixed blessing. People who moved away from their birth communities to take factory jobs felt culturally uprooted. They no longer knew their places or roles in society. They did not know where they belonged or which rules to follow.

French sociologist Emile Durkheim coined the term "anomie" to describe societies where norms had broken down and where individuals felt socially dislocated.

But he also used the term to describe a condition that afflicted individuals. In his book *Suicide* Durkheim described three causes of suicide: egotism, altruism and anomie.

In a normless or ruleless world, individuals lose their bearings. They do not know what to do or what not to do. They do not know what is right or wrong, good or bad. They do not know where they stand or where to sit. The result is anomie.

As I see it, there are four types of anomie.

In one, you arrive in a foreign community and feel disaffected because you don't know what the rules are. In that case you will learn the local customs.

In the second type, you live in a community in turmoil or in transition, where no one is honoring the old rules. In that case, you will try to fit into a subgroup while working to forge connections with the others.

In the third, you arrive at a foreign community and join a subgroup of people who were part of your community of birth. If you fail to assimilate into the larger group, you will feel, on the one hand, that you never left home, and on the other, that the dominant culture threatens your identity.

In the fourth, more virulent form of anomie, you try to adopt local customs but are rejected on racial or ethnic grounds.

In any case, the cure for anomie is getting along with other people. One does so by joining a community and participating in its rituals and ceremonies.

Some will find this solution; others will not. People who despair of finding a place in a group that is in turmoil might believe that they can only rely on themselves. They may believe that the group's normlessness leaves them with only one choice: to double down on anomie by asserting their authentic individuality.

Anyone who is in this position will find comfort and support in psychoanalysis.

In *Psychoanalytic Politics* Sherry Turkle described the difference between a functioning and a dysfunctional community. She explained why psychoanalysis appealed to people who were suffering from anomie:

> *When the individual feels himself to be a part of a network of stable social relationships with family, ancestry, and religion, he can use these relationships to make sense of experience, and when he feels himself in pain of distress, they become natural reference points for trying to understand what is happening and sources of support for finding a way out of the trouble. But with mobility of place, profession, and status, and a new instability of values, old ways of looking at the world no longer apply. The individual is thrown back on himself and may be more receptive to theories such as*

psychoanalysis which search for meaning in his dreams, wishes, fears, and confusions. In a stable society, people feel that they understand how things work. The rational and conscious are deemed trustworthy. When life is in greater flux, daily experience continually suggests the presence of processes hidden from awareness. Society appears more opaque, and the idea of an unconscious acquires greater reality.

When the Industrial Revolution began to change the world, some nations embraced it quickly. Others, fearful of social disruption decided to move more slowly.

Great Britain and Germany counted among the first group. France and Austria were among the latter.

Great Britain embraced the Revolution because it had invented it. It felt like a way to assert national pride. And yet, that nation also entertained a significant national debate over the value of industrialization. Thereby, it tried to reconcile the new industrial present with the aristocratic and genteel past.

Germany followed because it refused to see any nation gain a material advantage over it.

In France and Austria, things were different. These nations had excelled at pleasure, both sensuous and sensual. They loved the arts. When they had social problems, whether of injustice or inequality, they dramatized them in great events like the French Revolution. They believed, and still do, that dramatizing a problem is better than solving it. Why would they give it all up for factories and the free trade in ideas?

Moreover, they believed that they were in closer touch with spiritual truths and transcendent values. They rejected the crass empiricism and raw pragmatism of the Anglosphere in favor of a deeper appreciation of the soulful and religious side of life.

And they did not want to be judged by standards that had been imposed from the other side of the Channel.

For the French, national pride made it impossible to follow the lead of a nation that had executed *la Pucelle*.

The British dealt with anomie by reforming society. They tried to overcome normlessness by producing new rules to regulate social conduct. Taking their cue from classical ethics, they encouraged gentility, self-discipline, propriety, decorum, respectability and keeping up appearances.

In France and Austria industrialization came more slowly. These nations held fast to their traditional values and traditional norms.

The French, in particular, prided themselves on their ability to introduce enough industry to feel modern while retaining their indigenous culture.

Turkle described France at the turn of the twentieth century:

> *Although France had industrialized, the bourgeois social hierarchy was still based on traditional patterns of status, deference, and family ties. Although the state was secular, for many people the Catholic Church was a national presence that served to cement political and spiritual life. And although the French bourgeoisie ran corporations as well as the more traditional small businesses, they adopted many of the characteristics of the old aristocracy, in particular a disdain for the aggressive "entrepreneuring" associated with modern capitalism.*

In time, many Continental thinkers rebelled against the British solution to anomie. They rejected gentility and decorum in favor of an aesthetic that valued blood and soil, will and power, instinct and impulse, pleasure and desire, art and love. Preferring seduction to gentility, authenticity to self-control and the theatre to the market, they militated against liberal British economic and social policies.

Rejecting the gamesmanship required by the new world of industry and commerce, they wallowed in nostalgia for a dying or threatened past.

Their radical individualism appealed to the disaffected—it still does —but it was ultimately unworkable. There is no such thing as a human being living outside of all social groups. In time most radical individuals find themselves in subgroups comprised of people who despise the society they have rejected.

Feeling that their unique individuality is disparaged, they rebel against the larger society. Believing that they should be lionized for showing the way toward liberation, they set out to subvert the ungrateful surrounding culture.

To advance their cause many of those who were fighting the good culture war against the British hegemon took a cue from Freud. They claimed that the new industrialization, to say nothing of civility and liberal democracy, was built on sexual repression and was making people mentally ill. Worse yet, it had taken the drama out of life.

Freudian theory is a great story. It might not have produced many clinical benefits, but it made cultural history. Most of us, Freudian or not, have suffered its influence.

Herewith, I will tell the story of psychoanalysis, from the beginning to the end. I will not rehash its history. Many have done it before; most have done it well.

I will focus on Freud, the first psychoanalyst, and Lacan, the last. I will show how they, their apostles, their disciples and their students turned a pseudo-science into a pseudo-religion.

3

HUMAN BEINGS HAVE always been puzzled by dreams. How can we see images when our eyes are closed and the lights are out? Why do we feel so involved in our dreams, even, at times, mistaking them for reality?

For these among other reasons, people have long believed that dreams were especially meaningful.

To their chagrin, they had difficulty understanding what their dreams were trying to tell them. Before Freud came along, dreams were one of the mind's great mysteries. In many ways, they still are.

When his initial efforts to cure hysteria failed, Freud decided to become a new Joseph, a man who could interpret dreams.

Better a successful seer than a failed healer.

He began innocently by suggesting that dreams serve a purpose. Dreams, he asserted, are the guardians of sleep. We wish to remain asleep as long as possible, Freud suggested, and dreams help us to fulfill that wish.

Of course, this implies that our heart's desire is to be semi-conscious and in bed.

Regardless of whether Freud was right or wrong about dreams, he should not have suggested to his depressed patients that by withdrawing from life they were being true to their desire.

Consider an alternative to Freud's thesis. Perhaps dreams are preparing us to re-enter reality. They might be pointing us out of our minds and into the world. If a dream is alerting you to a nearby danger or even an opportunity, it is not telling you to stay in bed. It is telling you to get up and face the world.

When a dream refers to something that happened during the day, it is not necessarily trying to expose a repressed trauma. It might be helping you to weigh what just happened, the better to know where you were and where you are.

Often, we do not have the time or the inclination to think through all aspects of our experience. We might fixate on the trivial and ignore the essential. If dreaming points us toward what we need to know about the world and our lives, it might be helping us to function more effectively.

Ask yourself this: how long would the human species have survived if dreams had seduced us into avoiding reality in order to get a little more sleep?

Freud believed that dreams were the guardians of sleep, but it makes more sense to say that dreams are the guardians of us.

Of course, Freud was not a progressive thinker. He did not show his patients how to walk boldly into the future. He wanted them to fixate on the past.

Psychoanalysis has always privileged regression over progression. In truth, it has never had any use for progress.

Freud never encouraged his patients to face life's challenges. He often told them to avoid difficult dilemmas until they had fully integrated their past traumas.

By his theory dreams were drawing us back to the past, helping us to understand what went wrong. Freud saw dream images as clues to unsolved crimes and unprocessed traumas.

German-speaking people might have found the argument persuasive. Surely they noticed that the German word for dream, *Traum*, closely resembled the word for trauma, *Trauma*. Was this why Freud believed that the meaning of dreams lay in repressed traumas? Stranger things have happened.

In you believe that human existence is structured like a detective fiction this sounds like a good idea. If you do not, it is not.

There is more to Freud's theory of dreams, and we should examine the rest.

If dreams are trying to tell us something, why don't they say it clearly? Why do they use a congeries of inchoate images to express themselves? Why do they, like Salome, hide their truth behind veils?

Freud pondered the question and lit upon an answer. Your conscious mind does not want to hear the truth, so it obfuscates whatever your unconscious mind is trying to say.

Left to their own devices, he opined, dreams would speak clearly and directly. When their message is filtered through consciousness it becomes garbled.

At times, Freud almost suggested that unconscious ideas are too pure to be grasped by a profane, corrupting agency like consciousness.

He assumed, though not quite in these terms, that consciousness was having illicit relations with reality. Since consciousness makes mental images resemble real objects—the better to help you make your way in the world—it must be an uncertain guide to your hidden desires.

It makes some sense. If you are looking for your desire, you should not look at what you have. You can only desire what you don't have. If you have a Ming vase sitting on the mantle you cannot say that you wish you could have a Ming vase sitting on the mantle.

Since psychoanalytic treatment can only take place when the conscious mind is actively engaged, an analyst must deceive it. Or better, trick it.

He might, for example, pretend that psychoanalysis will help consciousness get into closer touch with reality. It isn't true, but the hope has lured many people into Freudian treatment.

Now, if dreams cannot express themselves clearly, why don't we just ignore them?

When someone says something you can't understand, you might think that he does not know what he is talking about. If so, you have good reason to ignore him. If he cannot make himself understood, why should you bother?

But, if a friend or even an acquaintance whispers something that you don't understand, you will still pay close attention. If his message is that important and that personal, you will make a special effort to find out what he is saying.

Since dreams feel more like whispering than conversing, you are less likely to ignore them.

People have always been intrigued by dreams. Often they haven't cared whether they found the right or the wrong meaning. Some meaning was better than none.

Throughout history humans have used all manner of prophetic arts, from symbology to astrology to necromancy, to decipher dreams.

Authors have written books that claim to reveal the secrets that are hidden in dreams. Often, these decoding devices tell us what we want to hear. Rarely do they tell us what we need to know.

No one should think that he understands a dream because he has learned that swimming in a lake represents a wish to return to the womb or that throwing a football points to a score.

Dream books offer the same interpretations to everyone, so they are ultimately unsatisfying. No one wants to be treated like just anyone.

Freud must have known it, because he personalized the process. He put the intimacy back into dreams. By his theory, dreams are telling you vitally important secrets about yourself.

Thanks to Freud we all believe that we should study our dreams in order to recall the forgotten past. It feels so natural to think that dreams are reconfiguring a lost past that we have failed to see that this theory makes very little sense.

In the book of *Genesis*, when Pharaoh asked Joseph to interpret his dream of seven lean cows devouring seven fat cows, he was not asking Joseph to help him rediscover his lost past in order to juice up his life story.

As you know, Joseph interpreted Pharaoh's dream as a prophecy. Your dreams, he told Pharaoh, are telling you that seven years of plenty will be followed by seven years of famine. By Joseph's reading, Pharaoh's dream was a crop forecast.

Joseph provided Pharaoh with actionable intelligence. The dream was instructing Pharaoh to stock up during the years of abundance, the better to save his people from starvation.

Where Freud saw dreams as crime stories, Joseph saw Pharaoh's dream as a policy proposal. As for Pharaoh's desire, Joseph assumed that the Egyptian ruler wanted to do right by his people.

Freud, however, wanted to do right by his ideas, regardless of what happened to the people. Where Joseph helped Pharaoh plan for the future, Freud remained mired in the past. Joseph read Pharaoh's dream in terms of an ethical obligation to care for his people. Freud believed that dreams were trying to expose a basic human depravity.

They are not the same thing.

Freud and Joseph cannot both be right. To decide who is which we can examine the way the word "dream" is used in everyday conversation.

Your dreams, such as they are, invariably involve your future aspirations and goals. It's normal to say that you dream of becoming a lifeguard or of visiting Nepal. Both count as desires and both point to possible futures.

If dreams are directing you toward the future, they are telling you to make plans and take actions. Isn't this what Joseph told the Pharaoh? When someone recommends that you pursue your dreams he is not suggesting that you dredge up your lost childhood.

If dreaming is like imagining, your dreams are inviting you to use your imagination to chart a path toward future goals. Even if, to take Freud's idea, they are helping you to solve a crime, they are really telling you to bring the perpetrator to justice.

There's more to it than expanded consciousness.

A good Freudian will reply that excavating the past will bring insight and awareness... preferably into your hidden motives, your "darker purpose." He will teach you how to use dream interpretation to discover your moral viciousness, your will to do ill.

But, don't we have other reasons for doing an inventory of past experiences? Sometimes we recollect our past successes in order to shore up our confidence. Recalling the times when we overcame adversity might help us to face a difficult challenge.

If you are looking to your past to find out why you wanted things to go wrong, the process will systematically demoralize you.

Being a pessimist Freud never imagined mining the past for good news. He failed to see that remembering past success improves morale and that obsessing about past trauma depresses.

If dreams are reworking past history, perhaps they are trying to help us to get beyond it. Perhaps they are trying to break our thrall to the past in order to help us see the future more clearly.

Freud believed that dreams were directing us to remember and to integrate unprocessed traumas. If we don't do it, he suggested, we will be condemned to repeat the past.

Believing, as an article of faith, that you cannot get it right unless you know why you got it wrong, Freud failed to see that knowing why you got it wrong tells you nothing about how to get it right.

If you learn why you got it wrong you will be making your mistakes meaningful. The more meaningful they are the more you will be attached to them. The more you are attached to them the more you will have difficulty building the confidence you need to succeed.

Undoubtedly, Freud would have agreed with George Santayana that: "Those who do not remember the past are condemned to repeat it."

But, why did Santayana and Freud assume that we are always going to repeat traumas? Why did they want us to dread the future? After all, if you are dreading the return of the repressed you will not be approaching the future with either confidence or optimism.

In truth, the future never really repeats the past. Freud notwithstanding, Heraclitus was right: you cannot step into the same river twice.

Freud deserves credit for having convinced so many people that looking backwards could be therapeutic. Apparently, he and his followers forgot what happened to Orpheus.

When applied to real people in the real world, Freud's theories make little sense. To make them make sense, we must move into the world of detective fiction.

Freud believed that human minds were haunted by unsolved crimes, thus, by ghosts. He asserted that we cannot move forward with our lives until we solve these crimes and send the ghosts to their eternal reward.

Yet, Freud had little interest in real police work. He was in it for the narrative, so he made literary detectives his role models.

It wasn't happenstance that Freud's favorite Greek tragedy was organized around a criminal investigation. As you know, Oedipus was told that he could only save Thebes from the curse that had befallen it by discovering who had murdered King Laios.

Freud tried to carry the process over into his consulting room. If it worked so well for Oedipus, why shouldn't it work for his patients?

Strangely, or not so strangely, people who try to overcome their mental health issues often do exactly what Freud did not want them to do.

They do it on their own, with friends and family, with religious or social groups, without introspection and without psychoanalysis.

Most especially, they do it by putting their traumas behind them. They work to forget what they cannot stop thinking about, not to remember what they never thought about.

If a bad experience is not relevant to your character, why cling to it as though it were. Why would you want to redefine yourself in terms of past pain?

Putting a trauma behind you is not an easy task. Hearing a reputable mental health professional tell you that it contains your truth can only make the process more difficult.

When an individual has been traumatized he will normally shift into trauma-avoidance mode. He will divide his world into people, places and objects that recall the trauma—and thus that might threaten him—and people, places and objects that will not.

If he has been subjected to a sexual trauma he will seek out and try to avoid or neutralize people, places and objects that he associates with a sexual threat.

In that way, he will move into a new fictional world where characters and actions are defined by the presence or the absence of sexual threats.

In time, he will extricate himself from this fiction by testing his hypotheses against lived experience. The more he sees that his fiction is alienating him from his life the more he will abandon it.

In the end he will not see trauma as a meaningful expression of a repressed fantasy. He will not retreat into his mind in order to avoid reality. Instead, he will refuse to allow the trauma to deconstruct his world. He will live as he would have if he had not been traumatized.

To overcome a trauma, you must resist the pull that wants to make the trauma the meaning of your life. You must fight off the temptation to reside in a fictional world defined by the trauma. And you must understand that your desire to withdraw from reality, to upend your life plans and to disrupt your routines really spells desperation.

It may feel like desire, but it's really despair—trying to take over your life.

Psychoanalysis does not want you to exit the fiction produced by the trauma. It will show you how to create a new world, defined in terms of sexual opportunities and the obstacles that prevent their realization. In his new world other people will become either potential love objects or impediments to *jouissance.*

You will still be living in a fictional world, but now every human encounter will be interpreted as furthering or preventing sexual enjoyment. Since the trauma will still be defining your being in terms of libido and aggression, psychoanalysis will declare that such is your human destiny.

Evidently, this will not make you feel more optimistic about the future. It will do nothing for your mental health or your emotional well-being.

Psychoanalysis is geared toward people who have either suffered sexual traumas or who have wanted to. By Freud's lights, that includes everyone.

Nothing about psychoanalysis can help people to overcome trauma. If we take it on its own terms, as a mental health treatment, it could not but fail.

When a clinician repeatedly fails his patients, he will suffer his own moral traumas. He will suffer, not for what has been done to him but for what he has or has not done to others. Knowing that he has failed them, he will be anguished about being found out to be a fraud.

He might persist in his error because he believes that the cargo planes will eventually land. He might even convince himself that it does not matter whether they land. Still, he will have to defend himself against the negative emotions that accompany repeated failures.

Before Freud tried his technique of dream interpretation on his patients, he applied it to one of his own dreams. As it happened, the dream was about his (and a friend's) professional responsibility for a treatment failure.

In the dream of Irma's injection, as it is commonly known, Freud was worrying about a bad clinical outcome. His close personal friend, the German rhinologist Wilhelm Fliess had botched a surgical procedure on a woman Freud called Irma. After the surgery, Irma suffered intense pains and nasal discharges.

Not knowing what was wrong, Fliess consulted with Freud. The Viennese neurologist declared that Irma was a hysteric. He was wrong. In fact, Fliess had left a long piece of gauze in his patient's nasal cavity during surgery. The doctor had committed medical malpractice.

Freud contributed to the negligence by saying that Irma's problem was in her mind, not in her head.

I will spare you more details and skip to Freud's interpretation:

> *The conclusion of the dream, that is to say, was that I was not responsible for the persistence of Irma's pains, but that Otto was.... The dream acquitted me of responsibility for Irma's condition by showing that it was due to other factors —it produced a whole series of reasons. The dream represented a particular state of affairs as I should have wished it to be.*

In the real world Freud, like his soul mate Fliess, bore responsibility for his patients. In his dream world, he escaped it.

But, what would it have meant to take responsibility? Surely, it would have required more than a new attitude and a few empty words.

If Freud had accepted that he had failed his patients, he would have modified his technique, radically.

Taking responsibility requires that you change what you were doing when you got it wrong. It has nothing to do with making your mistakes meaningful.

Psychoanalysts will counter that when Freud discovered that his treatment of hysteria did not work he changed his theory and practice.

True enough, Freud shifted his focus from forgotten traumas to repudiated desires. Yet, he still believed that patients could be cured by recovering their forgotten past.

He did not ignore the fact that someone might have been molested, but insisted that psychoanalytic work involved uncovering why the patient wanted it to happen.

Some will argue that when Freud became conscious of his own deplorable desire to escape responsibility, he overcame it. Yet, psychoanalysis does not tell patients to discard their worst as so much detritus. It forces them to integrate it into their personal histories.

Normally, taking responsibility involves changing behavior. If you are really going to take responsibility for lying to your neighbor, your apology must be followed by consistent truth-telling. It has nothing to do with how badly you feel, how well you understand why you did it or how you restructure your life story.

Did Freud's dream teach him moral responsibility? Apparently not. When faced with clinical failures, he always shifted the blame. Sometimes, he blamed his patients. Sometimes, he blamed civilization. Sometimes, he blamed human nature.

At its heart, Freudian psychoanalysis is an extended exercise in avoiding responsibility. It takes a long time because it is not very easy to overcome or repeal human nature.

If a patient has made a mistake psychoanalysis will show him why he wanted to do so. Then it will teach him how to do proper penance for his sin. It will not show him how to build character by doing the right thing.

When presented theoretically Freud's ideas have a certain gravitas. After all, Freud saw life as a tragedy. What could be more profound? When translated into clinical practice they become farcical. Examine a fictional case vignette.

Imagine yourself lying on a psychoanalyst's couch, analyzing a dream. You dreamt about taking a little blue pill called Viagra. Or was it Valium? You are feeling blue about your public speaking phobia. You wish there were a pill like Viagra or Valium that could make you a great orator. You would be happy to become a middling orator.

As you are chattering about Viagra or Valium you suddenly have a flashback. You see yourself at age 5 standing in front of your kindergarten class talking about your trip to Niagara Falls.

To your horror, you remember that during your presentation you wet your pants. You may not recall every detail, but your psychoanalyst will show you how to fill in the blanks.

If you only focus on the wet feeling running down your leg or the stain on your pants, your analyst will help you to conjure the image of your classmates laughing at you. From there you will recall the disappointment you saw on your mother's face when she picked you up from the nurse's office that day.

This work will produce a more complete account of a trauma that may or may not have been a life-altering experience of shame. Your analyst will remain unsatisfied.

He wants you to probe beneath the surface in order to suss out your repressed desire. What was your unconscious trying to say when it made you wet your pants in front of your school mates?

To him your self-wetting is a mystery waiting to be solved.

Were you trying to repress your lust for your irresistible kindergarten teacher? Perhaps her shapely legs reminded you of your mother's. Perhaps her hairdo caused you to remember the time when you saw your mother emerge, dripping wet from the swimming pool.

Eventually, your Freudian analyst will tie it all together with an interpretation. He will announce that you have been repressing your desire to do to your mother what your father was doing to her. Now you know why you wet your pants and why you are suffering from a phobia.

Does it make sense? Yes, it does. Will it help you to overcome your phobia? No, it won't.

Miraculously, your analyst will have transformed an experience of shame into one that involves guilt and punishment. He will have shown you how to mitigate some of your psychic pain without changing your behavior.

Thanks to psychoanalysis, you no longer need to go out and take lessons in public speaking. You can cancel your membership in Toastmasters.

If you want to be a good Freudian patient, you will take your analyst's interpretation, assume the attendant guilt, do a little personal penance and inject it all into your new life history. By owning the trauma you will make it meaningful.

Unfortunately, it might become so meaningful that it reinforces your fear that any time you step before an audience you are destined to repeat the kindergarten incident.

But, let's be charitable. Let's say that you now know why you have so few friends and why you are terrified to speak in public. You might also believe that you understand why you chose to become a urologist, a firefighter, an arsonist or a dry cleaner. Isn't insight grand?

Will this knowledge set you free? Will it make you a great orator? Will it make you a better urologist? Will it cause you to lose interest in arson? Will it diminish your attraction to arses?

Experience says that it will not. No serious psychoanalyst would assert that it could.

Even if your fear of public speaking began with your unfortunate experience in kindergarten, the knowledge will not make you a great public speaker. Nor will it make you more gregarious. It is just as likely to make you introverted and self-absorbed.

As treatment, psychoanalysis had to fail. You might be a great urologist who fears public speaking. If your psychoanalysis reveals a disturbing trauma associated with urology, you might feel so self-conscious about your career choice that you become a lesser urologist.

If it teaches you to associate public speaking with a humiliating experience you might feel compelled to avoid all similar engagements.

If you learn that the kindergarten accident drove you to choose a career in dry cleaning, you might be tempted to give it up in favor of a profession that is not tainted by trauma.

If you use your new self-knowledge to blow up your life, that's your problem. Your Freudian analyst will not feel responsible for a bad treatment result.

Normally, he will not feel ashamed for having let it happen, but if he does, he will expiate it with a few rounds of self-criticism, or better, of self-analysis.

Freud held fast to the idea that remembering your forgotten past, embracing your repressed desires, and rewriting your life story would benefit you. It was an original thought. It made for a coherent theory. It established Freud as a genius.

In that and only in that sense, it worked. It might not have done anything for his patients, but it did everything for Freud.

Yet, the truth will out. Psychoanalysis has been falling into desuetude because more and more people have come to agree with Freud —yes, with Freud himself—that it has no future as a clinical practice.

4

WHEN FREUD ARRIVED in Paris in 1885 he was hoping to learn about the most recent advances in neurology. In particular, he wanted to study hysteria. He felt privileged to work under the world's leading authority, Jean-Martin Charcot at the Paris hospital, *La Salpêtrière.*

For six months Freud attended Charcot's lectures and witnessed his clinical case presentations. Being a physician he had ample opportunity to interview the hysterics himself.

Hysteria mostly afflicts young women. The original Greek term meant: "wandering uterus." Hysterics are prone to emotional outbursts and histrionic behaviors. They suffer a variety of somatic disturbances, from inexplicable paralyses to hyperesthesias.

In Freud's day hysteria was something of an epidemic. Young women were complaining of bodily pains, bodily sensitivity and bodily numbness. Medical science, such as it was, could not find a physiological cause for the symptoms.

Some physicians believed that a biological cause would eventually be found. Others concluded that these women were suffering from toxic ideas. If the symptoms had no physical cause, they must have had a metaphysical cause.

During his sojourn in Paris Freud also discovered the erotic side of hysteria. After he returned to Vienna, he reported that Charcot had told him that hysteria always involved *"la chose génitale."* Fascinated and probably puzzled by an experience that was largely foreign to him, Freud started theorizing that hysteria and anxiety neuroses were caused by bad sex.

He soon convinced himself that anxiety neuroses were caused by sexual abstinence, sexual inhibition, prudery, virginity and coitus interruptus.

Freud believed that hysterics had been condemned to sexual frustration by a repressive culture. Yet, *mirabile dictu*, their sexual impulses had found alternate paths to gratification. Eventually, Freud concluded that the sexual impulse could not be denied.

During Charcot's case presentations hysterics often entered into rapturous states. Sometimes they even suffered seizures and convulsions. Many spectators believed that these young women were experiencing something like sexual enjoyment, without the benefit (or detriment) of copulation.

Some of the physicians on Charcot's service concluded that if fantasy-driven sexual release was not a cure, perhaps these patients needed the real thing. They began offering a treatment that Freud described as: *penis normalis, dosim repetatur.*

Freud never alluded to the extracurricular "healing" that was happening in Paris. To my knowledge, it was first mentioned publicly by Surrealist writers Louis Aragon and André Breton in 1928.

In a short essay celebrating hysteria as a great fiction they concluded that it was no longer a viable medical diagnosis. As for the extra-curricular liaisons that had been taking place under Charcot, they challenged Freud to tell what he knew and when he knew it.

They wrote:

> *Freud, qui doit tant à Charcot, se souvient-il du temps où, au témoignage des survivants, les internes de la Salpêtrière confondaient leur devoir professionnel et leur goût de l'amour, où, à la nuit tombante, les malades les rejoignaient au dehors ou les recevaient dans leur lit?*

My translation:

> *Does Freud, who owes so much to Charcot, remember the time when, according to those who were there, the residents at the Salpêtrière confused their professional duty with their taste for love? [Does Freud remember when] at nightfall*

patients got together with their doctors outside of the
hospital or received them in their beds?

If Freud knew about this, he might have imagined that, as a "therapy," it contained a kernel of truth.

If sexual experience was not curing Charcot's hysterics, it must have meant that they were so emotionally damaged that they could not enjoy coitus.

So, Freud seems to have decided that the residents had the right idea, but the wrong organ. They had failed to see that seduction really takes place in the mind.

Good-bye, fornication. Hello, transference love.

Freud came to believe that he could liberate his hysterics' sexuality by seducing their minds. By removing the mental impediments to sexual gratification—that is, their failure to think dirty thoughts—he would show them the way to sexual flourishing.

More literally, where Charcot recommended that physicians apply manual pressure to the women's ovaries Freud applied it to their foreheads.

Apparently, Freud was trying to inject sexual ideas into these women's minds. In his dream of Irma's injection, he saw his friend introducing a substance called Trimethylamin into Irma's head. It is commonly found in seminal fluid.

If this is true, psychoanalysis began as a sublimate of the ineffective treatment that Charcot's residents were offering to hysterics.

At this early stage in his career, Freud believed that hysteria was produced by traumatic sexual abuse. Since proper young ladies did not discuss or even think about such matters, they could not process their traumas normally. Thus, memories of bad sexual experiences had taken up permanent residence in their unconscious minds, there to function as toxins.

Some time after he returned to Vienna, Freud saw that his theory needed revision. The more his hysterics told him that they had been sexually molested the more he doubted their word.

He should also have been suspicious when they eagerly told stories that, by his theories, they should have been trying to repress.

For the first and last time, Freud corrected himself. If his hysterics were not telling him what had happened, they must have been telling him what they had wanted to happen. If they were not recounting facts, they must have been exposing their desires.

In particular, they were exposing desires that they refused to accept as their own.

Hysterics who said that they had been molested against their will were denying their depraved desire. They were pretending to be saintly martyrs, victims of sexual predators. In truth, they were witches consorting with devils.

In Freud's new fiction, hysterics had not been sexually abused by real men. They had been fornicating with phantoms. Naturally, they wanted to forget it.

Freud invented psychoanalysis when he declared, in so many words, that hysterics were sinners who refused to accept their sinfulness. Naturally, his technique came to resemble a criminal investigation—or inquisition—that would force these women to admit to having practiced witchcraft.

He did not put it in these terms, but Freud's new theory implied that conversion symptoms were marks that the devil had left on a hysteric's flesh. If they were signs of the hysteric's desire, not for God, but for the devil, they were the inverse of the invisible stigmata borne by St. Catherine of Siena.

Freud's initial victim narrative had allowed hysterics to retain a shred of their dignity. In his new theory they lost even that.

True Freudians will tell you that the shift from the seduction theory to psychoanalysis was a momentous event.

Sometimes they explain it by saying that Freud changed his mind because he had undergone a pre-psychoanalytic treatment, a self-analysis.

But, why did Freud need therapy? Was he anguished to see that the talking cure continued to be ineffective? Did he believe that he had unconsciously wanted to fail?

Did he really want these young women to be healthy and sane? Or, did a "darker purpose" obstruct the path to cure?

Freud acted as though he had been inspired by a text from the Gospel according to Luke: "Physician, heal thyself!"

Of course, he might have wanted to try his new therapy on himself before he foisted it on an unsuspecting public. He would not have been the first physician to experiment on himself.

Yet, there was something different about Freud's quest for his unconscious desire.

By directing his self-analysis toward the question of his desire he made it clear that he was not a scientist. How many scientists believe that their experiments fail because they do not really want them to succeed? How many physicians believe that a medicine does not work because they do not want it to work?

To be fair, it is also possible that Freud was suffering from an emotional problem of his own. One suspects that this chronically pessimistic man was depressed.

Since psychoanalysis had not yet been invented, Freud enlisted the services of his rhinologist friend, Wilhelm Fliess. The latter lived in Berlin, so the doctors had to communicate via letters. In his missives Freud explored his mind by analyzing his dreams. The letters are commonly referred to as his writing cure.

Did Freud's writing cure help? It seems that it did not. At the least, it failed to teach him optimism. By convincing him that the human mind was structured like a Greek tragedy it mired him more deeply in the slough of despond.

Had Freud's writing cure relieved his depression he would not have had to medicate himself with massive doses of a powerful anti-depressant: nicotine. Addicted to cigars, he smoked upwards of twenty a day.

While doing his writing cure Freud recalled a childhood memory of his alluring half-naked young mother. Counting it an epiphany, he concluded that his unconscious was trying to tell him that he really wanted to copulate with her.

Dubbing himself a "budding Oedipus" he drew the logical conclusion: he could only fulfill his wish by removing the obstacle that was standing in his way. He had to murder his father.

In a strange *argumentum ad anecdotem* Freud reasoned that if the Oedipus complex explained his motives then it also explained everyone else's.

Leaping effortlessly from a childhood memory to a Greek tragedy to a theory that explained human motivation, Freud declared that the Oedipus complex had to be universally true because all people at all times in all places had responded emotionally to a single play.

He was assuming that all people at all times in all places possessed a high level of intellectual sophistication. *Oedipus Tyrannos* is not pop culture.

Freud never justified choosing the Sophoclean tragedy and not another piece of dramatic literature. It was certainly not the only work of art that had moved large numbers of people.

Unabashedly proud of his discovery, Freud announced that he had solved the riddle of the mind's intentions. By his lights, we only want one thing in life, we have only wanted one thing in life and we will only want one thing in life... but we cannot have it.

That thing is... to copulate with our mothers!

Why can't we have what we want? Our fathers have forbidden it.

According to Freud, this idea tells you all you need to know about human motivation.

Reducing the dizzying complexity of human motives to a single narrative sounds too good to be true. It is.

The Oedipal formula is simple to the point of simplemindedness. If my rendition reads like a caricature, it's because the theory is a caricature. If a single idea explains everything, it explains nothing.

When he first discovered the Oedipus complex Freud must have believed that it would be an effective psycho-surgical instrument. As more and more of his patients confessed to having an Oedipus complex he probably became suspicious. When they did not get better, he must have doubted his theory.

It must have appeared that his initial failure to cure hysterics was being repeated in his properly psychoanalytic work. Could it have been a return of the repressed?

Freud could not accept that he had failed. He could not accept responsibility, either. So, he lit on an alternate explanation.

He surmised that his patients were just pretending to embrace the Oedipal truth. They were trying to trick him, even to patronize him by paying lip service to his ideas, and not in the good way. In more vulgar terms, Freud suspected that they were faking it.

Since he could not use the power of the Church to extract confessions, he decided that he needed to give his patients more time to convince themselves that he was right. He averred that the cure for ineffective psychoanalysis was more ineffective psychoanalysis.

In a late essay, "Psychoanalysis Terminable and Interminable" he wrote that some people might require endless psychoanalysis. Apparently, some patients preferred death to Freud's interpretations.

Either way, Freud's followers were thrilled with the concept of endless analysis. With one stroke their guru had provided a pseudo-theoretical argument that "confirmed" the correctness of his interpretations while shifting the blame for poor results on to his patients. If treatment could last forever, there was no point in time when one could say definitively that it did not work.

With his concept of endless treatment Freud also made psychoanalytic patients into living annuities. His followers were overwhelmed with gratitude.

Psychoanalysis may not have been foolproof, but Freud made it failproof. Thereby, he fulfilled his fondest wish. He absolved himself of responsibility for bad clinical results.

But, why did patients continue treatment for years, even decades without receiving any therapeutic benefit? It's puzzling.

We can solve this enigma by seeing psychoanalysis as a religious experience, not as a medical treatment.

Waiting to be cured is one thing; waiting for forgiveness and absolution is something else.

Like it or not, psychoanalytic treatment is rooted in the sacrament of confession. Like penitent sinners psychoanalytic patients feel duty bound to spend their session time speaking ill of themselves. They believe that it is pointless to waste their time recounting good news.

Once they get in touch with their guilt, they learn to do penance and submit themselves to bouts of moral self-flagellation, that is, to self-criticism.

They are awaiting something that, heretofore, had only been given by priests. That is: absolution. Sadly, psychoanalysts have convinced their patients that if they do not receive Freudian absolution, they will continue to be haunted by their repressed depraved desires, thus, their sins.

If the ploy seems ignoble, that's because it is.

Many psychoanalysts will object to my comparing their pseudo-science to a religion. If so, they will not be happy to learn that, from the beginning, Freud saw himself as a father confessor. In *Studies on Hysteria*, he described his role as a therapist:

One works to the best of one's power, as an elucidator (where ignorance has given rise to fear), or a teacher, as the representative of a freer or superior view of the world, as a father confessor who gives absolution, as it were, by a continuance of his respect after the confession has been heard.

Truly zealous patients have never been satisfied with mere absolution. They have felt that their superior dedication to the Freudian cause should merit a higher reward: indulgences.

Traditionally, Roman Catholics have received indulgences from the Church. Roughly speaking, indulgences are get-out-of-jail-free cards. Sinners who possess them go straight to Heaven without having to pass through Purgatory.

When, in days of yore, Church officials were selling indulgences, those who purchased them could, effectively, go out and sin with impunity. The Church stopped selling them in 1567, but the faithful can still earn them by performing charitable acts.

It has been left for psychoanalysis to restore the darker side of the practice. And, thanks to Freud, it has infiltrated the culture at large, in the guise of permissiveness. Many people feel empowered by their analysts and therapists to indulge their appetites, their whims and their fantasies.

If the ambient culture tends toward permissive parenting, we owe it, perhaps indirectly, to Freud. If parents tend to indulge their children's desires, we owe that also, perhaps indirectly, to Freud. If we have all accepted, rather mindlessly that we have no right to judge anyone for anything, we are living in a culture that has suffered the influence, however indirectly, of Freud's ideas.

Psychoanalysis began by masquerading as a science, but it has survived by becoming a stealth religion.

It has sacraments, rituals and ceremonies. It has sacred texts, dogmatic truths, true believers and cult followers. In some places it even has an Index of forbidden texts. And it has created and sustained its own communities, real and virtual. Some of its patients and practitioners have even martyred themselves for the Freudian cause.

Obviously, the Freudian pseudo-religion differs radically from Judeo-Christianity. Psychoanalysis promotes permissiveness and devalues character. It glorifies histrionic displays of emotion over more temperate expressions. It produces people who are more prone to indulge their appetites than to discipline them. It prefers empty assertions of self-esteem to earned self-confidence. It has never encouraged humility and has always been at war with modesty.

In the Freudian pseudo-religion the "content of your character" is far less important than what you can get away with.

The Freudian cult also differs from real religions because it does not create a real congregation, a community or a fellowship. You cannot found a social group on the principle that everyone wants to aggress his neighbor and to copulate with his neighbor's wife.

Lacan imagined that psychoanalysis had created a new way for people to form social connections. He should have added that it would feel very much like living theatre or permanent psychodrama.

Unfortunately, characters in a play do not connect. In trying to make life imitate art psychoanalysis has only produced asocial discon-nections.

Lacan did not see that newness is not necessarily a sign of goodness or truthiness. If no one thought of it before, that might mean that the idea was not worth thinking.

5

FREUD DID NOT discover just any old meaning. He did not discover the meaning of life. He did not want to make your life more meaningful. He never sought the golden mean.

Instead, he fixated on meanings that scare us half to death or make us sick to our stomachs. Good deeds and good intentions have no place in Freudian theory.

Some people see the glass half-full. Some people see it half-empty. Freud saw it as empty.

The only "mean" that comports with Freud's attitude is: mean-spirited. It is hardly what you would expect from a member of a healing profession.

Freud said it himself:

> *I have found little that is 'good' about human beings on the whole. In my experience most of them are trash, no matter whether they publicly subscribe to this or that ethical doctrine or to none at all. That is something that you cannot say aloud, or perhaps even think.*

Freud believed that people suffered mental illness because they refused accept their malign nature. Those who thought they were performing good deeds were denying their evil wishes.

To Freud, the meaning was the motive, and the motive was to do ill.

It is neither healthy nor helpful to see human beings in such a negative light. Lost in his theories, Freud failed to see that his relentless focus on life's tragedies could only make people depressed.

If life is a Greek tragedy, why not give up? If an effort to live a decent and honorable life is an exercise in futility, why bother? The Chorus in *Oedipus at Colonus* sounded Freudian when it concluded that, for human beings, the best was never to have been born and the second best was to die as soon as possible.

Freud did not allow his train of thought to reach this destination. Nevertheless, the inference is logical.

In *Learned Optimism* Martin Seligman explained that people become depressed when they give up trying. Convinced that life is a lose-lose proposition, they withdraw into themselves and introspect.

If Seligman was right—and I believe he was—Freudian psychoanalysis has produced a lot more depression than it has cured.

This should not come as news. If life is a Greek tragedy writ large, happiness must be an illusion. As Freud himself said: "...the goal of psychoanalysis is to turn neurotic misery into ordinary, everyday unhappiness."

It's a distinction without a difference. And it is decidedly self-serving. If human beings are destined to be unhappy they cannot blame psychoanalysis for failing to make them happy.

Freud could not accept that true happiness was achievable. His followers have driven his argument to its logical terminus. If you are happy, healthy, sensible and serene they will say that you are in denial. If you like other people and are liked by them, true Freudians will take it as an offense against their theory.

For that they will make you pay.

Whatever your ostensible reason for stepping into the *sanctum sanctorum* of a psychoanalyst's office, once you are there you will encounter someone who feels morally obligated, not to help you to solve your problems or to show you the way to happiness, but to undermine your character.

However heroic you think you are, however charitable you have been, however honest and decent you claim to be, your Freudian psychoanalyst will tell you that you are up to no good.

You think you have acted courageously. Through the lens of Freudian theory you want to murder your father.

You think that you are the soul of charity. A Freudian will say that you gain a sadistic thrill watching other people suffer.

If you pride yourself on your industriousness a Freudian will tell you that your work ethic is disguising your repressed anal-erotic instincts.

If psychoanalysis convinces you that these are the meaning of your life, you will not end up feeling very good about yourself.

The more Freud's ideas were disseminated the more they became self-fulfilling prophecies. Patients who knew about Freud's tragic vision tailored their communications to fulfill their analysts' expectations.

Those who did not get the memo might have started treatment by presenting their good, their bad and their ugly. When their wily psychoanalysts ignored the good in favor of the bad and the ugly, they eventually got the message.

In Freudian practice, patients who brought good news were bad patients. If they got better too soon, they were told that they were resisting the truth. If they were proud of the way they were conducting their lives they were pronounced unanalyzable.

Psychoanalysis has always diminished, demeaned, debased and degraded human beings. Why else would its practitioners systematically give people "the silent treatment?"

Giving someone the silent treatment for no reason is extremely rude and morally corrosive. Anyone who does so is inflicting emotional harm.

Psychoanalysts do not see it this way. They believe that sitting there like deadwood makes them a silent audience. Thus, they are encouraging their patients to turn their lives into drama.

Other analysts see their sessions as psychic hazing, an initiation into a cult. If the process numbs you to abuse, you can become a true Freudian.

Under normal circumstances you would never accept being treated as badly as a psychoanalyst treats his patients. You would quickly dissociate yourself from someone who shunned you because you asked him for help.

If you are undergoing psychoanalysis you do not have the option. You are not allowed to see your analyst's behavior as insulting. You must think that it's meaningful. If it tastes bad it must be good medicine.

To be a good patient, you must accept that your analyst is mistreating you because you are unworthy of anything else. Surely, he knows something about you that you do not know. If he didn't, why would you be paying him?

In treatment, you will be tasked with making the silent treatment make sense. You can do it by revealing the worst about yourself, whether in word, thought or deed. You will hope that once you make your analyst feel that he was right to treat you rudely, he will talk to you.

The more you slander yourself the more you will absolve your analyst of his bad behavior. Your self-derogating comments will allow your analyst to believe that he is not doing anything wrong.

If you want to be a good patient—who doesn't?—you will become an association mill, filling the dead air of your analyst's office with all manner of wretched blather.

This can continue for weeks, months or even years. With any luck, your analyst will eventually tell you what it all means. Invariably, his interpretation will expose your mind's repressed criminal tendencies. I promise you, it will not make you look good.

When your analyst interprets, he will expect you to provide confirming material. You must conjure up a memory or a fantasy that demonstrates, to his satisfaction that he was right. If you don't, you will be sentenced to three more years of treatment.

If you want to complete the process you must fulfill your appointed task: to rationalize your analyst's blind faith in Freud. Then he will grant you absolution and perhaps an indulgence or two.

Psychoanalysis is a drawn-out process. It seeks to draw you out of your life and into psychoanalysis. A good Freudian will want your work with him to be your most meaningful life experience.

If you want to excel at it, you should withdraw from your world. Of course, this will make you more dependent on your analyst's approval. If he is the only person who stands between you and social oblivion, you will feel compelled to think as he wants you to think.

The process will impact your everyday life. The less your analyst cares about your life, the less you will. If he ignores your real dilemmas you will come to believe that they don't matter.

Clinically speaking, it cannot work. If you, as a patient, pour out your soul to someone who is only interested in what is wrong with you, you will eventually believe that mistakes define you.

After a time, you will sink into a mild chronic depression and will become more dysfunctional.

If you alienate friends and family, you will find yourself increasingly isolated. Getting rejected by your entourage will make it appear that your analyst was right to mistreat you.

When Freud invented psychoanalysis he prescribed one session a day, six days a week. He could not have done much more to make psychoanalysis central to his patients' lives.

Not wanting his patients to become too involved with reality Freud invented the rule of abstinence. (It resembles a vow of chastity.) He told them to abstain from making major life decisions until they completed treatment.

By imposing this rule Freud thought that he was doing his patients a favor. He believed that their minds were so contaminated by unanalyzed neurosis that they could not possibly make sane decisions about important matters.

The less a patient cared about his everyday life the more he would feel attached to his analyst. He might, in the best cases, even come to love him... as the one and only. Thus, he would develop what Freud called transference.

Freud thought he could cure a patient's inability to form durable love relationships by inducing him to get involved in yet another disappointing, unfulfilling and dysfunctional love relationship... this time, with his psychoanalyst. He called it transference and declared it to be love.

Later psychoanalysts, drunk on analogies, compared this new relationship to a specimen that could be examined under the psychoanalytic microscope. They pretended that it was the perfect way for a patient to learn why he kept failing at love.

Freud based his theory on a dubious assumption. He believed that transference would replicate a patient's relationship pattern, or better, that it would reenact the repressed fantasy that was causing him to fail at love.

But, what if transference is merely a contrivance, an artifice that has nothing to do with the way the patient conducts his real life? Why would the stressful and abusive experience called psychoanalysis reveal anyone's truth?

Here's how transference is supposed to work.

Imagine that you, as a patient, are angry with your perfectly blank analyst. Normally, you feel anger because of something that someone has done. When you express the anger to the other person, he will accept that he provoked it and will apologize. When you, decent human being, forgive him, your anger will dissipate.

As you know, psychoanalysts do not believe that they are responsible for their patients' emotions. They underwent years of training in order to learn never to say they're sorry.

They tell themselves, and at times they tell their patients that since they are just sitting there silently, like blank screens, they have nothing to do with their patients' emotional reactions. Psychoanalysts are very good at protesting their innocence. Some even see themselves as saints.

Obviously, they are posturing. Their claim of innocence is a ruse. Only a dupe would believe it.

Think about it. When someone gives you the silent treatment for no reason, you will normally feel anger. It is an appropriate emotional response.

When you get angry at your analyst, he will explain that you cannot possibly be angry at him. You must be transferring unprocessed anger from your past onto poor innocent him. He might tell you that you are angry at him because you are afraid to get angry with your father.

By definition, an important emotion expressed in analysis is always transferred from somewhere else. Your analyst will teach you that your feelings toward him, be they anger or even lust, are always misdirected. If you disagree, he will tell you that you are resisting and will prescribe five more years on the couch.

By the rule of transference you are expressing your anger to the wrong person at the wrong time in the wrong place under the wrong circumstances. If so, psychoanalysis has given you yet another chance to get things wrong. By interpreting your transference, your analyst will try to make it meaningful, but a meaningful bad habit is still a bad habit.

Once you spend a lot of money making your bad habit meaningful, you will, as the saying goes, own it. It will feel like an integral part of your being. Try breaking it then.

Nothing about the process will teach you how to obey the Aristotelian imperative: to say the right thing to the right person at the right time in the right place under the right circumstances.

Unfortunately, transference is not the only bad habit that psychoanalysis teaches. It also forces you to learn free association.

It would have been bad enough if Freud had *recommended* that his patients master the arts of being boring and obnoxious. Instead, he took a step into ignominy by making free association a condition of treatment. Were it not for Freud I doubt that very many people would try to master such a useless skill.

Most of us temper our verbal offerings in order to connect with our friends and neighbors. If an injudicious thought pops into mind, we often choose not to share it. We respect the feelings of others and do not make a fetish of our own.

Instinctively, we are programmed to get along with other people. Getting along becomes impossible when you express whatever is passing through your mind. Most of it is not worth sharing, anyway. You do not make a habit of blurting out insults or making offensive and tedious comments in normal conversation.

It ought to be self-evident, but no one can conduct his life successfully by saying whatever comes to mind. Who would want to associate with someone who, when he is not boring you to tears or giving offense is revealing his wife's secrets?

Freud rationalized free association by saying that normal speech was censored speech. Seeing himself as an intrepid culture warrior, he thought he was freeing his patients from culturally imposed censorship.

To his discredit, Freud tricked people into believing that thinking out loud was healthier than tailoring their speech to maintain harmonious relationships. If you should be foolish enough to try this at home you will discover that it will turn your relationships into recurring psychodrama.

Many people have accepted this idea, uncritically. Yet, it is far from obvious that uncensored verbiage is more truthful than conversational speech. Words that you expel under stress might just be neuronal static.

Free association is mindless meandering. If you do it right, you will produce a string of incoherent and distasteful verbal fragments. In principle, these are the verbal equivalent of your rebus-like dreams.

Freud believed that free association would allow patients to access their unconscious thoughts in nearly raw form. He thought that it would show them how to let their unconscious minds speak.

A psychoanalyst might object to my presentation here. He certainly does not encourage his patients to free associate outside of session. He expects that they will revert to normal speech once they step into the real world.

But, if a patient has one tactful Self and another tactless Self, how can he tell which is his real Self? Since a Self divided against itself cannot stand, as soon as a psychoanalytic patient rises from the couch he will face a dilemma: his psychoanalysis or his life?

Will he go back to a habit that his analyst told him was contributing to his neurosis or will he continue to bed down with the truth?

Obviously, free association is as much a problem as a solution. Lacan offered the most serious attempt to justify it. Or better, to redeem it. Wanting to make tactlessness into an art form, he suggested that learning to associate freely would help you to access your inner poet.

He even implied that speaking more poetically would equip you to seduce people. When you say what you mean and mean what you say you are not being mysterious.

Language that refers to objective realities contains no mystery. Telling someone that the cat is on the mat does not invite sleuthing. To be a great seducer, you must surround yourself with mystery.

Isn't that what analysts do? Isn't their blank screening an effort to be mysterious? Isn't their failure to converse a lure, intended to incite their patients to seek a hidden meaning in their every gesture?

In the psychoanalytic process patient and analyst never converse and never connect. Their world is defined by desire—by wishes, dreams and imaginings. In such a world there are no objective facts that can serve as common ground.

The best they can do is to inhabit the same fiction, the same play. In some cases they will become characters in the great historical drama called Freudian psychoanalysis.

With his analyst's help a good patient will find the meaning in his verbal meandering and will turn his associations into stories.

More often than not, his analyst will be unsatisfied with his efforts. This will incite him to tell more and more stories. Beyond the challenge of keeping his analyst awake, he will be looking for the story to end all stories, the one that will gain him absolution and liberation... from analysis.

Truth be told, psychoanalysis is overpriced storytelling. It is *Scheherazade* without the happy ending.

6

IF, AS FREUD believed, the tragedy of Oedipus is the meaning of our lives, we are all destined to be sacrificial victims, as in, scapegoats.

Since the Greek word for tragedy, *tragoidia*, means the "goat's song," it makes sense that the tragic hero is a scapegoat, someone whose punishment will atone for someone else's sin.

True, Oedipus was brought down by his own hubris, but he was also atoning for his father's sin.

When Laios, the father of Oedipus, was a young man, he tutored Chryssipus the youngest son of Pelos, king of Pisa. One day Laios kidnapped and raped the boy. Later, Chryssipus committed suicide and the gods cursed the descendants of Laios, beginning with his son Oedipus.

Trapped in a script that was not of his making, Oedipus lived it as a tragic hero.

Many heroes do not live tragedies. Some set an example that inspires or encourages us. When we follow their lead we put ourselves on the road to success. Freud notwithstanding, all roads do not lead to doom.

Like Oedipus, tragic heroes have no real choice in what will happen to them. Since the outcome of their stories seems inevitable, they are portrayed as lacking free will.

Epic heroes are not fated to be brought down by their hubris. Whether they compete in the arena or set off on a quest their ending does not feel predetermined.

Case in point: Odysseus.

Think about it: what would psychotherapy and its culture look like today if Freud had fixated on Odysseus instead of Oedipus.

A reader might be inspired by Odysseus. He might emulate the great hero in order to build his own character. He might work at achieving a comparable success.

If you see yourself as a budding Odysseus you will direct your energy toward competing in the marketplace or the arena. You will know that you might, by using your cunning and your wits, overcome adversity and live happily ever after.

The Odyssey is a comedy. It ends with a loving reconciliation between Odysseus and his wife, Penelope.

Oedipus Tyrannos is a tragedy. No member of Oedipus's family achieves anything that resembles happiness. His story ends when his youngest child, Antigone, hangs herself.

No spectator has ever been inspired by the story of Oedipus. No one wants to emulate his example. People dread ending up like Oedipus.

That was why the morose Dr. Freud chose him.

Unlike Oedipus, Odysseus had choices. True enough, he was cursed by a god, in his case by Poseidon. Even though Poseidon delayed Odysseus's return to Ithaka, he did not make the great voyager into a tragic hero.

As opposed to Oedipus, Odysseus exercised free will. He was not cursed to be sacrificed for someone else's sin.

When the Homeric hero rejoined his wife Penelope, he earned a moral triumph. It was not a scripted event.

By calling Odysseus "cunning," Homer was saying that the hero's wits determined his destiny. Things could easily have turned out differently for him and Penelope.

The same cannot be said of Oedipus, King of Thebes. Cursed by a god, Oedipus was trapped. The story makes it appear that nothing could have prevented the god's curse from being fulfilled.

When Oedipus, as a young man, learned of his fate, he tried to run away from it. When he did, he ran into it. Presumably, resistance was futile.

Oedipus and Odysseus both saved their respective cities from corruption and pollution, but they used radically different means.

Oedipus saved Thebes from a plague by becoming a sacrificial victim. Thereby, he expiated his and his father's crimes.

Odysseus rid his home of the unruly and depraved suitors by the force of his arms. He shot them, one by one.

Oedipus and Odysseus faced markedly different challenges. Thebes was suffering from an unpunished crime. Ithaka had fallen into chaos because its leader was absent.

Oedipus was a criminal. Odysseus, we might say, was derelict in his civic and conjugal duties.

Oedipus sacrificed himself to assuage guilt. Odysseus restored group pride by acting decisively and forcefully. His leadership brought order back to his city.

Oedipus atoned for his and his father's guilt, but he also brought shame on Thebes. Odysseus restored community pride.

No one would imagine emulating Oedipus or Jocasta. Everyone would do well to emulate Odysseus or Penelope.

The story of Oedipus shows neither virtue nor cunning. In the *Odyssey*, virtue and cunning are rewarded.

For Oedipus life was a tragedy whose ending was beyond his control. Odysseus saw life as a game. In many ways he was its master.

The cunning Odysseus invented the ruse that ended the stalemated Trojan War. For him war was more game than drama. On its chessboard he made a decisive move with his horse.

Oedipus was a murderer; Odysseus was a warrior. Oedipus committed crimes; Odysseus competed on the battlefield.

Odysseus fought in someone else's war, but he was not cursed to play a role in someone else's drama. Whether it was the Trojan War, his phantasmagorical voyages or his encounter with the suitors, he was involved in games whose outcome was uncertain.

Oedipus was given his wife by the grateful citizens of Thebes. Odysseus had to win back his wife by drawing the great bow and engaging in mortal combat against her many suitors.

Odysseus and Penelope have no place in Freudian storytelling. Their exploits and their travails cannot be reduced to polymorphously perverse impulses.

Moreover, their story does not induce you to look back into the past. It points you toward future success.

Freud had no use for an epic hero like Odysseus. He did not and could not see human existence as a game.

Preferring tragic certainty to comic uncertainty, Freud accepted that it would all end badly. He thought that it was the tough-minded thing to do. He must have believed that it was better than not knowing how it would end.

By seeing life as a tragedy Freud attained a degree of certainty he could never have found in a competitive arena. If you believe that life always ends in death there is no chance that you will be proved wrong. If you want always to be right, death can be your helpmate.

If death is both inevitable and tragic, every new day brings you closer to an unhappy ending. You can slow down the process by reversing the forward motion, but that is the best you can do.

If that is your goal, you can make good use of regression. By going back in time you can convince yourself that you have put off the inevitable. Eventually, the process will remove you from your life.

If death is the ultimate human certainty, the afterlife must be the ultimate uncertainty. No one knows for certain what comes after death or even whether anything comes after death.

How should people negotiate the uncertainty? Pascal recommended that we think of it as a gamble. He suggested that we should see ourselves as players whose actions might influence the outcome.

As you know, Pascal recommended that we wager on the possibility of eternal life. By his calculus, if we accept God and act virtuously we have relatively little to lose and everything to gain.

If we are wrong, we will have sacrificed a few cheap thrills. If we are right, we will be rewarded with an eternity of bliss.

If there is a God and if He has a say in what comes after life, rejecting Him in favor of sin will put your soul at grave risk. If you are wrong you will be punished with hellish pain. You might ask how a just God could punish a lifetime of frivolity with an eternity of pain, but that is off the topic.

If you can wager on (or against) Paradise, you are free to influence the outcome, for better or for worse.

Once you accept the uncertainty that shrouds the afterlife, you will leave the theatre and enter the arena. You will be assuming a greater risk, but you will also be accepting more freedom and more responsibility.

Such is life when life is not scripted. If there is no script and if your decisions are not being directed by another mind, you are responsible for them.

When actions are chosen freely, you cannot know the outcome. Therefore, Jean-Paul Sartre said, you will always, upon taking action, suffer some anxiety while awaiting the results. It is, he suggested, the cost of freedom.

For Freud, however, anxiety was a form of guilt. When you are overcome by anxiety, you are anticipating punishment for a sin of word, thought or deed.

In psychoanalysis, anxiety bespeaks an awaited, but inevitable punishment, not an uncertain outcome.

By making anxiety a function of guilt, Freud offered an easy and private way out. You can do penance; you can submit yourself to self-criticism; you can try to discover why you wanted to fail.

If your action was not engaged freely you do not need to address the consequences. You do not need to make a public apology, to make amends or to change your ways.

Freud might have thought he was solving the problem of anxiety. In truth, he was begging the question.

7

PSYCHOANALYSIS WANTS YOU to think the worst of yourself. According to Freud, your worst is your truth.

Freudians believe that those who think the worst of themselves are morally superior. By their reasoning, those who think ill of themselves are superior to those who think well of themselves. They are even superior to those who do not think about themselves at all.

Call it false pride if you like, but it's better than no pride.

Freud seemed to believe that, by disparaging human nature, he was being original. He even declared that his concept of infantile sexuality had corrected the age-old illusion that children were innocent.

About this he was either wrong or deceptive. Augustine and Aquinas had long asserted that children were born sinners and that their sins involved concupiscence or libido.

Protestant theologians also embraced the concept of a sexual original sin.

Martin Luther declared that: "...all men are full of evil lust and inclinations from their mothers' wombs...."

In his turn, John Calvin added:

> Original sin, therefore, seems to be a hereditary depravity
> and corruption of our nature, diffused into all parts of the
> soul, which first makes us liable to God's wrath, then also
> brings forth in us those works which Scripture calls "works
> of the flesh" (Gal 5:19). And that is properly what Paul often
> calls sin. The works that come forth from it – such as

71

adulteries, fornications, thefts, hatreds, murders, carousings – he accordingly calls "fruits of sin" (Gal 5:19–21), although they are also commonly called "sins" in Scripture, and even by Paul himself.

Whatever Freud did or did not know about the theology of original sin, the concept haunts his theories... in strange ways.

Remember, Freud began his career by insisting that hysteria could only be cured by unearthing an initiating, original sexual trauma.

Decades later, when he was fully engaged in psychoanalytic work, he argued that one of his patients had become neurotic because he had, as a baby, witnessed a traumatic primal scene.

Where Christian thinkers, both Catholic and Protestant, believed that human depravity could be redeemed through God's grace, Freud took a different tack.

To the gullible he offered the prospect of cure. To intellectuals he offered enlightened self-knowledge. For everyone else he intimated that he could free them from Western civilization itself.

Since Freud believed that Western civilization, through its institutions, was producing neurosis by repressing libido, he must have believed, somewhere in his heart, that psychoanalysis could not offer its own version of grace—that is, cure—until it had its own alternative church, that is, its own counterculture.

Freud wanted to draw people away from religions that demanded instinctual renunciation. He wanted to help create a new culture where they could live in accord with their more degenerate impulses, much as the pre-Christian Romans did.

Having begun as a physician treating mental illness, Freud eventually realized that his method would be put to better use if he aimed at civilizational transformation.

Of course, he did not use the term "civilization." His British translator, James Strachey, chose the word to render the German, *Kultur*. We usually translate that word as "culture."

Normally, we see civilization as a stage of cultural development. We believe it to be an advance over savagery and barbarism.

When Freud was referring to culture or civilization, he must have been thinking primarily of Western or Judeo-Christian civilization.

When we speak of a culture, we are referring to the principles and precepts, customs and mores, rules and values that organize human community. Living in a culture means following certain rules, holding certain values and participating in the rituals and ceremonies that affirm them.

In Freud's time Austrians would also have associated the word *Kultur* with the *Kulturkampf* or culture war that German Chancellor Otto von Bismarck had been waging against the Catholic Church.

Everyone knows that Freud grew up in an epoch that was defined in Europe by the person of Victoria, Queen of England. Yet, a man who lived in Austria during the latter half of the nineteenth century must have suffered the influence of the Iron Chancellor.

In 1871, when Freud was fifteen, Bismarck launched a culture war. In particular, the Protestant Bismarck wanted to repress Roman Catholicism in Germany. Thereby, he wrote a new chapter in the centuries-old struggle between Protestantism and the Catholic Church.

Before declaring culture war, Bismarck had won real wars against two of his most powerful Catholic neighbors, Austria and France. By winning the Austro-Prussian War in 1866 Bismarck established Prussia's power over Austria. Four years later Bismarck defeated France in the Franco-Prussian war.

After demonstrating Prussian military superiority, Bismarck started a *Kulturkampf* to assert another kind of dominance.

While Great Britain and Prussia had embraced the Industrial Revolution, France and Austria had chosen not to rush into industrialization. Holding fast to traditional community structures they had staked their prestige on their prowess at art and leisure, dancing and perfume, cheese and pastry.

By rapidly industrializing, Prussia increased its military power. It followed naturally that the nation would become more bellicose.

Industrialization and militarization fit together, even culturally. If industrialization produces anomie, military mobilization provides an antidote. It offers membership in a social organization that possesses a clear set of rules.

When you join a military organization, you know who you are, what the rules are, what you have to do and what your purpose is. For many people it is vastly better than anomie.

People fight wars to gain or defend territory and to compete for status against other cultures. But military service also imposes order on society. This may be more important than a will to destroy.

Freud did not see psychological distress in social terms. An inside/out thinker, he believed that an inner mental conflict between ego and libido was being projected onto the world stage in a battle between civilization and sexual desire.

In this conflict, Freud sided with libido. Yet, he barely distinguished between different attitudes toward sex. Surely, different modern cultures see and practice sexuality differently. Whatever its discontents, civilization is not the same throughout the world. It is not even the same across Europe.

Occasionally, Freud expressed contempt for American Puritanism and Victorian prudery, but he did not distinguish between Catholic and Protestant attitudes toward libido. He rarely referred to the sexually repressive Jewish culture in which he had been raised.

Freud must have believed that Protestant cultures, with their Puritanism and their work ethic had wrung the pleasure out of sex. He must have judged that British and German cultures, in particular, had purchased economic prosperity and military success at the expense of sensual delight.

Freud's theory could have consoled his fellow Austrians. Even if they were falling behind in the marketplace and in military competition, they were having better sex.

For Austria's cultural enemies, his theories might have functioned as psy-ops. Freud was telling the denizens of the Anglosphere to abandon their principles, their factories, their freedoms and their sense of propriety, and to return to their instinctual roots.

By all appearances, Protestant cultures discouraged the free and open expression of sexuality. Valuing modesty and humility over histrionics and public eroticism, they disapproved of shameless self-exposure and excessive psychodrama.

It may not seem intuitively obvious, but if Freud had wanted to lead the march toward greater sensuality, he should have embraced Roman Catholicism.

It is relatively easy to grasp the cultural differences between the two most important branches of Christianity.

Take two of their leading European capitals: Paris and London.

Where Paris has been associated with high fashion, London is known for bespoke tailoring. That does not mean that there are no great tailors in Paris or that there is no fashion in London. It means that these cultures value sensuality and its public expression differently.

Obviously, France has excelled at cuisine. Its greatest restaurants have long been temples to gastronomic delight. It is difficult to forget the *canard au sang* at the *Tour d'Argent*. London has had some great restaurants, but no one travels to London for the steak and kidney pie.

Sensuality and sensuousness have been more at home in Catholic cultures. Distinct from many other religious rituals, the Catholic mass engages all five senses. The Church did not always have a celibate priesthood, but its priests have never lacked sexual desire. In many ways their vow of chastity seems to have intensified their concupiscent longings.

Catholic cultures have promoted erotic public rituals. They have the Viennese waltz, the Argentinian tango and Mardi Gras. Protestant cultures have no comparable displays. Queuing up is not an erotic ritual.

The Church's greatest theologians were anything but prudish about sexual matters. Their writings were not widely available to the faithful, but the Church did not repress the discussion of sex.

I have already mentioned Augustine's analysis of the mystery of the phallus. In later years Bernard de Clairvaux sermonized at length on the erotics of the "Song of Songs." And Thomas Aquinas importantly offered a rational solution to one of his time's great mysteries. Why, when witches fornicated with devils, did they report that the devil's semen was cold?

The Church has long permitted its penitents to discuss sex, including the perverse variety, in the confessional. In *The History of Sexuality, Volume 1*, Michel Foucault explained that when medieval priests were learning how to take confession they studied manuals that described every manner of deviant sexual behavior.

When Giotto rendered the Last Judgment in Padua's Arena Chapel he depicted perverse sexual acts. The Church discouraged these practices, but it did not banish them from consciousness.

Catholic cultures have produced erotic masterpieces like Boccaccio's *The Decameron,* along with the works of the Marquis de Sade and Giacomo Casanova. Protestant cultures, not so much.

It is doubtful that the Catholic Church would want to take credit for Casanova, but it has long been on good terms with sin.

Of course, the infamous inquisitor's manual, *The Malleus Malefi-carum,* authored by two Dominican monks and published in 1487, was an important and influential book about sexual dysfunction.

Used widely to persecute witches, the *Malleus* placed a special emphasis on the ways these women interfered with male sexual functioning. It explained, for example, that only a witch could cause a man's genitals to disappear.

Freud's Vienna was hardly a sexual wasteland. In *Adventures of a Bystander* Peter Drucker explained:

> ...*sexual repression did not exist in the Austria in which young Sigmund Freud grew up and in which he started to practice. On the contrary, late nineteenth-century Vienna was sexually permissive and sex flourished openly everywhere.*

Drucker explained that Vienna had been an: "...erotic whirlpool... with its constant balls, its waltzes, its intense sexual competition...."

Austria might have lost a war or two. It would lose other wars during Freud's lifetime. It always had the waltz.

When Freud denounced sexually repressive cultures, he could not have been referring to Vienna. He may, however, have been thinking of the repressive Jewish culture in which he grew up. Even psychoanalysis could not free him from its chains.

As a Jew in libertine Vienna, Freud was like the poor boy whose face was pressed against the window of the candy store. Unable to enter, he could only yearn for delights that were available to others. Perhaps that's why his theory emphasized desire more than gratification.

His own asceticism notwithstanding, Freud's theories aligned with Roman Catholic Austria against Lutheran Prussia or Germany.

Of course, the Iron Chancellor did not symbolize nineteenth century sexual repression. That honor belonged to Victoria, Queen of England. The nation that had given the world the Industrial Revolution was ruled by a model of instinctual renunciation.

During most of Freud's life Great Britain was the world's leading industrial power, military power, political power, trading power and imperial power. British economic, social and political success had made it the world's alpha culture.

British culture is defined by tea ceremonies, strict rules of etiquette, queuing up and the stiff upper lip. Great Britain has had its aesthetes and its decadents, but it has never been identified by the sophisticated eroticism of *Les Liaisons Dangéreuses* or *The Story of O*.

A good Freudian might find a hidden meaning in the British stiff upper lip, but, as a moral precept, it is decidedly anti-Freudian. Maintaining a stiff upper lip means not expressing emotion openly. It is, literally, an imperative to save face.

British culture valued character, honor and respectability. It placed industry ahead of pleasure, commerce ahead of dances, military might ahead of aesthetic sophistication. It encouraged gentility and produced rules that defined gentlemanly and ladylike behavior.

Ironically, the ethos associated with Queen Victoria was decidedly manly. It must have looked like a threat to cultures that valued feminine and maternal values.

Since no one associated Queen Victoria with effulgent femininity, it made sense for physicians in France and Austria to believe that the Victorian ethos was hurting young women. They might well have believed that a cult to British manliness was inimical to feminine sensual flourishing.

Then again, men on the Continent might have feared that their women might find British gentlemen more attractive. To ward off the danger, they chose to master the art of romantic love.

Some tried to learn it through Freudian psychoanalysis. The treatment would not have cured their emotional distress directly. It would not have made them better competitors. Yet, if it taught them how to love, it might have been worth the price.

When hysteria broke out in Great Britain in the nineteenth and early twentieth century, physicians did not treat it with romantic love, transferential or real. Eminently practical, they sought to relieve sexual frustration with a method that was less socially disruptive: manual stimulation of the female genitalia.

Freud understood that the Industrial Revolution had produced considerable emotional distress.

Like Nietzsche before him, he suggested that Europeans needed to get back in touch with their primal instincts. Faced with the prospect of reconstructing their societies according to imported British customs, many Continental thinkers yearned for a return to the days when blood ties were more important than social links, when agriculture and cottage industries were more valued than manufacturing, and when kinship and tribalism trumped rules and customs.

They wanted to go back to a time when people were born, grew up and died in one community. Some had rebelled against a decadent aristocracy and a hereditary monarchy, but they all preferred entitled leisure in the salon or boudoir to competitive striving in the marketplace.

Continental thinkers also believed that industrialization, capitalism and liberal democracy were systematic attempts to deny the dark truth about human nature.

While Freud and Nietzsche, among others were bemoaning the ravages caused by the Industrial Revolution, Great Britain and America were healing the anomie by creating a new set of rules.

In the Anglosphere, civility became more important than blood, decorum prevailed over drama, and social harmony replaced internecine conflict. In such a culture your relationships depended less on the accident of birth and more on good behavior.

Freud set off in the opposite direction. His theories were biased toward the family. He had little to say about peer groups, friendship or neighborliness.

Had he been asked to explain exogamous marriage Freud would have said that it repressed the most basic human desire—to keep sex in the family.

The ethos of a culture that makes blood ties primary differs significantly from one that grants more value to voluntary social ties.

Family ties do not depend on showing up on time, returning phone messages or chewing with your mouth closed. If you behave badly you will still be your mother's son and your sister's brother.

But, if you insult and offend your friends and acquaintances, you will inevitably lose them.

Freud's family-centered vision devalued work, competition and achievement in favor of motherly love. He did not see a child earning pride by competing successfully in the classroom or on the playground. He saw some children receiving what would have been called, in another context, supervenient grace, from their mothers.

Freud wrote:

If a man has been his mother's undisputed darling he retains throughout his life the triumphant feeling, the confidence in success, which not seldom brings success along with it.

Freud should have added that a child whose mother believes that he can do no wrong might also grow up to be an adult who cannot take responsibility for failure.

Worse, if a child has nothing more than his mother's love to buoy his confidence, no one else will understand its basis. Other people might end up believing that he is a self-important fraud.

A doting mother will love her child, no matter what. She will find him lovable even when he is at his worst. To a Freudian that is the crux of the issue.

If people believe that their romantic love should be unconditional, and if they test it by showing themselves at their worst, they are asking their lovers to love them as their mothers did.

While Freud wanted to keep it all in the family, Aristotle constructed his ethic around friendship.

Freud wanted people to get in touch with their worst, but Aristotle, who saw humans as social beings, believed that friends should wish the best for their friends.

The philosopher never suggested that friends should act badly in order to see who loves them unconditionally. He wanted them to manifest good character and to offer generosity of spirit.

In the *Nicomachean Ethics* Aristotle said:

To be friends, then, they must be mutually recognized as bearing goodwill and wishing well to each other....

While Freud believed that his patients could be cured by engaging in the sublimated love affair called psychoanalysis, Aristotle suggested that the best cure for despair was to make a friend.

He wrote:

For without friends no one would choose to live, though he had all other goods; even rich men and those in possession of dominating power are thought to need friends most of all; for what is the use of such prosperity without the oppor-

tunity for beneficence, which is exercised chiefly and in its most laudable form towards friends.

In his *Eudemian Ethics*, the philosopher said:

...men believe a friend to be the greatest of goods, and friendlessness and solitude to be the most terrible, because all life and voluntary association is with friends.

It may be mere coincidence, but when Alexis de Tocqueville observed American life, he noted in particular that American society was often organized around "voluntary associations," that is, around non-familial social groupings.

Like Aristotle, Tocqueville noticed that we choose our friends, but not our parents or children. Thus, when we make or unmake friendships we are exercising free will.

If you are free to begin or end friendships you are less likely to insist that your friends change their errant ways. If they behave badly, you can cut off ties.

When you are related to someone by blood, it is far more difficult to cease all intercourse. If a blood relative becomes insufferable you cannot ignore him or avoid him. When weddings and funerals and holidays come around, he will be there, in all his obnoxious glory. You might conclude that everyone's life would improve if he became someone else.

Psychoanalysis is less about relieving human anguish and more about making blood relatives less insufferable.

In France and Austria family ties prevailed over social ties. In the more developed liberal democracies of Great Britain, and especially in America, the opposite pertained. One understands why Freud did not harbor warm feelings toward anti-aristocratic America.

8

IN HIS LETTERS and private conversations Freud disparaged America.

Ernest Jones reported that Freud once told him: "America is a mistake, admittedly a gigantic mistake, but a mistake nevertheless."

And Freud told Hanns Sachs: "America is the most grandiose experiment the world has seen, but, I am afraid, it is not going to be a success."

What was so wrong with America, or even Great Britain? It was not just the steam engine, the cotton gin, free enterprise, free speech and liberal democracy.

Both Great Britain and America valued empirical evidence and pragmatic truths. Both preferred real achievement to wish fulfillment. Both believed that hard work was necessary for success and that success would bring happiness.

Freud paid lip service to the value of work, but ultimately he was promoting a love ethic. In his clinical practice he was trying to treat mental illness with romantic love.

As a man of his culture, Freud must have believed that a regimented environment was not the best place to cultivate love. By his theory, cultures that tamped down public displays of sensuality were repressive.

It is a dubious, but commonly made assumption.

Considering how many times France fought wars against England, it is not surprising that Continental Europe, often led by France, was predisposed to reject most of what came from across the Channel.

Among the reasons for French (and Continental) enmity toward Albion must have been a single, strange British custom. The custom dated to before the Industrial Revolution. It threatened everyone's sex life.

As you may know, the Anglosphere led the charge in replacing traditional arranged marriages with what is commonly called love marriage.

For most of human history marriage has been an arrangement, an alliance between families. Most human cultures have been loath to allow callow young people a free choice in such an important matter. Thus, they have refused to grant young women the freedom to choose their husbands.

Great Britain changed all that. By giving a woman an important say in her choice of a husband, it expanded the practice of human freedom. For reasons that are probably not too mysterious, this new custom made romantic love an essential component of marriage.

It is no exaggeration to say that the change was revolutionary.

Love marriage was first institutionalized in perfidious Albion, but it seems first to have been practiced by Martin Luther and his followers.

When Luther and his band of defrocked religious decided to marry, they could not marry for power or property. Upon entering holy orders they had renounced all worldly possessions.

Having nothing of material or social value to offer their potential spouses, they could only give one thing: their love.

Significantly, theirs was also a free choice. Having been excommunicated, they were detached from their communities. They had to choose their spouses freely.

A little more than a century later, Anglo-American Puritans made love the basis for marriage. Historian David Hackett Fischer stated: "The Puritans cherished true love, and insisted that it was a prerequisite for a happy marriage."

Everyone denounces Puritans as sexual scolds, but their practice of love marriage, coupled with a more severe attitude toward adultery, must also have threatened those who had been finding their sexual pleasure outside of marriage.

Since America had dispensed with all vestiges of aristocracy, it practiced a purer form of love marriage than even the British.

The new custom remained so culture-specific that a sophisticated nineteenth century Frenchman like Alexis de Tocqueville found it to be intriguing and foreign.

Writing in the early 1830s, he described the American custom:

> *In a country in which a woman is always free to exercise her choice and where education has prepared her to choose rightly, public opinion is inexorable to her faults. The rigor of the Americans arises in part from this cause. They consider marriage as a covenant which is often onerous, but every condition of which the parties are strictly bound to fulfill because they knew all those conditions beforehand and were perfectly free not to have contracted them.*

As Tocqueville recognized, the new custom increased human freedom, but not human license. It freed women to choose their husbands and also to take responsibility for their actions.

More often than not, arranged marriages were not based on romantic love. If a woman's father chose her spouse on socio-economic and political grounds, he was probably not giving very much weight to her feelings. She might have been granted a veto if the man was intolerable, but she would not have expected to be madly in love with her husband.

Of course, the custom of arranged marriage had not killed romance. It exiled true love to a domain outside of the conjugal estate. For centuries, Europeans who practiced arranged marriage had cultivated romantic love as an extramarital diversion.

Men had mistresses, courtesans, concubines, lovers and favorites. Married women reveled in courtly love.

The Decalogue had proscribed adultery and the book of Leviticus had pronounced it a capital crime. No less than St. Paul admonished its practitioners severely. Yet, Europe had kept it alive. Good Christians found that forbidden lust could revive flagging libido. They had no reason to abandon it.

Priests cooperated by granting absolution, thus, palliating the attendant guilt. In the best cases the sanctions, especially confession and penance, remained private.

With the advent of love marriage, problems arose. Institutionalized adultery could not easily co-exist with the new custom. After having been more-or-less tolerated for centuries, adultery became a serious threat, especially to wives.

A woman who had chosen her husband freely and who expected to have ongoing carnal knowledge of him would have seen his adultery as a threat to her home, her family and her health.

Thus, communities that made love marriage the rule and not the exception had to introduce new sanctions to discourage extra-marital dalliances.

Since guilt for having transgressed the Seventh Commandment had proven to be relatively powerless in stopping adultery, people lit on a stronger sanction: shame.

When love marriage became customary, adulterers were threatened with public humiliation and a loss of face. They could not have overcome either by doing penance.

We associate this sanction with the scarlet letter worn by Hester Prynne, but adulterous men in Puritan America were also publicly shamed.

Making shame more important than guilt did not merely change the cost basis of adultery from self-punishment to the loss of reputation. It also redefined the nature of marriage.

Having a sense of shame does not mean that you repress your sordid desires because you fear the consequences of acting on them. It does not assume that people act well only when they fear being punished for acting badly.

People with a sense of shame do the right thing because they enjoy doing the right thing. As Aristotle put it, they act virtuously for the sake of acting virtuously.

Inhabitants of a shame culture enjoy following community standards and living according to the rules. They enjoy getting along with their friends and neighbors. They do not believe that "hell is other people."

When the new culture set out to shame adultery it was not only telling people what not to do. It was telling them what to do: to love their spouses, more actively and more lustily.

Anyone who lived in such a community had an incentive to choose a desirable and desiring spouse.

If you are following the Freudian model and are merely trying to avoid, let's say, castration, you can obey a taboo against adultery (or incest) without making love to your spouse.

Once adultery became shameful the issue was not about breaking or not breaking the law. It was about honoring or dishonoring one's vows, keeping or going back on one's word.

Promoting intra-marital sexuality also proved to be socially and psychologically beneficial. Keeping sex (for the most part) in the conjugal bed produced fewer bastards and less relational confusion. In a community that practiced love marriage more people knew with a higher degree of certainty who their parents were and what their place in society was.

Thus, the new Anglo-American custom sustained social order better than the decadent pleasure principle.

Prior to the invention of love marriage, sophisticated Europeans, especially aristocrats, had risked very little when they had relationships with mistresses and courtesans. Adultery might have produced some bastards, a twinge of conscience and perhaps even an infection or two, but it did not put anyone's reputation at risk.

Women who had entered into arranged marriages often countenanced their husbands' adulterous liaisons. They were happy to be left alone. Or better, they felt freed to enjoy their own extramarital dalliances, discreetly.

In a culture that accepted adultery, a man who had many lovers was affirming the strength of his sex drive. If he was a Freudian he would have seen it as a sign of good mental health. He might even have believed that it made him an alpha male. It is especially important to look like an alpha male when you aren't one.

Once adultery was stigmatized, the moral balance changed. An adulterer risked being exposed as someone who, having gone back on his word, possessed weak character.

By shaming adulterers Anglo-American cultures turned a sexual transgression into a character flaw. Previously, those who sinned had only to answer to their consciences and God. When adultery became a character flaw, sinners risked public exposure.

The new sanction against adultery created an important problem. Under the old rules, a married man who ceased to desire his wife or had never really desired her could sustain his libido by finding a comely mistress. If the option was no longer viable, marital bed death would spell sexual repression.

Such was the case of Sigmund and Martha Freud. From his letters we know that Freud's marriage was a love, even a lust match. Unfortunately, the fire burned out of his marriage when he and his wife were relatively young.

If we are to believe what Freud told other people, he suffered sexual deprivation. We assume that, for him, adultery was not an option. He chose to sublimate his libido in his work.

Despite his personal experience, Freud clung doggedly to the belief that marriage should contain and sustain romantic love and good sex. He knew that he would never enter the Promised Land but he wanted to show others the way.

Examine the way Freud handled the case of Ernst Lanzer, aka the Rat Man.

When he consulted with Freud in the first years of the twentieth century Lanzer was suffering from a neurosis that dramatized the conflict between arranged marriage and love marriage.

Torn between his mother's wish that he contract an arranged marriage to a wealthy heiress and his own desire to marry the poor, but penniless woman he loved, the Rat Man became neurotic.

Since Lanzer's parents had had an arranged marriage, such a match was customary within some Austrian communities in the late nineteenth century.

Failing to grasp his patient's moral dilemma, Freud believed that Lanzer was suffering because he refused to embrace his desire to undergo a sadistic rat torture. In American argot the torture involved tossing salads.

In a different place and time Lanzer would have accepted the arranged marriage and spent his newfound fortune on an official mistress. Freud never considered the possibility.

Wanting the Rat Man to marry the woman he loved, Freud seemed to believe that marrying for love was a sign of mental health. After less than a year of psychoanalysis Lanzer fulfilled Freud's wish.

Strangely, the case reads more like a romantic comedy than a Greek tragedy. Worse yet, it feels perfectly American.

When he wrote about the Rat Man, Freud pronounced the treatment a success. We do not know how the marriage ultimately worked out because, soon after his analysis ended, Lanzer was killed in World War I.

Was Freud suggesting that he believed in the power of romantic love? Was he telling the world that the best way to achieve mental health was through a fulfilling love marriage?

Perhaps he believed it. Stranger things have happened.

Yet, we should not ignore the possibility that Freud was using the case to promote psychoanalysis. Knowing that the future of his "dangerous method" depended on its ability to infiltrate Great Britain and America, he might have tailored his approach to appeal to their sensibilities. After all, he did publish the case.

It is also possible that Freud did not want to pick a quarrel with those who favored love marriage and who believed that it represented progress. He might have believed that promoting adultery would have discredited his enterprise.

As a rhetorical ploy, Freud's approach was persuasive. Everyone who reads the case agrees, reflexively that Lanzer should have married the poor girl he loved. If the Rat Man hesitated to do the right thing, he must have been neurotic.

But, for all we know, and for all Freud knew, the answer to the dilemma might not have been quite so easy.

Even if we believe that the correct decision was self-evident, we do not need to accept Freud's hypothesis, namely, that in order to choose the right wife, the Rat Man needed to get in closer touch with his anal eroticism.

It's very difficult to see clearly with your head up your....

As was his wont, Freud made the Rat Man's psycho-cultural problem into a mental health issue. The great doctor believed that his patient's inability to make up his mind was a sign of a mental illness. He also believed that once psychoanalysis removed mental obstacles, his patient would naturally marry the girl he loved.

And yet, if arranged marriage offends our sensibility, we also recognize that if a young married couple has nothing but romantic love, their prospects for a long, happy marriage are not very bright, either.

There are other ways to read of Lanzer's moral dilemma. For all we know, he might have been anguished because he had fallen in love with Miss Wrong. He might have known that he was making a mistake. He might have been seduced into making a commitment that he could not honorably renounce.

Also, his manly pride might not have allowed him to accept his mother's advice, however good it was.

We know nothing of the heiress his mother wanted him to marry. Was she interesting, engaging, attractive, intelligent or sociable? Was she a woman of good character? Would her presence have facilitated his career? Or was she bland, boring, asexual and unprepossessing?

Aside from the fact that he loved her, we know nothing about the woman the Rat Man married. Was she charming and brilliant, devoted to the man she loved? Or was she using her Rat Man to advance herself socially?

We do not know the answers to these questions. And yet, when choosing a spouse they are vitally important. By all appearances, Freud ignored them.

If Freud believed that romantic love would suffice, he failed his patient and his readers. If he refused to allow the Rat Man to examine his dilemma objectively and to weigh his options, he himself was acting irresponsibly.

By insisting that the Rat Man's problem was all in his mind, Freud misled his patient and his readers.

Whatever Freud's reasoning, a few decades later a sophisticated French sybarite like Jacques Lacan saw adultery as an acceptable way to express his libido.

After all, adultery had traditionally been the cornerstone of sexual desire. What could be more Freudian than illicit love affairs? If Freud's theoretical blinders prevented him from seeing it, Lacan took upon himself the task of fulfilling the theory.

While Freud held out hope for sexually fulfilling love marriages, Lacan wanted to make the world safe for adultery. He refused to allow Anglo-American Puritans to block his or anyone else's path to *jouissance*.

In the Left Bank subculture that Lacan inhabited romantic dalliances were easily tolerated. The woman who became his second wife was nominally married to someone else when she bore him a child in 1941.

No one much noticed or cared.

In later years, Parisian psychoanalysts knew and accepted that Lacan regularly sought the sexual favors of women who were not his wife.

He was commonly seen as a man who loved women, a ladies' man. It was part of his aura.

The British gentleman was a man's man. He did not assert his manliness by seducing women. He claimed no special expertise in the boudoir and was not a connoisseur of female flesh. A gentleman knew how to conduct himself in a salon, but he sought validation in the marketplace, the arena or the battlefield.

Whatever the truth about Lacan's adulterous liaisons, when he sought the cultural prototype for transference love, he found it in one of Europe's most peculiar forms of institutionalized adultery: courtly love.

Dating to the early Middle Ages, courtly love was one of the few forms of adultery where the adulterers were adulteresses. It took root most easily in communities where people had formed cults to the Virgin Mary.

Courtly love entered Europe from North Africa at around the time of the Crusades. When Europe's warriors rode forth on extended trips to the Holy Land they left their wives alone in their castles, attended by male adolescents who were too young to fight but not too young to love.

With little else to affirm their sexual being, these ladies amused themselves by seducing their male servants. Given the disparity of age and experience, the process must have been didactic. The ladies taught their pupils the art of love.

In courtly love a teenage boy courted his Lady, most often referred to as his "Lord," by writing plaintive love poems and songs. Some of these boys were troubadours, or, as we would call them, guitar heroes.

A youth who desired his Lady's favors proved his love by suffering a series of ordeals. Most of them were commanded by the Lady herself. These trials amounted to an eroticized, mock-heroic version of the ordeals a knight endured to prove his manliness.

Through courtly love a boy became a Lady's man... but only if he didn't get caught. Courtly love poets always insisted that they had not consummated their love. In their stories, Ladies always withheld the ultimate gift of *merci*.

Clearly, courtly love was all about sustaining desire.

One suspects that the rule was breached more often than anyone dared admit. It was better to dissimulate than to die.

Of course, if the courtly love had been consummated, the Lady would have transformed her husband, the manliest of men, a knight in shining armor into a cuckold.

That being said, Lacan believed that courtly love was just like psychoanalysis. Both engaged libido, generated desire, and could never be consummated. Both were sublimated love affairs.

If the analogy holds, a psychoanalytic patient is like an aspiring troubadour, trying to seduce an analyst who is playing the part of Lady/Lord.

But, Lacan added a twist. If a patient, when he begins treatment, thinks that he must seduce his reticent analyst into speaking to him, he will, in the best of cases, learn that his analyst is not really the unattainable Lady.

If a psychoanalyst is really a father confessor, as Freud called him, perhaps he cannot answer anyone's prayers without the intercession of a Lady.

Lacan was one of the few psychoanalysts who did not share Freud's bourgeois values. He did not emulate Freud's example. He lived a Freudian life, but he did not live Freud's life.

Lacan had come to fulfill the Law, thus, to live the Freudian dream. If the uxorious Freud, as Lacan called him, could not do it himself, his theories had laid down the predicates.

As the first psychoanalyst, Freud wrote the theory. Afflicted by his culture, he could not live it himself. He could not even promote it overtly.

As the last psychoanalyst, Lacan did not have the same scruples. Wanting to return psychoanalysis to its roots in Catholic culture, he refused to appease the Anglosphere. In that he was more Freudian than Freud himself.

9

IN *ADVENTURES OF a Bystander* Peter Drucker explained that Freud's first hysterics, like Freud himself, came mostly from small Jewish towns outside of Vienna.

In so noting, Drucker was emphasizing the socio-cultural causes of mental distress.

Here, he described the Jewish culture where many of Freud's patients had grown up:

> *In these small ghettos, sex was indeed repressed—for both men and women. Marriages were arranged by a middleman when both bride and groom were children. They married as soon as they reached sexual maturity—and until then they had never seen each other.*

When young women brought up in such a culture moved to Vienna, Drucker continued, they were thrown, unprepared, into a sexualized world.

In the great capital city there were constant balls where women competed with each other for male attention. Having been raised to expect that their fathers would choose their husbands, these young women did not know how to find husbands on their own.

If emotional distress is caused by not knowing how to do something, it does not spell neurosis. It manifests inexperience.

Culturally dislocated, these women were suffering from anomie. Eventually, they expressed their psycho-cultural problem through symptoms that were most likely to attract the attention of the medical profession.

Freud and his wife had overcome their anomie—such as it was—by embracing the more modern and more British custom: they married for love. By Freud's admission, their marriage soon lost that sexual feeling.

We possess very little information about the intimate life of Sigmund and Martha Freud, but we can speculate about their marital problems. Would it not be ironic if these problems had been caused, not by neurosis or by civilized morality, but by Freud's weak character? Or better, by his tyrannical disposition.

Martha Freud was an observant Jew. She believed herself duty bound to light Sabbath candles on Friday evenings. Yet, throughout her marriage her godless husband prevented her from doing so. (Perhaps Freud was not as uxorious as Lacan believed.)

We learned this from an Oxford philosopher. One Friday in 1938, soon after Freud had arrived in England, this philosopher spent an afternoon conversing with him.

Peter Gay described what happened next:

> As it came to be around five in the afternoon, Martha Freud joined them and said to the visitor: "You must know that on Friday evenings good Jewish women light candles for the approach of the Sabbath. But this monster—Unmensch—will not allow this because he says that religion is a superstition."

Both Gay and the Oxford philosopher thought that the Freuds were amusing their guest with some slapstick comedy. They should have taken Martha Freud's words more seriously. For an observant Jewish woman, being forbidden to light Sabbath candles was not a joking matter.

Also, if a man sees himself as an *Ubermensch* and his wife sees him as an *Unmensch*, he is an *Unmensch*. It's the first rule of marriage.

Could Freud's repressive action have extinguished Martha's desire? Did she, forbidden to light the Sabbath candles refuse to light Freud's fire? Women have withdrawn from their husbands for less.

It would be ironic for a man who held an enlightened anti-religious attitude to suffer sexual deprivation because he had forced his wife to abrogate an important religious duty.

Moving from the sublime to the farcical, the Freuds' marital problems might also have been caused by toothpaste. For reasons that defy reason Freud forced his wife to put the toothpaste on his toothbrush, every night.

One doubts that Freud would have missed the sexual symbolism of the act he was forcing his wife to perform. For all we know, she did not miss it either. Understandably, she did not consider it to be enticing foreplay. When it came to her husband's more Freudian tube, she appears to have left it in his own hands.

These anecdotes suggest that Freud behaved like a domestic tyrant in his home. You need not have had too much human experience to understand that such behavior does not put you on the royal road to conjugal bliss.

Now, you will be asking, what about Minna? Many serious scholars, especially Peter Swales, have argued that Freud was really an adulterous and incestuous scoundrel. They have asserted, based on compelling evidence, that Freud was having a love affair with his sister-in-law, Minna Bernays.

Naturally, Freud's most loyal followers have defended him vigorously from the charge that he had been unchaste. Yet, if they did not think it was Freudian to lust after a forbidden sexual object, they missed an important part of psychoanalytic theory.

The unmarried Minna moved in with her sister and brother-in law when Sigmund was around 40. She functioned as a second mother to the many Freud children and lived with the family for four decades.

We know, at the least, that Freud lusted after Minna in his mind. No one knows with certainty whether they ever consummated their longings. If desire, as Freud believed, is produced by the incest taboo, perhaps the next best thing to your mother is your sister-in-law.

If the presence of the comely and spirited Minna provoked Freud's desire, he failed to transfer it to his wife. Freud may have felt like a randy old satyr, but his wife was apparently not enticed by the idea that he was craving her sister.

It is impossible to believe that Martha Freud would not have noticed an extended flirtation between her husband and her sister.

Whatever the truth about Sigmund and Minna, their "affair," real or imagined, was decidedly Freudian. If Freud's fantasies were filled with images of the lusty Minna he might have considered them to be "empirical" proof that he was right: sexual desire was more intense when it was directed toward a forbidden woman. He might also have concluded that he no longer desired his wife, or vice versa because carnal relations between them were not tabooed: they were prescribed.

As long as he refused to accept adultery as a way to restore libido, Freud was in a quandary. He believed that the difficulty, and thus the solution lay in the human mind. He might have reasoned that if the problem was more general than particular and if the fault lay in the human mind, he could help people to sustain their sexual desire by showing them how to use mental fetishes, fantasies and psychodrama.

Even today, sustaining sexual desire within a long term marriage remains a great challenge.

If Freud, as Lacan insisted, did not believe that sexual attraction was natural, he would have been looking for some unnatural ways to keep it alive. And he would have begun his quest by referring back to his theory of infantile polymorphously perverse sexuality.

He would have concluded that sexual desire is sustained by fetishes and fantasies. Many of us would agree, but we must also note that Freud's theories deviated markedly from the common-sense understanding of these sexual aids.

Obviously, the world did not need Freud to learn about the erotic potential of fetishes and fantasies. Most people had long since known that sexual fantasies often accompany sexual arousal.

Still, Freud did make an original contribution to the concept of fetish objects. In most of human history fetishes have signified fertility and availability. If they provoke fantasies, these seem more like rehearsals of something that might come to pass than like a compensation for something that can never come to pass.

Until Freud came along to addle our minds, sex was considered a natural process whose purpose was to reproduce the species. Fetishes and fantasies contributed to the process.

Saying that the sex drive is organized around an instinct to procreate is not the same as saying that your desire is sustained by a taboo against incest.

When Oedipus married his mother/wife she was old enough to have an adult son. Yet, she had four more children with her son/husband, without the aid of reproductive technology.

Jocasta's fecundity is the MacGuffin of *Oedipus Tyrannos*. It obscures the fact that if sons were really programmed to crave intimacy first with their mothers, their desire would spell species suicide.

Freud confused the issue further when he declared that the power of fetish objects could be traced to an initial frustration at not being able to copulate with one's mother.

If he had seen a man turning away from his wife and toward a young mistress, Freud would have emphasized that the mistress was forbidden. Had you pointed out that the man had chosen a younger, more fertile and perhaps more available woman, Freud might have replied that the husband was denying his wish to ravish his mother.

Most rational individuals understand that men choose mistresses for their youth and availability. As often happened, Freud's theory was denying the obvious.

A theory that bases sexual attraction on an incest wish and that sees sex as polymorphously perverse will conclude that people can only sustain their desire by entertaining all manner of sordid fantasies. When psychoanalysts say that they want you to have a rich fantasy life they are not encouraging you to get lost in reveries about pastoral idylls.

Freud was suggesting that psychoanalysis could solve the problem of a sexless marriage by teaching people to fantasize about perverse sexual activity. Once they filled their minds with depraved fantasies the spouses could act them out with each other, the better to achieve *jouissance*.

It did not work out very well for Freud, but he seems to have held out hope that it might work for others.

When a psychoanalyst suggests that you chose your wife because she reminds you of your mother, he is making your wife tabooed. If you believe him and if the incest taboo produces sexual desire, you should feel a rush of desire for your now-forbidden wife.

As an intrapsychic solution, this leaves much to be desired. As soon as a man's wife gets wind of the fact that her husband is taking her for someone else, she might well turn away from him, however ardent his desire.

But we are well within our rights to question Freud's theory of how desire was generated. Does a child really feel the first stirrings of desire when he learns that he will never be allowed to copulate with his mother?

Is it true that once his father says No to incest, a child will want nothing else?

According to this theory, desire can only flourish when based on a taboo. As soon as sex becomes a conjugal duty, desire will diminish.

Is there any way to know whether Freud was right? Is a father's No the *sine qua non* of concupiscence? How can you tell?

Try a thought experiment.

In olden days a gentleman who wanted to get married would ask the permission of his intended bride's father.

For the sake of argument, imagine a situation where her father says No. Will our rejected suitor immediately become consumed with desire for the now forbidden object of his lust? Or will he feel demoralized and desperate?

If the unhappy couple does not elope, we can easily imagine our young suitor falling into despair. If he mistakes his desperation for desire, he might convince himself that he loves her so much that he cannot live without her.

This does not signal a desire. It is an effort to produce desire out of nothing. After all, the absence of desire is a hallmark of depression.

One suspects that a great deal of Freudian theory is based on the confusion between desiring something and being desperate to have it.

However much Lacan was obsessed with the power of No, human experience tells us that people are more aroused by Yes. Better yet, they feel the most desire when they hear: Maybe... since that is the mean between the extremes.

Some people are aroused by No, but we normally classify them as psychopaths. The point is strangely consistent with Freud's theory.

When called upon to provide a rationale for the Oedipus complex, Freud's followers usually explain that the incest taboo is universal. If incest is universally tabooed, they reason, everyone must want to do it.

This is not the same as saying that the taboo generates the desire, but why quibble?

In *How the Mind Works* Harvard psychologist Steven Pinker debunked Freudian theory. Taboo or no taboo, Pinker asserted, people are not attracted to their close relatives. He explained:

Avoiding incest is universal; taboos against incest are not.

Responding to the notion that brothers and sisters, for example, find each other sexually attractive because they are forbidden fruit, Pinker wrote:

> Brothers and sisters simply don't find each other appealing as sexual partners. This is an understatement: the thought makes them acutely uncomfortable or fills them with disgust.... Freud claimed that the strong emotion is itself proof of an unconscious desire, especially when a male claims revulsion at the thought of coitus with his mother. By that reasoning we may conclude that people have an unconscious desire to eat dog feces or to stick needles in their eyes.

Obviously, Pinker is correct. Disgust is adaptive. Saying that it masks a desire is sophistry.

And yet, many cultures have laws against incest. Does this mean that everyone wants to commit incest or does it tell us that no one really wants to do so?

Why, for all of human history, would people obey laws whose primary purpose is to restrain, constrain and repress the expression of their heart's desire? Are human beings really that masochistic?

Does anyone really believe that we follow rules and obey laws because, as Freud intimated, we are happy to accept being joyless ascetics?

For all we know, people respect the incest taboo, among other constraints because they do *not* want to commit such heinous actions. They understand that some depraved creatures do things that no one else wants to do, but that does not mean that all human beings are longing to commit incest.

Laws must command respect. People follow them because they make sense. Human beings experience satisfaction, not only for living in a harmonious society but for following rules successfully.

Admittedly, we are all capable of committing appalling acts. We are capable of committing murder, and we are capable of cannibalizing our neighbor's remains. (At least, some of us are.) But these are extremes; they are not necessarily anyone's truth.

In the end Freud was living at a time when arranged marriage was giving way to love marriage. And he must have seen that sustaining desire for a single individual over a long period of time was... as they say... challenging.

Where Freud failed to find a way to sustain desire within a marriage, recent therapists have done better.

If you accept that a natural sexual attraction exists, you do not need to manufacture an artificial desire out of nothing. Your desire does not depend on your ability to fill your mind with fantasies about repulsive sexual activities. No one will say that such thoughts do not sometimes arouse people, but they are more often a sign of desperation, not desire.

Couples who want to sustain their desire might begin by working to get along with each other. It doesn't feel quite as exciting as fantasies of BDSM, but you can't have it all.

To sustain desire couples often do what Freud did not do in his own marriage.

They act to build trust and confidence. They show respect and courtesy toward each other, mixed with an occasional kind gesture. If you cannot trust your spouse, and if your spouse does not respect you, your desire will eventually turn to gall.

If depression causes desire to diminish, contemporary therapists treat the depression by showing their patients how to build character through better behavior and how to build pride through achievement. Desire will follow.

It is not intuitively obvious that enhanced pride sustains desire. It is easier to believe that we can produce lust by entertaining sadomasochistic fantasies.

If enhanced pride is the solution to waning concupiscence, we are quickly confronted with another problem.

Freudian psychoanalysis treats individuals as individuals. Yet, pride does not merely belong to individuals. The face you save is never just your own.

Like shame, pride is a social emotion. If your team wins a game or if your country wins a war, you will share in the group pride. If either fails, your pride will be diminished. With diminished pride comes diminished desire.

When a parent succeeds the entire family will feel proud. When a child succeeds his parents and siblings will share the pride.

Unfortunately, this pride is another casualty of Freudian theory. If, as Freud believed, sons normally hate their fathers and if siblings are bitter rivals, no one can share pride.

If Freudian psychoanalysis inevitably diminishes pride, it must also dampen desire. No wonder psychoanalysts have wanted to produce desire artificially.

When a leader fails and his nation suffers an ignominious defeat his subjects lose pride. When a football player drops the ball his team and his fans suffer.

If a child learns in school that his nation has achieved great things, he will gain pride. If his teachers emphasize his nation's crimes and faults, its failures and flaws he will become demoralized.

All things being equal, people who live in a successful community feel greater pride than will those who live in a community that is losing status and influence. When nations become more powerful and prominent, their citizens are less likely to be depressed.

Like it or not, nations, like civilizations compete. They compete in ways that can be quantified objectively. Winning a war or achieving prosperity builds more pride than does a refined aesthetic sensibility. In many cases, the latter seems to be a compensation for the absence of the former.

When Great Britain and America became hegemonic powers their people felt more optimistic, more accomplished, more confident and more proud. If their citizens did not advertise their sexuality, perhaps they did not need to manufacture and sustain desire artificially.

In a declining nation like Austria the psycho-cultural forces were aligned differently. It makes sense that Freud, coming of age in the midst of a Long Depression and a military defeat, should have felt demoralized. More so since, as a Jew, he did not feel like a full member of Viennese society.

It also makes sense that a declining nation would have made social life into a sustained exercise in eroticism. Threatened by a loss of desire, it must have needed to work much harder on keeping it alive.

While he lived in Austria Freud had little to say about national pride. Once he arrived in England he discovered the advantage of living in a proud and powerful nation.

In a peculiar passage from *Moses and Monotheism* Freud compared the feelings of two people who found themselves stranded in a foreign country during an insurrection. One was a Briton and the other was a citizen of a small state. The Briton, Freud said, would feel more secure and more confident.

He explained:

> For the Briton counts on the fact that his Government will send along a warship if a hair of his head is hurt, and that the rebels understand that very well—whereas the small state possesses no warship at all. Thus, pride in the greatness of the British Empire has a root as well in the consciousness of greater security—the protection—enjoyed by the individual Briton.

We forgive Freud his exuberance and his clumsy example, but he was correct to see that national pride was stronger in Great Britain than in Austria. Having been forced to leave a defeated and occupied Austria for Great Britain, he had a right to raise the question.

If national despair causes libido to wane, neither the problem nor the solution is all in your mind. Both lie outside of your mind, in the culture.

Harvard psychiatrist Richard Mollica once stated that: "the best anti-depressant is a job." Allow me to qualify his point: the best anti-depressant is doing a good job in a profitable company that is part of a successful nation.

10

IN THE BEGINNING Freud called psychoanalysis a science and claimed that it could treat mental illness.

It never fulfilled his wish, but that does not mean it has never helped anyone. Some people insist that psychoanalysis has done wonders for them.

Then again, some people swear by scientology and EST.

It is worth emphasizing that clinical psychoanalysis has almost always been reserved for elites. Its practice has been confined to large cities where patients often see treatment as a badge of honor, even of status. Doubtless, this boosts self-esteem. Of course, it was also used, in watered-down form, in the psychiatric hospitals associated with these cities.

Moreover, when orthodox analysts saw their patients four days a week for roughly an hour, they did not have very large caseloads.

Psychoanalysts have always fudged the question of cure. They have defined treatment goals in terms of acquired insight and sexual liberation. Surely, these were more accessible than symptom relief, mental health and/or normality.

Lacan was more honest than most. He once argued that if anyone got better through psychoanalysis, it was fortuitous. Having seen patients get better without acquiring any insight and having seen patients not get better after learning about their repressed motives, he concluded, reasonably, that good clinical results were incidental to a patient's ability to access his unconscious desires.

If that's the best case, Freud's critics were correct to believe that his "dangerous method" was only producing placebo cures. To be fair, for some people a placebo cure, however transitory, is better than no cure.

But, how does psychoanalysis produce placebo cures? At the least, and despite Freud's defense of lay analysis, it can only do so if its clinicians are recognized as healers.

If a patient lives in a culture where everyone believes in the power of medical treatment, he might get better by being told that he is receiving a new medicine.

But, if a primitive tribesman who knows nothing of modern medicine receives a sugar pill offered in a strange place by a man in a white coat he will not respond as he would to a shaman's ritual.

Placebo cures are like phantoms. When they first appear, they dazzle. As soon as you try to grab hold of one, it vanishes.

In *Shame and Guilt in Neurosis* psychoanalyst Helen Block Lewis wrote about a group of patients who had completed psychoanalysis but had later suffered severe breakdowns. Their cures had not lasted because psychoanalysis, she argued, had deprived them of their ability to deal with shame. Theirs were surely placebo cures.

More broadly, if psychoanalysis had really been clinically effective it would not have spawned so many different varieties. We do not have twenty-two different schools of neurology, each based on the teachings of a single guru.

Of course, if psychoanalysis and its cognate therapies had worked, our world would not be awash in psychiatric medication.

If Freudian psychoanalysis were an effective treatment, the nation where it has the greatest influence—France—would not be leading the world in the per capita consumption of psychoactive medicines.

If psychoanalysis worked, the well-analyzed French would not, as economist Claudia Senik has shown, count among the unhappiest people on the planet.

Many psychoanalysts take offense at the suggestion that their practice is just another sugar pill. Allow me to correct the misapprehension. Psychoanalysis is not a sugar pill. It is a bitter pill. It took genius to convince people that if it tasted bad it had to be good medicine.

Even though Freud was reputed to be, in Peter Drucker's words, "a master healer," many of his colleagues had their doubts. Speaking for them, Drucker asked: "what explained the fact... that so many of its patients became permanent patients, or... came back to the psycho-analyst again and again?"

Besides, other Viennese physicians saw their patients getting better without receiving treatment. This has been called the waiting-list effect.

Drucker explained:

> *Every Viennese doctor saw obviously "neurotic" people in his practice; a large number of them got better without any treatment—especially, of course, adolescents.*

Beyond his unshakeable arrogance, Freud had one thing that most other physicians lacked. He had charisma.

Like a modern day faith healer Freud cultivated an aura and made it an instrument of cure. He worked long and hard to transmit it to his disciples.

Cure by charisma is not the same as cure by insight. To be cured by charisma you must partake of the leader's mystical aura. You do not need to understand yourself and you do not need to improve the way you conduct your life.

If Freud's aura was producing placebo cures, the future of clinical psychoanalysis depended on his transmitting it to his disciples.

To ensure the transmission of his aura Freud oversaw the establishment of numerous psychoanalytic institutions. He brought them together to form the International Psychoanalytic Association, the IPA. Members of the IPA were presumed to possess the great man's aura.

Among later psychoanalysts Lacan disputed the IPA claim to ownership of Freud's charisma. He intimated that he himself had inherited the better part of it.

Someone who has suffered a cure by charisma might show signs of exceptional creativity and/or idiosyncratic individuality. Often, he will continue to be burdened by anguish. He may even retain his tics.

Some analysts have understood that they are not treating or curing their patients. They have compensated by dismissing the idea of cure and by declaring that they are helping their patients to transcend normality.

Placebo cures required more than charisma. They could only work if people, especially the cognoscenti and the literati, created an expectation that psychoanalysis was therapeutic. Psychoanalysts and their enablers did not, at first, need to produce such a culture for an entire nation. They were happy to limit themselves to educated, cosmopolitan urban elites.

Here again, Freud led the way. He acted as though he knew that, for psychoanalysis to survive, it had to transform the culture.

He was acting like a conquistador, not like a scientist.

Peter Gay explained:

> Whatever the historians' verdict on his plight as a revolutionary, Freud behaved more like a general marshaling his forces and mapping his movements than a scientist willing to let his ideas carry their own conviction.

Freud's ideas entered Western culture on two fronts: medical and artistic. In many places they first attracted artists and intellectuals. Later they became part of psychiatric practice. In other places the order was reversed.

In many European countries psychoanalysis was first promoted by artists and intellectuals. In practical-minded America, it was first embraced by psychiatrists and psychologists. Having little else to offer those who were suffering from mental illness, they were happy to give Freud's method a trial.

Eventually, the American model came to dominate and psychoanalysis took its place among the mental health professions. It may not have produced many successes but, for a long time, it was the only game in town.

In France, and, to a lesser extent England, psychoanalysis was first presented as a way to escape conformity and to enhance creativity.

In 1920s Paris, for example, people in high society played with Freud's ideas as though they were toys. Parisian salonistas amused themselves with Freud's ideas. They mocked its pretense to be a therapy.

In the second volume of her magisterial *History of Psychoanalysis in France*, Elisabeth Roudinesco described the scene in 1922:

> Stylish salons hurriedly began to comment on the Viennese works much as when Mesmer's tub had been a source of excitement among the city's courtesans. Elegant ladies became fascinated with the alchemy of dreams and thought they detected in the complicitous eyelid of the neighbor at table the ultimate explanation of a repressed tendency, slip of

the tongue, silence, or pun. From receptions to alcoves, a variety of charlatans dismantled the figures of a sexuality whose perversions they flaunted with as much delight as their ancestors had elicited voices from tables. Couches invaded boudoirs to which exalted souls fallen prey to their own dereliction hurried. All recounted their fantasies while devouring petits fours, and conversations waned beneath the weight of their own insipidity or jargon.

This description brings to mind an old French proverb: *Plus ça change, plus ça reste le même.*

At about the same time, Surrealist artists and writers were promoting the Freudian cause. They went the salonistas one better; they redefined the concept of cure.

Foreshadowing the British anti-psychiatry movement, they asserted that hysterics were expressing, through their symptoms, truths that society was trying to repress. As I mentioned, Aragon and Breton believed that hysteria was a fiction.

In 1928, André Breton wrote a novel about psychotherapy. He called it *Nadja*. In a deft reversal, Breton did not show a psychiatrist curing a hysteric. He showed a hysteric saving her psychiatrist.

Being in closer touch with her desire, Nadja could liberate her dour psychiatrist from his slavish devotion to bourgeois values and conventional notions of cure. The moral of the story was that banal notions of mental health had to be transcended.

Roudinesco summarized the novel:

> ...Nadja *is the story of a therapy in which the narrator occupies the position of a psychiatrist who cannot manage to cure his patient.... The madwoman allowed him to attain his desire to write and to achieve the convulsive beauty of which he dreamed while contemplating the iconography of the Salpêtrière.*

French intellectuals saw psychoanalysis as an enterprise that would validate their culture and allow them to luxuriate in a "convulsive beauty" that, I suspect, had something to do with spasmodic *jouissance*.

France was not the only place where artists and intellectuals brought psychoanalysis into the culture. In England psychoanalysis first gained influence through the work of the intellectuals who formed the Bloomsbury group.

More a grouping than a constituted group, its most prominent members were Virginia Wolff, E. M. Forster, John Maynard Keynes and Lytton Strachey.

Virginia Wolff's brother, Adrian Stephen and his wife were psycho-analyzed by Freud, as were Lytton Strachey's brother James and his wife Alix.

French Surrealists had mocked Freud's pretense to cure, but some Bloomsbury intellectuals, like the Stephens and the Stracheys became practicing psychoanalysts.

James Strachey eventually produced a standard English edition of Freud's writings whose authority, for the faithful, compared to that of the Biblical translation associated with another James.

Freud had not won over the Viennese medical establishment, and he did no better with British physicians. Yet, he enjoyed great success in Cambridge and central London. From there his ideas entered British culture.

In their introduction to *Bloomsbury/Freud* Perry Meisel and Walter Kendrick explained:

> *In England psychoanalysis lingered longer in a stage of generous dilettantism.... Anthropologists, art historians, economists, as well as doctors of various persuasions—even literary types like Lytton [Strachey]—dabbled in psycho-analysis, seeing it as a contribution to their chosen specialties, not a profession in itself.*

Bloomsbury intellectuals also did their part by living Freudian lives. In that way, they too helped change the goal of treatment.

Situated on the political left, the group opposed traditional British and Victorian culture. Its members made common cause with the countercultural movement that had been initiated by British Romantic poets a little more than a century earlier.

If mental health involved conforming to social norms, the Bloomsbury group was not interested. Its members felt alienated from a rule-bound and well-normed society. They readily accepted Freud's view that such a culture stifled creativity and sexuality.

John Maynard Keynes described the attitude that might have drawn them to Freud:

We repudiated entirely customary morals, conventions and traditional wisdom. We were, that is to say, in the strict sense of the term, immoralists. The consequences of being found out had, of course, to be considered for what they were worth. But we recognised no moral obligation on us, or inner sanction, to conform or to obey. Before heaven we claimed to be our own judge in our own case.

At a time when the British were developing new rules of decorum, Bloomsbury intellectuals took pride in defying them. They were more like today's celebrities than today's corporate executives.

Since the Bloomsbury group was sexually liberated its members must have seen Freud as someone whose theories validated their way of life.

Psychoanalysis provided moral cover for people who believed that their polymorphous and polyamorous escapades put them in a cultural vanguard.

Besides, the Viennese neurologist was offering something they could not find in England: indulgence.

In exchange for indulgences they helped Freud to enhance his reputation and his aura. Being adopted by British intellectuals at a time when England was a great power gave Freud cachet.

And then there was Berlin. After World War I psychoanalysis thrived in Germany. The Weimar Republic was fertile ground for Freudian theory, and the analysts who lived in the German capital happily embraced its decadence.

Meisel and Kendrick described the cultural ambiance of Berlin in the 1920s:

Enough has been written about Berlin in the twenties to stock a library; most accounts emphasize, with varying degrees of sensationalism, the "decadence" of the place, its incitement to all forms of excess, primarily the sexual, in the shadow of a nameless malaise.

Working under the aegis of Freud's pupil, Karl Abraham, German psychoanalysts found the time to partake of the Weimar spirit. They demonstrated publicly that psychoanalysis had freed them to enjoy that doomed culture's delights.

By frequenting the same cafes and bars as George Grosz and Berthold Brecht they made psychoanalysis a presence in the culture.

But they, like French Surrealists and the Bloomsbury group, were also modifying the concept of cure.

It's far easier to produce placebo cures if you define your goal in terms of adolescent rebelliousness, aesthetic refinement, creative self-expression and shameless self-indulgence.

In France, England and Germany psychoanalysis did not become fully integrated with psychiatry until after World War II.

America was the exception. Before Bloomsbury, before the French Surrealists and before Weimar Germany American psychiatrists and psychologists had been working with psychoanalysis. Some had started before World War I.

Freud traveled to America in 1909. Lecturing at Clark University, outside of Boston he discovered that Americans were taking his ideas seriously. The distinguished psychologist William James traveled from Cambridge to Worcester to hear him.

Within a few years psychoanalytically inspired techniques were being used to treat patients in prestigious institutions like the Menninger Clinic in Topeka and the Austen Riggs Clinic in Stockbridge. The former was founded immediately after World War I. The latter, just before it.

In places like Menninger and Riggs different variants of psycho-analysis were used as a therapy, especially on patients who suffered from severe mental illness.

Shortly thereafter, major American psychoanalytic institutions deci-ded to restrict training to physicians. Thus, they asserted that theirs was a healing profession. It you want to go into the business of producing placebo cures, it is good to fill your ranks with physicians.

The American Psychoanalytic Association decreed in 1926 that all psychoanalysts had to be physicians. It continued the policy until it was sued for restraint of trade in the 1980s. Only then did it fully open its institutes to psychologists and social workers.

Since the important biochemical treatments for mental illness did not arrive until well after World War II, psychoanalysts could at least claim that their something was better than nothing.

To establish themselves, they had to bring the "good news" to their patient population. They needed to produce a climate of opinion in which their strange method was believed to be a therapy, not merely an amusing intellectual pastime or a way to enhance creativity.

Even if most psychoanalysts were physicians, it did not make intuitive sense that talk could cure. In order to produce placebo cures, psychoanalysis needed to provide what Shakespeare called "ocular proof."

It would happen, at first, in the movies.

It was inevitable that Freud would be adopted by the movie industry. Hollywood films were a perfectly modern way to proselytize the Freudian faith.

Members of the film industry were ripe for Freud. By the nature of their business they lived in a state of free-floating anomie.

Sometimes they worked; sometimes they didn't. Sometimes they worked with the same people; often they didn't. Theirs was a business that fostered chronic rootlessness. Whether they were celebrities themselves or were surrounded by celebrities, they had more than a passing acquaintance with rulelessness.

Filmmakers happily portrayed psychoanalysts as white knights doing battle with disease. It made for a compelling narrative and did not even have to be true.

If you, as a prospective patient, saw a movie or a television show where a character was cured by psychoanalysis, you might have come away believing that psychoanalysis was therapeutic. You might even have believed that it could produce Bible-worthy miracles. If so, you would have been more apt to respond to a placebo.

In 1945 Alfred Hitchcock made *Spellbound*, still one of the best films about psychoanalysis. In it Ingrid Bergman played a psychoanalyst who used dream interpretation to treat a character played by Gregory Peck.

Peck's character had forgotten an adult trauma because it reminded him of a painful childhood experience. After receiving the proper psychological ministrations, he recovered his repressed memories and was magically cured.

Those who saw the movie learned that people could be cured by remembering forgotten traumas. It made dramatic sense; it told a good story. Who would dare dispute it?

By placing the action in a psychiatric clinic, Hitchcock made Freudian treatment appear to be a medical practice. The great director's name also enhanced the treatment's prestige.

Other film directors also promoted the Freudian cause. In 1959 Joseph Mankiewicz directed *Suddenly, Last Summer*. It told of a woman, played by Elizabeth Taylor, who had been hospitalized for mental illness.

The story unfolded in a medical facility. Taylor's character was so ill that her psychiatrists saw only one option: a lobotomy. In a desperate attempt to avoid surgery they gave her a truth serum. Under its influence she recalled a forgotten trauma and was miraculously cured.

The film portrayed a stark choice: lobotomy or psychoanalysis. If those were your options, which would you choose? Freud himself could not have created a better ruse.

These were not the only post-war films that touted clinical psycho-analysis. Hitchcock's less successful *Marnie* and Nunnally Johnson's *The Three Faces of Eve* did the same.

Strictly speaking, these movies caricatured Freudian practice. No psychoanalyst believes that recollecting a trauma will produce a miracle cure. No psychoanalyst uses truth serum to jog memory.

Nonetheless, the films created a cultural climate that influenced the way patients experienced treatment. They helped psychoanalysts to offer more placebo cures to a growing patient population.

At a time when movie-going was becoming a secular substitute for attending religious services, Hitchcock and the others were offering a public ritual that could complement the private ritual of individual therapy.

In truth, psychoanalysis needed Hitchcock and the others because it could not show a passel of patients who would attest to its therapeutic effectiveness.

Few does not mean none. Among those who claimed to have been cured by psychoanalysis was Joanne Greenberg who authored a book called: *I Never Promised You a Rose Garden*.

Published in 1964 the book was a relatively late arrival on the Freudian scene. We grant that psychoanalyst Frieda Fromm-Reichmann helped Greenberg, but no one today believes that the treatment was really psychoanalysis or that she cured her patient of schizophrenia. No psychiatrist today would diagnose Greenberg as schizophrenic.

Be that as it may, the book helped to enhance the reputation of psychoanalysis as an effective clinical treatment, even for severe mental illness.

After World War II, the American media, in particular, discovered the commercial potential of psychoanalytic storytelling. Newspapers and magazines enlisted expert therapists to explain the mysteries of human motivation.

Joyce Brothers and Rose Franzblau wrote newspaper columns that offered plausible explanations for all things psychological. Later, Oprah Winfrey became the greatest public therapist. In turn, she begat Dr. Phil McGraw, another master of the genre.

And then there were the forensic psychiatrists. Their names are less familiar, but they happily offered to explain why serial killers killed and cheating spouses cheated. Often, they made oblique references to Freud.

Since Freud saw human beings in singularly repugnant terms, monstrous criminals seemed to prove him right. Yet, those who trotted out such explanations were more adept at proselytizing the Freudian faith than showing how to treat psychopaths.

The general public was pleased to read pseudo-scientific explanations of appalling and horrific behavior. It found comfort in the idea that someone could explain the inexplicable and make the strangeness more familiar.

Inevitably, savvy medical experts implied that if psychopaths had gained a full understanding of their unconscious motives they would have been cured.

All mental health professionals know that this is untrue. Yet, citizens who listen to the stories can be forgiven for coming away with the impression that self-awareness can cure psychopathy.

In post-war America, the psychoanalytic insights that appeared in the media were off-the-rack. People who read them were induced to think that if they consulted with therapists individually they could acquire bespoke insights.

It almost goes without saying, but media psychologists were rarely giants in the field. They excelled primarily at communicating via the media. Very few of them were trained psychoanalysts.

This produced a dilemma for psychoanalysts. Not wanting to leave the field to Joyce Brothers and Co., they had to find a way to disseminate their new ideas and show off their brilliance. At the least, they needed to present them to the urban intelligentsia and wanna-be cognoscenti.

Since most American analysts were physicians they were ill-equipped to present an intellectual case for Freud.

And, they could not report their own cases. The information was too sensitive and too personal.

So, they enlisted the services of various academic and non-academic intellectuals. Together they decided that they could, at least, show everyone how brilliant Freud was. Since Freud's mind and Freud's charisma were the basis for their practice, it was the least they could do.

They began by showing that psychoanalysis could help everyone to understand important historical figures. Freud set the process in motion by analyzing Leonardo da Vinci and Dostoevsky among others. Later analysts and non-analysts have worked over the psyches of Sylvia Plath, Martin Luther, Marilyn Monroe, George W. Bush and Adolph Hitler... among others.

Many analysts were uneasy with psychobiography. They believed that it was beneath their dignity to pretend to understand the mental life of people they had never met. They decided that it was more honorable to analyze literary characters. In that, they were enabled by literary scholars.

Just as Hollywood directors contributed to the Freudian cause by making movies about psychoanalysis, and just as historians and biographers promoted Freudian theory by applying it to historical figures, literary scholars advanced psychoanalysis through their critical studies.

Whether they were performed by analysts or scholars these studies could create the impression that if a character had been properly analyzed he would have solved his problems and not made a mess of his story.

For true Freudians the literary field was *terra firma*. Freud did not discover the Oedipus complex in a laboratory. He did not see it through the lens of a microscope. He found it by conjuring a personal memory and relating it to a Greek tragedy.

Since Oedipus was unanalyzable, Freud chose Hamlet, Prince of Denmark as his first fictional patient. Among tragic heroes Shakespeare's melancholy Dane seemed to have had the most obvious mental health issues.

It made sense. Freud convinced himself that he had demystified human motivation. How better to show it than to solve the greatest literary psycho-mystery in Western civilization: Prince Hamlet's procrastination.

After Freud, Ernest Jones and Jacques Lacan did extensive work on Hamlet's case. In time, the play became a proving ground for how well psychoanalysis could explain the inexplicable.

Without quite saying it, Freud and his followers implied that if Hamlet had known what they knew, his play might have had a happy ending.

It made for a good, unwritten story. If Prince Hamlet had undergone psychoanalysis, he would have overcome his neurosis, murdered his uncle, married Ophelia and lived happily ever after.

Strict Freudians analysts should have recoiled at the notion that psychoanalysis could produce happy endings. Yet, they could never have sold Freudian treatment if they had not dangled the possibility in front of their prospective patients.

Forget that Hamlet is not a human being. Forget that psychoanalytic critics were creating a fiction about a fiction, and a rather silly one at that. Forget that they were trying to do for *Hamlet* what Nahum Tate had done for *King Lear*.

Following Freud's lead, they wanted to produce a culture where people believed that psychoanalysis could cure. If psychoanalysis could solve Hamlet's problem, it would surely be able to help you to "unpack" your heart "with words."

You know the Hamlet enigma. Why did the prince, upon learning that his uncle had murdered his father, not exact swift and certain revenge? Why did Hamlet procrastinate?

Just as Oedipus was told that punishing the murderer of King Laios would lift the curse on Thebes, Hamlet was told to clean out Denmark's rot by punishing his father's killer.

If Hamlet had motive, means and opportunity to do as he was told, why did he not do it? Did he have a psychological impediment or was he stymied by real obstacles?

To answer these questions and to establish his claim to genius Freud argued that Hamlet was procrastinating because he was denying his Oedipus complex.

By Freud's logic, Hamlet was paralyzed because he could not accept that Uncle Claudius had done what he himself had wanted to do. Through a Freudian lens Hamlet's is the tragedy of the unanalyzed.

Freud and his followers deserve credit for turning one of the world's greatest art works into a marketing tool. They have used Shakespeare to suggest that if people do not hie to the nearest couch and pursue treatment to the bitter end they will end up like Hamlet.

In their zeal to promote Freud, psychoanalysts and Freudian literary critics have accepted several dubious assumptions. They have assumed that the ghost was telling the truth, that he was giving actionable advice, that Hamlet was obliged to follow the advice and that assassination was the only way to achieve justice.

Perhaps it's an occupational hazard, but psychoanalysts have always believed that Hamlet was suffering from mental health issues. They have dismissed the notion that Hamlet was stymied by external obstacles.

Predating even Freud, the obstacle theory did raise important questions.

When the ghost told Hamlet that his uncle murdered his father he told him in confidence. Hamlet's companions knew about the ghost, but they did not hear him speak. King Hamlet's ghost spoke only to his son; his son kept the message secret.

Initially, Hamlet doubted the ghost's word, but he became convinced when he saw how the King reacted to the play-within-a-play. We take it for granted that the King's reaction proved his culpability, but Hamlet never said anything about it. What was obvious to him might not have been obvious to anyone else.

Even if the play-within-a-play had been an investigation, it would only have been persuasive to someone who had been privy to the ghost's words.

If Hamlet had murdered Claudius because a ghost (that may or may not have been reliable) told him to do it, and if he had done so without having conducted a public investigation, he would have looked like an unhinged displaced heir. His action would not have been justice; it would not have avenged a murder; it would have been a palace coup.

Such theories were known in Freud's day and were disputed by the leading Shakespearean of that time, Oxford professor A. C. Bradley.

In *Shakespearean Tragedy* Bradley argued that Hamlet had not been impeded by real obstacles. If such were the case, he said, the prince would have mentioned it himself. Hamlet never complained about external constraints, so the issue could not have been very important.

Bradley believed that since Hamlet showed no concern about how his action would be interpreted, his problems lay in his mind, not in circumstances.

On the other hand, Bradley noted, Hamlet said this in his last soliloquy:

> *How all occasions do inform against me,*
> *And spur my dull revenge!*

Bradley's argument is cogent and persuasive. Yet, anyone who is facing insurmountable obstacles might put them out of mind. A depressed individual, in particular, might not want to think about seemingly insoluble problems.

He might retreat into his mind in order to deal with his personal issues, blithely imagining that once he solves his mental problems he will easily be able to do what needs to be done.

If we accept, for the sake of argument, that there were no external obstacles preventing Hamlet from taking revenge we still need to know whether the ghost's command, taken as a whole, was actionable.

The ghost did not merely tell Hamlet to murder Claudius. He told him that he should not, in taking revenge, harm his mother.

Would this have been possible? If Claudius deserved to die for murdering his brother and for conniving with his sister-in-law to assume the throne of Denmark, Hamlet could not have taken revenge without implicating his mother.

Even if no one at court knew that King Hamlet had been murdered, everyone did know that Queen Gertrude had contracted an overly hasty marriage. At worst, she was revealing her complicity in a murder. At best, she was disrespecting her late husband's memory.

No one should have needed a ghost to tell him that: "the funeral baked meats did coldly furnish forth the marriage tables." If Hamlet was the only one who saw it, he was indeed: "benetted round with villainies."

Unfortunately, the ghost of King Hamlet was so caught up in his passion for revenge that he gave his son instructions that could not be executed quickly or easily.

Moreover, the ghost was commanding his son to do something that he himself had motive, means and opportunity to do... but did not do. During his lifetime King Hamlet knew that his wife had made him a cuckold. He did nothing about it. He was murdered because he failed to defend his honor.

By not acting, Hamlet was emulating his father's example. Hamlet's dilemma had less to do with wishing he had murdered his father and more to do with not being able to shame his father.

The ghost found his son to be "apt" for the task, but the play suggests that Hamlet was miscast as the avenger.

When his father was alive the thirty-year-old Hamlet had been packed off to the university at Wittenberg. By the standards of the day, he was too old to be a student, so perhaps he was preparing for a career as a scholar. In that case, Hamlet might not have been sufficiently adept at palace intrigue to engage a political action and to control its meaning.

It is also odd that the thirty-year old Hamlet was unmarried and childless. When it came to assuming his manly roles, Hamlet was running late. Perhaps, even there, he had procrastinated.

Hamlet could act impulsively, but he could not take decisive moral action. He did not suffer from a neurosis, a desire gone awry. He was crippled by anomie.

The play's true question is why King Hamlet's sole heir (and apparently his only child) had been passed over in the succession.

True enough, Claudius named Hamlet his successor in the first scene at court, but, that raises the question of why Hamlet had not inherited the throne from his own father.

Hamlet himself declared it to be one more reason why he despised Claudius. In Act V he confided in Horatio:

> *He that hath killed my king and whored my mother,*
> *Popped in between th' election and my hopes,*

We may also ask whether Hamlet, when he failed to succeed his father, began to doubt that he was really the crown prince of Denmark.

When Gertrude helped make Claudius king by marrying him, she seemed to be complicit in a plot to deprive her son of the throne. But that would only have been true if Hamlet was really his father's son. Wasn't she the best placed to know who fathered her son? Didn't her adultery cast doubt on the identity of Hamlet's father?

This reading is more consistent with Bradley than with Freud. Bradley believed that Hamlet could not act because he had suffered a massive trauma when he discovered that his mother was not the woman he thought she was.

Hamlet's problem was not whether the ghost was a true ghost. His problem was whether he was who he had been told he was. You can't be true to yourself if you don't know who you are.

If Freudian theory is to be judged on its ability to elucidate the mystery of Hamlet, it falls seriously short.

Be that as it may, psychoanalysis could not have helped the prince. Let's assume that Hamlet had been lying on Freud's couch. How could psychoanalysis have cured Hamlet's procrastination when it itself is therapeutic procrastination?

Hamlet's play is not the tragedy of the unanalyzed; it is the tragedy of the well-analyzed. It shows what happens when someone tries to use psychoanalysis to solve a moral dilemma. And it shows what happens when a placebo cure wears off.

If Hamlet had been Freud's patient, he would first have learned the rule of abstinence. He would have been instructed to delay all major life decisions until he fully grasped his Oedipus complex.

Procrastination, anyone?

Had he been undergoing psychoanalysis Hamlet would have learned to introspect and to think out loud. Has any literary character so fully explored his mind and mastered the art of soliloquy?

If Hamlet had been a psychoanalytic patient, he would have spent more time trying to understand his unconscious mind and less time trying to strategize an effective revenge. Isn't that what he did?

Throughout his play Hamlet tormented himself over his relationships with his parents. To a psychoanalyst he would have been resisting the truth of his Oedipus complex.

Sometimes Hamlet embraced his Oedipal longings; sometimes he fought them. Sometimes he was crippled by the attendant guilt; sometimes he even acted out. Wasn't he doing what psychoanalytic patients are supposed to do: working through an interpretation?

And Hamlet was also fulfilling a wish that more recent psycho-analysts have expressed: he was making himself the author of his own tragedy.

Despairing of ever becoming a real hero or a real ruler, Hamlet rewrote the script to make himself a tragic hero. Apparently, he preferred it to becoming a real hero.

In a different context, he said as much:

> *Ere I could make a prologue to my brains,*
> *They had begun the play—I sat me down,*
> *Devised a new commission, wrote it fair:*

When his play began Hamlet was neither the central character nor the tragic hero. In the first scene at court, he was a sideshow.

His first line was an aside. Hearing Claudius's reference to him, Hamlet thought: "A little more than kin and less than kind."

Is there a better definition of anomie and its accompanying melancholy?

Depression does not necessarily entail inactivity. A depressed individual will not be able to do the right thing at the right time in the right place under the right circumstances, but he might dramatize his problem by doing too much and too little. He might vacillate between impulsive over-acting and cowardly inaction, between trigger-happy and gun-shy.

Unable to murder Claudius at his prayers, Hamlet quickly stabbed Polonius through the arras. When he discovered that the King had put out a contract on him, he did not procrastinate. He rewrote the order and had Rosencrantz and Guildenstern executed. He didn't give it a second thought.

Despite his prior hesitation about murdering Claudius, Hamlet acted decisively when he discovered that he himself was dying at his uncle's hand.

When the play began, Hamlet's antic disposition made him a central character, not as a hero but as an object of concern. Unable to say a word against a man he hated, Hamlet became the center of dramatic tension.

Later, after Hamlet murdered Polonius, the King decided that his nephew was a threat to the crown. Critics disagree about whether Hamlet knew who was standing behind the arras when he thrust a dagger into it, but his uncle saw the action as a declaration of intent.

By murdering Polonius, Hamlet shifted the play's action away from his duty to avenge his father and toward Laertes' duty to avenge his own murdered father.

Thus, the play dramatizes Hamlet's transformation from bit player into doomed hero.

Readers are also fascinated by Hamlet because he seems, in distinction to other tragic heroes, to have free will. Being introspective, Hamlet sounds as though he pondered his action. Where Oedipus seemed compelled to do what he did, Hamlet appeared to have other options.

Of course, Hamlet's free will is a mirage. Being a tragic hero, Hamlet does not have free will.

Just as Oedipus was cursed to murder his father and marry his mother, so was Hamlet cursed to murder his step-father.

Bradley explained:

> ...whatever may become of Hamlet, and whether he wills it or not, his task will surely be accomplished, because it is the purpose of a power against which both he and his enemy are impotent, and which makes of them the instruments of its own will.

In the final analysis, Hamlet did avenge his father's murder. Yet, by making it appear that he was avenging his own murder, he remained the play's true hero.

Hamlet also fulfilled the second part of the ghost's instructions. He succeeded in murdering Claudius without harming his mother. When Hamlet killed the King, Queen Gertrude was already dead.

Hamlet thought like a philosopher and spoke like a poet. Had he been alive in Freud's day he would have felt more at home in Bloomsbury than in Whitehall. Had he been living in Paris he would found the ambiance in the Latin Quarter or Montparnasse congenial. A studious soul, he would have been more drawn to the young scholars on the *rue d'Ulm* than to the aspiring politicos at the *ENA*.

For Hamlet, it was not just the time that was out of joint. He himself was ill-suited to the challenge he faced. A poet among assassins, a philosopher among thieves he was the wrong person in the wrong place at the wrong time.

Hamlet might have studied history and politics. Surely, he knew something about philosophy. Being a student in the city that was most closely associated with Luther's Reformation he must have known about defying corrupt authority.

Before he suffered the trauma of his father's murder and his mother's remarriage, Hamlet seemed to enjoy good mental health.

When Ophelia first encountered Hamlet's antic disposition she recalled who and what he had been. To her, the loss was palpable:

> *Oh, what a noble mind is here o'erthrown!*
> *The courtier's, soldier's, scholar's eye, tongue, sword*
> *Th' expectancy and the rose of the fair state*
> *The glass of fashion and the mould of form,*
> *Th'observed of all observers, quite, quite down!*

Presumably, Hamlet was faking madness. But, even if he was pretending, he told his friends Rosenkrantz and Guildenstern that he was depressed:

> *I have of late (but wherefore I know not) lost all my mirth,*
> *foregone all custom of exercises; and indeed, it goes so*
> *heavily with my disposition that this goodly frame the earth*
> *seems to me a sterile promontory....*

Hamlet might have been a good student and he might in the past have been more jovial than dour. When faced with a moral dilemma that surpassed him, his good mental health disappeared. Despite all his learning, all his awareness and all of his good feeling, when reality came calling, Hamlet's prior health turned out to have been a mirage. It's as though the placebo suddenly stopped working.

Anyone who uses psychoanalysis to resolve a real world dilemma will find that what felt like a cure was nothing more than a placebo. The reckoning will be as pitiless as it is certain.

11

PSYCHOANALYSIS DID NOT die with Freud. Or, if it did, its ghost lived on.

Coming so soon after the horrors of World War I, the catastrophe of World War II enhanced Freud's credibility by making him look like a prophet.

For most Americans, World War II was a heroic enterprise. Having defeated Nazi Germany and Imperial Japan, America's "greatest generation" applied its experience to the task of revitalizing the American economy.

The war united most of America's cultures in a successful enterprise. It brought the nation together and gave it a common purpose. Americans had no problem translating the ethic that brought victory on the battlefield into commercial and industrial activity.

Postwar America was not an especially fertile ground for the advancement of psychoanalysis. Some mental health professionals were trying to use it as a clinical tool, but, culturally speaking, most Americans did not buy the pessimism that psychoanalysis was selling.

The exception was the relatively small American Jewish community, joined by academics, artists, intellectuals and celebrities.

For American Jews victory over the Third Reich was emotionally confounding. With the end of the war they learned the full extent of the Final Solution and discovered that many of their friends, family members and co-religionists had been exterminated.

Belonging simultaneously to a group that had suffered an unspeakable atrocity and to a nation that had won a great victory they suffered a type of anomie.

For the first two postwar decades Freudian psychoanalysis mostly touched people who lived in large cities and around college campuses. Having entered the nation as a mental health treatment, it continued, after the war, to advance in the world of psychiatry.

In 1946 a young neurology resident named Aaron Beck, doing a rotation in psychiatry at the Veterans Administration Hospital in the Boston suburb of Framingham, MA, found himself surrounded by psychoanalysts. Basking in what he called "the psychoanalytic mystique" Beck felt like he was being lured into an "evangelical movement."

Initially, he was impressed by the psychoanalysts. As he explained, they:

> ...had theories for everything. They could understand psychosis, schizophrenia, neuroses. Every single condition that came in, they could get a good, sound—apparently sound—psychoanalytic interpretation for.

When Beck asked the analysts what evidence they had to support their theories, they told him he was suffering from unanalyzed resistances.

So it went, until the late 1960s. When the Vietnam War sent America into cultural turmoil, psychoanalysis escaped from the captivity imposed by psychiatrists and the urban intelligentsia.

When America failed in Vietnam, the nation divided against itself. Post World War II social cohesion seemed to dissolve, almost overnight.

With the debacle of Vietnam came a counterculture that, in the words current at the time, brought the war home. It proved to be fertile ground for Freudian thought. Herbert Marcuse and Norman O. Brown, among others, helped disseminate Freud's radical and negative psychology.

Given the spirit of the time, countercultural intellectuals had little interest in treating mental illness. They wanted to transform American culture.

In particular, they wanted to undermine the Protestant work ethic and the 1950s culture of conformity. In many ways they were advancing the efforts of French Surrealists and the Bloomsbury group. They extolled the virtues of creative self-expression, sexual liberation and adolescent rebelliousness.

In fairness, Americans were ill-suited for decadence. Most of them embraced it as mental hygiene. Evidently, they missed the point.

After World War II the French confronted a different psychosocial reality. For one, they did not know whether they were on the winning or the losing side.

After fighting for around six weeks, France surrendered to the Nazis in 1940. During the war many French citizens actively collaborated with the Vichy government and the Nazi occupiers. Marcel Ophuls seized the nation's anomie and its shame in his film: *The Chagrin and the Pity.* Yet, when the war ended France was treated as an ally.

Dwight Eisenhower seized the French anomie: "They are very volatile. They think they are a great power one day and they feel sorry for themselves the next day."

You can see why psychoanalysis was destined to thrive in France.

After the war, France, led by Charles de Gaulle, chose to Americanize. The indigenous culture that had staunchly resisted Anglo-American influence had not served the nation well on the battlefield, so France began to emulate the Anglosphere.

Sherry Turkle described the transformation:

> *The traditional French family business gave way to new industries based on the American corporate model, and the percentage of the population working in agriculture and living in rural villages fell from fifty percent before the war to less than fifteen percent in the mid-1970s.*

These reforms added another form of anomie. As France transitioned from family-centered businesses to a more corporatist system its people felt socially and culturally dislocated.

Before the war psychoanalysis had exercised a limited cultural influence in France. After it, as the nation floundered in despair, Freudian thought began to flourish.

It is also possible, as some have suggested that pre-war France rejected Freud because he was an Austrian Jew. After the war, embracing Freud was a way to expiate wartime sins.

According to Turkle, psychoanalysis did not fully enter French culture until the student revolt of May, 1968. In that, the French experience resembled what happened in America.

By rebelling against the government of Charles de Gaulle, French students were fighting against someone who had been trying to Americanize France.

With America failing in Vietnam the students believed that France should reject Anglo-Americanism. Wanting to be on the winning team, they chose to emulate the Viet Cong and the Viet Minh.

Sophisticated young revolutionaries also idolized Mao Zedong. They did not know what was going on in China, but they eagerly embraced Mao's Great Leap Forward and his Great Proletarian Cultural Revolution. Some of them formed Maoist truth squads to invade university classrooms and sow disruption. Radical French psychiatrists traveled to China to learn about the latest in mental health treatment.

And yet, France did not become truly Freudian until a charismatic Catholic Frenchman made psychoanalysis feel quintessentially French. His name was Jacques Lacan.

After 1968, Lacan gained cultural prominence for being a brilliant thinker and a charismatic speaker. He was decidedly strange but inalienably French. Better yet, he was not a run-of-the-mill bourgeois physician.

Like a cult leader, Lacan bewitched and beguiled young people and induced them to follow him... even when they had no idea what he was saying.

Many of them took his inability to speak clearly as a sign that he was channeling God.

A credentialed psychiatrist, Lacan had also studied philosophy. In his spare time he frequented Surrealist poets and artists. Rumor had it that Picasso sent his ex-mistresses to Lacan for treatment.

Seeing Freud more as a philosopher than a scientist, Lacan set out to rework Freudian theory, the better to produce what one writer called a "French Freud."

Occasionally, Lacan hinted that it would be good to improve clinical practice, but he never wrote up case histories and never offered guidance on how to conduct treatment.

He might have believed that those who saw Freud's Ideas clearly would magically become better clinicians, but he never argued the point.

When the post-war period started Lacan was as much an outsider to the world of international psychoanalysis as Hamlet was at the beginning of his play. Like Hamlet, he set out to rewrite the story.

In his version Lacan was a savior who would redeem Freud's sins. Alone among psychoanalysts he did not have an Oedipus complex. He suffered a Jesus complex.

Clearly, Lacan saw himself as Freud's one true intellectual heir.

As a psychoanalytic Jesus, Lacan would save psychoanalysis from the illusion that it was medical science and would free it from the need to produce positive clinical results.

However useful it was for analysts to call themselves men and women of science, Lacan, like Freud himself, knew that it was only a matter of time before people would see through the ruse.

Stories have a beginning, middle and end, usually in that order. If Freud was the first, the alpha analyst, Lacan cast himself as the omega analyst, the last of a breed.

The alpha was the first, the unanalyzed analyst. One might call him the unmoved mover.

With the omega analyst the movement stopped, the story ended and a new testament began.

In this new phase psychoanalysts could still practice, but they would no longer attempt to cure mental illness. They would aim at cultural re-education.

No longer would people believe that psychoanalysis was a thera-peutic experience. They would see it as a one-on-one initiation into the Freudian mysteries.

No longer would patients ask what psychoanalysis could do for them. They would ask what they could do for psychoanalysis.

No longer would patients expect psychoanalysis to help them to understand their issues. They would use their issues to gain a better grasp of Freudian theory.

No longer would psychoanalysis pretend to be helping people to conform to society's customs and values. It would incite rebellion against a repressive civilization and would offer membership in a cult of true-believing Freudians.

Members of the cult could gain access to the Freudian truth through his one true son, Lacan.

Psychoanalysis would no longer pretend to make people happy, healthy or respectable. It would offer absolution and sell indulgences.

This would incite patients' creative spirits. Since psychoanalysts would also allow their patients to sin with impunity, their work would subvert the dominant culture and make the world more Freudian.

In return, patients would show their gratitude by proselytizing the one true Freudian faith.

Throughout the better part of his career Lacan was happy to pretend to be a clinician. In his last years he changed course, in order to initiate a new Freudian testament.

Before he could do so, he had to neutralize the dangers that were still lurking. He had to chase out the practitioners who still saw analysis as a clinical enterprise.

Fearing that his death would provoke an atavistic reaction that would portray psychoanalysis as a clinical practice, Lacan tried to ensure that no one would ever again mistake it for a therapy.

To forestall the eventuality he chose to speak the truth. He wanted to be so unambiguous that no one could possibly misunderstand him.

It was a daunting challenge. When you have spent your life obfuscating, your listeners will have been conditioned never to take your words at face value.

In early 1977, to the shock of many, Lacan declared, during a lecture in Belgium that psychoanalysis was... a scam. He added, for emphasis, that he was sick of it. One assumes that he was thinking of what Kierkegaard called the sickness-unto-death.

As a parting gift, Freud had offered his followers a theoretical rationale for endless treatment. Lacan left his students with an admonition: they should cease thinking of themselves as clinicians.

Knowing that his words would be widely reported, Lacan was also telling the French patient population to stop expecting something that psychoanalysis could not deliver.

Of course, "scam" is a strong word. Lacan's disciples did not know what to do with it. Was their dear leader telling them to close up shop and surrender to the authorities?

If Lacan wanted them to change their errant ways, what would their new practice look like? Surely, he did not want them to become behavioral psychologists!

When Lacan's students first heard his Brussels statement, they were gobsmacked. Coming from a man who had done everything in his power to become the living embodiment of Freudian theory, it was too much to absorb.

So, no one did. Everyone repressed it.

Here is what they repressed. As quoted in a 1981 issue of the *Le Nouvel Observateur* Lacan said this in 1977:

> *Notre pratique est une escroquerie, bluffer,... les éblouir avec des mots qui sont du chiqué, [...] Du point de vue éthique, c'est intenable, notre profession ; c'est bien d'ailleurs pour ça que j'en suis malade, parce que j'ai un surmoi comme tout le monde. [...] Il s'agit de savoir si Freud est oui ou non un événement historique. Je crois qu'il a raté son coup. C'est comme moi, dans très peu de temps, tout le monde s'en foutra de la psychanalyse."*

My translation:

> *Our practice is a scam... we bluff... we dazzle them with words that are bullshit. [...] Ethically speaking, our profession is untenable. That's why I am sick of it, because I have a superego like everyone else.... We need to know whether Freud is or is not an historical event. I think that he blew it. Like me, very soon, no one will give a fuck about psychoanalysis.*

I am translating Lacan's expression, "*du chiqué,*" as "bullshit" but it has a different connotation in French. Specifically, it refers to the spittle that accumulates in your mouth when you chew tobacco.

Clearly, the French metaphor is more apposite than its English translation.

For those who care about such things, the last two sentences in the paragraph can be punctuated differently:

> *I think he blew it... like me. Very soon, no one will give a fuck about psychoanalysis.*

To my mind this new punctuation makes more sense.

Lacan was saying that psychoanalysts should cease worrying about whether or not their practice was clinically effective. It was not. End of story.

When he said that the only open question was whether Freud had made history, Lacan was suggesting that psychoanalysis would be judged in the context of cultural history. Were Freud's ideas influential? Had they changed the culture? For Lacan, that was the question.

When Lacan's comments made their way to Paris, some of his disciples were shaken, not stirred. Sensitive to their feelings, Lacan retracted it a few weeks later. To soothe their anguish he obfuscated the truth by wrapping it in double talk.

He was well qualified for the task.

Unfortunately, this prevented him from exploring the larger issue. Had he done so, he would have asked whether clinical psychoanalysis was a scam or a failure.

You can fail by not being up to a task. Or you can fail by making an honest mistake. Failure brings shame, but it does not necessarily bring guilt. Scamming people exposes you to both shame and guilt.

A clinician can fail to heal his patient without perpetrating a scam. If he offers the best available treatment, he might fail, but he will not be scamming anyone.

If, upon discovering that his method does not and cannot work, he continues to practice it, he will be scamming his patients.

A psychoanalyst who feels ashamed because he is not helping his patients can solve the problem by changing his practice. He will not mitigate his shame by doing penance, asking forgiveness and going back to doing what he was doing.

By confusing shame with guilt psychoanalysis shows people how to numb psychic pain. Of course, it's only a placebo cure. The pain will return, at times with a vengeance.

Lacan's word notwithstanding, his minions did not instantly stop practicing psychoanalysis. They kept doing what they were doing, shamelessly.

They seem to have reasoned that if patients persisted in believing that treatment could cure them, psychoanalysts had to permit them their illusion.

This implies that the new post-Lacanian psychoanalysis should be curing people of their mistaken belief in cure. It can fulfill itself by offering a cultural reeducation in the guise of a mental health treatment.

12

NO ONE KNOWS when Lacan discovered that psychoanalysis was a scam. He might have seen it late in life or he might have suspected it much earlier.

Either way, Lacan never believed that psychoanalysis was science. In his theoretical work he cleansed Freudian theory of its references to science and medicine.

To eliminate Freud's empirical references Lacan tried to rewrite the theory in the language of symbolic logic. Constructed out of letters and symbols, this logic does not refer to anything real. Since it does not contain words, it is ultimately unspeakable. One suspects that its "darker purpose" was to free people from the need to compromise themselves by engaging in conversation.

Lacan was not the first to try to reduce human knowledge to a concatenation of letters and symbols. Throughout the twentieth century great thinkers had been trying to logify knowledge. It wasn't a return to Freud. It was a return to Plato.

They were not looking for a new way to navigate reality. They wanted to gaze directly on the pure Forms. They believed that this provided a purer knowledge.

Bertrand Russell and Alfred Lord Whitehead tried to do it for mathematics in their ill-fated *Principia Mathematica*. In his "salad days" Ludwig Wittgenstein made common cause with this movement by writing the *Tractatus Logico-Philosophicus*.

Walter Gropius and Co. brought it all to a larger public through the work of the Bauhaus. By using geometric forms and unnatural materials Gropius and his colleagues aimed to produce structures that would embody Platonic Ideas.

Some of the structures were magnificent. Others were unfit for human habitation.

What impelled twentieth century philosophers and artists to undertake this grand project? Why did they imagine that formal logic could offer a purer knowledge, one that, strictly speaking, was perfectly useless? Perhaps they imagined, unconsciously, that formal logic, especially the predicate calculus could give them access to the mind of God.

Having lost the God of organized religion they might have been trying to get back in touch with Him by other means.

If God had a mother tongue, it could not be one of the languages that He had handed out after the debacle at Babel. By definition, God's language would, for humans, be unspeakable. It would be a language that transcended language.

To great thinkers, it made sense that this language could embody pure thought in a script comprised of letters and symbols.

A man of his times, Lacan attempted to write a Freudian logic. He used letters and symbols, charts and graphs, but he never produced anything resembling a logic. He wrote down a few abbreviations, scribbled a few symbols, drew some squiggles and doodles, threw in a few charts, added some predicates and declared that it was a formal logic.

It wasn't.

When it came to logic, Lacan talked a better game than he played.

Lacan was correct to see Freudian theory as a logical construct. He was right to see that it should not be judged by the clinical practice it engendered. And he was right to see that it could never account for human psychology.

To spare you the squiggles and doodles I will examine how Lacan theorized about speech and language. After all, he is best known for emphasizing the importance of speech and language in psychoanalysis.

Significantly, Lacan was more interested in the idea of language than in the way people used real words to communicate with each other.

Moreover, for all his interest in linguistics he had nothing to say about the important modern work in the field of transformational grammar. Perhaps it was too real for him.

Lacan thrilled to Martin Heidegger's musings about the *Logos*, the Greek word that appears in the original version of the expression: In the beginning was the Word.

He had little to say about Ludwig Wittgenstein, the greatest modern philosopher of language. He commented briefly on the *Tractatus* but ignored the *Philosophical Investigations*, Wittgenstein's later, more important work on language games.

Living at a time when philosophers like J. L. Austin and Gilbert Ryle were studying everyday language Lacan wagered the future of Freudian theory on a superannuated Swiss linguist named Ferdinand de Saussure.

By analyzing the way people used words Austin and Ryle were respecting the marketplace of language usage. They believed that meaning lay in the usage, not in anyone's philosophical lucubrations. They did not scavenge through fragments by Heraclitus to discover the "original" meaning of words.

For his part, Lacan was trying to shore up Freud's intellectual credibility. If psychoanalysis could not command respect for being a science, it could do so by being perfectly logical, like the first order predicate calculus.

If Freudian theory could not be validated by referring to objective realities, the next best thing was to show that it was logically consistent, coherent and complete.

By revealing that Freudian theory only cohered as logic, Lacan was admitting that it did not refer to reality. The truth value of sentences in symbolic logic does not depend on a reference to reality.

To make it sound easy, if someone says—"tomorrow it will either rain or not rain"—the truth value of the sentence does not depend on tomorrow's weather.

Lacan was implying that even if Freud contributed nothing to our knowledge of human psychology, he opened our eyes to transcendent ideas. Freud's theory did not involve human beings as they are, but as they might become.

Obviously, formal logic has more in common with fiction than it does with science. The value of a fiction does not depend on whether its statements can be proved empirically.

Lacan believed that if reality did not fulfill Freudian theory, then reality needed to be changed. Thereby, he was joining a group of people who wanted to remake the world into something that more closely resembled a fiction. Refusing to negotiate with reality, such people have worked feverishly to impose their ideas on it.

It is, dare we note, an exercise in futility, but that has not prevented a lot of people from trying.

At times, they have even tried to transform human nature. If human beings, as currently constituted, cannot function within a new culture or social order, they have to be transformed.

Radical psychoanalysts have wanted their discipline to contribute to this metamorphosis. If you cannot deal with people as they are, why not deal with people as they might be.

Lacan and Freud wanted to produce a new culture where the aesthetic mattered more than the ethical, where drama mattered more than responsibility, where desire prevailed over respect.

The old rules, the ones that valued good character and social harmony would be replaced by new principles that would value free self-expression, great sex and creative enterprise.

In the new world people would live according to their desires and not care about how they looked to others. They would no longer care about connecting with others. They would play their roles and recite their lines... with authentic feeling.

By speaking more poetry than prose they would undermine the marketplace of commerce and industry and turn life into a series of seductions. They would master the art of manipulating people, not getting along with them.

By trying to create a new form of human being, one that would feel at home in an unreal or fictional world, psychoanalysts were acting more like demiurges than like men and women of science.

Aiming to create a new humanoid creature they saw no reason to study the current version scientifically.

Even before Freud, philosophers had drawn the outline of these new beings.

They would, of course, be radically individual. They would be perfectly autonomous and independent. They would answer to no one and be responsible for no one. If they were disconnected from their fellow humans they would see it as a sign of superiority.

No longer needing to negotiate or compromise with other people, they would be beyond right and wrong. They would no longer allow anyone to judge them, even by the content of their character.

If they succeeded in overcoming the rules of social intercourse they would become perfectly amoral.

Historically, psychoanalysis began with an effort to cure people. Given its failures, its practitioners eventually understood that they would first have to transform the culture. When their patients did not get well, intellectually sophisticated analysts decided that the fault lay in the ambient ethos, the one that was imposing sexually repressive values. Worse yet, modern liberal society did not allow people to live their lives as though they were actors in a play.

The groundwork for the new Freudian culture lay in the structure of fiction.

In a literary fiction, actions matter when they advance the plot, sharpen the dramatic conflict and lead to a satisfying conclusion.

In a fiction right and wrong become aesthetic considerations. How well does the plot cohere? How consistent are the characters? How intelligible are the actions? What emotional response does the work elicit in readers or spectators?

A character might embody traits that we consider to be evil, but we cannot put him on trial. His value as a character involves the way he functions in the world he inhabits. Does his behavior make sense? Do the responses of other characters fit his actions?

Freud, of course, privileged the special type of fiction called Greek tragedy. By all appearances, it contains unique qualities. It does not point outside of itself. It does not provide guidance about how to function in the real world. In the largest sense, it captivates and ensorcells. When it takes you into its world it does not seem to offer directions for going anywhere else.

Even if a fictional character can serve as a role model, an artwork's aesthetic value does not depend on what happens when you draw a lesson from it. The aesthetic value of *The Odyssey* has nothing to do with how you act the next time you encounter a Cyclops.

Surely, literary fictions can teach moral lessons. They can contain characters who represent virtue and/or vice. Nevertheless, their value as guidance must take second place to their aesthetic value.

Since psychoanalysis aims at changing minds, not behaviors, Freud was right to base his theory on a play that will not encourage you to change the way you behave.

Of course, not all stories rise to the level of literary fictions. Some are specifically designed to teach lessons.

Some stories teach moral precepts by showing them in action. Some seek to make abstract ideas intelligible. Some project the possible consequences of an action or a policy.

Freud ignored them in favor of fictions whose characters were unworthy of emulation.

Freud believed that tragic heroes, being radically individual, dramatized the truth of human motivation. He wanted to induce people to use them like a drug... to regulate the psyche without changing behavior.

You might be thinking now that Freud did promote a reality principle. Didn't he want us all to come to terms with a recalcitrant reality? Doesn't the reality principle contradict the idea that Freud was aiming to turn human beings into fictional characters? How is it consistent with the notion that psychoanalysis wants to make the world a stage?

To answer these questions, we turn to Lacan. The French analyst accepted the reality principle, but he limited its scope.

Like Freud, he defined it as a speed bump, that is, as something that delays gratification. If you are trying to live your dreams by becoming a dramatic persona and turning your world into a stage, real objects are anything that gets in the way.

Lacan saw reality as an obstacle preventing you from becoming a new fictional being living in a new fictional world. He did not believe that Freudian psychoanalysis should be helping anyone to negotiate with reality.

To be a true Freudian, one had to impose one's ideas on reality, not to make deals with it.

Science is about what is. Psychoanalysis is about wish fulfillment, about what might be. Wish fulfillment is never about facts. There are no scientific facts about what might be or what might have been.

Many psychoanalysts have missed this point. They believe that if their patients tear away the veils of repressed wishes they will be more open to reality. They imagine that patients who overcome the lure of appearance will one day see things as they are... in their noumenal form.

Of course, a multi-year excursion into your mind is more likely to get you lost in the mental funhouse.

When he referred to the analytic process itself, Lacan said that, for a patient, the real was anything that did not fit the narrative. If, in the course of analysis, a patient found a piece of evidence that did not fit the story he was telling, he should have been motivated to reconstruct the narrative until the little object found its proper place.

Eventually, he should discover that the little piece of reality is not a meaningless chunk of inchoate substance, but a meaningful piece of evidence that fits perfectly in the right narrative.

If life is—as many people believe, even today—nothing but a narrative, once you change your story you will transform yourself.

You might also be thinking that Freud's reality principle is a call for deferred gratification. Didn't Freud suggest that adults need to learn to live with a certain level of frustration? Didn't he say that the ability to defer gratification is a sign of maturity?

Here, the answer is yes and no. According to Lacan, a being of desire can never achieve complete satisfaction. You might achieve some satisfaction by fulfilling some of your wishes, but there will always be something left to desire. If there were not, you would cease to desire. If you are a being of desire, ceasing to desire would mean ceasing to exist.

If Lacan was right to see Freud's theory as a logic—he could have been right without being able to write the logic himself—attempts to use psychoanalysis to access reality are doomed to fail.

If we want a slightly imprecise dramatic rendering of the disconnection between logic and reality we can find one in Zeno's dichotomy paradox.

Zeno was referring to a runner running a race, but I will take a liberty and apply it to the task of shooting an arrow at a target. Zeno discussed bows and arrows in another paradox; at the least, it feels more Freudian.

By this reformulated paradox, when you shoot an arrow it must first traverse half the distance to its target. Then it will travel half of the remaining distance. Then it will bisect the remaining space... and so on.

A half of a half of a half of a half... the sequence can and will go on forever.

Since an infinite number of spatial divisions separate the arrow from the target, the paradox "proves" logically that it will only reach its destination at infinity.

And yet, logic notwithstanding, a real arrow will hit its target in a finite time period. Zeno's paradox shows that logic can remove you from reality. Or better, it shows that once you detach from reality, it is devilishly difficult to get back to it.

You may believe, as an article of faith that logic gives you access to a higher truth, but don't try to prove the point by standing in front of an archer's target. You may be the truest of Freudian believers and you may feel perfectly secure in your knowledge that the arrow will traverse an infinite number of spatial divisions before it hits the target, but, trust me, reality will out.

You can see why Freud and Lacan did not want to deal with empirical or pragmatic truths. If they had given reality a say it would have undermined their logical deductions, overthrown their fictions and sent the Freudian enterprise crashing into the real world.

This explains why the great minds of psychoanalysis have always preferred mythology to archery.

And yet, if we see the arrow as forever desiring to reach a goal that is forever unattainable, the paradox might well offer a picture of desire. To some people, desire fulfilled counts as true love. Perhaps that is why true love often feels like it will last forever.

In the mythic image that most clearly renders that state the god of love, Cupid, pierces a lover's heart with an arrow.

Strangely, for all his talk about love, Freud rarely mentioned Cupid. He, like Lacan after him, referred to the Greek version, the god or *daimon* Eros.

One understands why. If you want to lure people into a bright new world of desire, you shouldn't suggest that you are leading them down the royal road to cupidity.

13

WITH JACQUES LACAN the Freudian Word became flesh. With him Freud's *Logos* took on a bodily form and the theory came to life.

More than any other psychoanalyst, Lacan tried to live the Freudian dream, thus to fulfill the Freudian law.

Since Freud could not bring himself to live a Freudian life, someone had to do it.

Freud had resigned himself to repression. In 1915 he told the American neurologist James Putnam: "I stand for a much freer sexual life. However I have made little use of such freedom."

Lacan, however, was irrepressible. Freud's theories had promised a smorgasbord of erotic delights. Lacan tried to enjoy them.

To do so he needed to be in touch with both his Oedipus complex and his narcissism. After all, Freud's theory is based on two Greek myths, the myth of Oedipus and the myth of Narcissus.

Obviously Lacan did not want to repress or abolish these complexes. He had come to fulfill them.

According to Freud, the Oedipus complex inscribes a child's polymorphous perversity in a family narrative. As the French say: *il ne manquait que cela*. The narrative served to produce and sustain sexual desire.

Were we to ask how someone could fulfill Freud's drive theory we would answer: by indulging his sensual appetites shamelessly. He would openly and honestly engage in forbidden and dangerous liaisons. He would relish decadence, with impunity.

And then there is narcissism. A late addition to Freud's theoretical ecosphere, narcissism is a form of self-love. In the original myth, the youth Narcissus fell in love with the image of his own beauty, as he saw it in a reflecting pool.

Freud believed that narcissism would eventually become object love. A child who loved himself and his image would eventually transfer that love to another person.

For his part, Lacan did not want to repress or abolish narcissism. He wanted to fulfill it.

What could it mean to fulfill one's narcissism? If narcissism begins as an infatuation with one's image, it is fulfilled when an individual loves himself, not because he is enthralled by his pretty face, but because he is unique and exceptional, one of a kind.

Someone who fulfills his narcissism and his Oedipus complex will live his sensuality fully and will not be ashamed to let other people know it. He will transform himself into the kind of being—or is it a mirage?—that fascinates and captivates others, drawing them into its lair.

A perfectly fulfilled narcissist will allow other people to love him, in a worshipful way, but he will never love them as much as he loves himself. He will draw people to him with his charisma, but will give little in return.

We do not have very much concrete evidence of Lacan's private decadence. We have heard enough rumors to feel confident that he did not emulate Freud's example of joyless asceticism.

But we do know how he created a public persona that showed narcissism fulfilled. Unlike most other psychoanalysts, Lacan was not shy about promoting himself.

Michel Foucault once invented a parable to help people understand Lacan as a man and a teacher. He explained it to me in a private conversation.

Imagine, Foucault said, a diligent student who spent years attending Lacan's seminar. He took copious notes and hung on Lacan's every word. As assiduous as he was dedicated, he worked the theory and did all the recommended reading.

Then, one day, this student screwed up his courage and presented a seminar report, or perhaps just a few remarks about one of Lacan's grand ideas.

Lacan, upon hearing it, would invariably reply: I never said that!

But, Foucault continued, if a scholar who had never heard of Lacan or psychoanalysis one day made an important discovery in his field, Lacan, upon hearing about it, would respond: I have always said that!

Shamelessness, anyone?

Lacan made his professional life a public spectacle. In a world of dour clinicians Lacan cut a dashing figure. Idiosyncratic, eccentric and dandyish, he did as he pleased, when he pleased, where he pleased and with whom he pleased. His was not a conventional or even a normal life.

In the postwar period most psychoanalysts emulated Freud's demeanor. Lacan chose not to. He knew that, to live the theory, he would have to be more Freudian than Freud.

Most importantly, he knew that he would have to abandon the idea that treatment was going to make people normal.

Why, he must have asked himself, would anyone undergo years of psychoanalysis in order to arrive at something as banal as normality? Why would anyone submit to such an ordeal in order to become like everyone else?

Lacan did not suggest that psychoanalysis would make people abnormal. He intimated, without saying it that at its best Freudian treatment could make people supernormal.

Lacan never claimed to be Nietzschean, but his work and his behavior were consistent with Nietzsche's idea that normality was something to overcome.

Everyone knows what normal looks like. Many people aspire to it. Most people know what abnormal looks like. Few people seek it out. But, how many people know what supernormality looks like?

Lacan knew that preaching the gospel of supernormality would not suffice. He had to set an example.

Rejecting the modesty that had shackled other analysts, he made himself a public figure. He became the first and most prominent celebrity psychoanalyst. If there had been psychoanalytic tabloids in France Lacan would have been perfect fodder. He would have accepted the exposure.

After all, he had come to create a new cult, not to heal the sick.

If you are going to found a cult to your person, you will need to manifest a palpable charisma. Of course, one might use charisma to produce placebo cures. After overcoming that temptation, one might do what Lacan did: to offer charisma as a quality that brings order to a chaotic life.

Max Weber offered the now-standard definition of leadership through charisma:

> *Charisma is a certain quality of an individual personality by virtue of which he is set apart from ordinary men and treated as endowed with supernatural, superhuman, or at least exceptional powers or qualities. These are such as are not accessible to the ordinary person, but are regarded as of divine origin or as exemplary, and on the basis of them the individual concerned is treated as a leader.*

When Lacan was alive, and even after his death, Parisian psychoanalysts and other itinerant intellectuals were intensely interested in his life. They gossiped about him constantly. They knew who his patients were and who his friends were. They suspected that they knew who his mistresses were. In his Freudian School, talking about him was almost a course requirement.

Some of the talk was rank gossip; some of it might have been projection. Yet, researchers have discovered that much of it was true.

Those who were not privy to Parisian gossip also had access to Lacan's supernormality. The charismatic psychoanalyst happily displayed his eccentricity in his clinical practice and public performances. By behaving strangely during his sessions, he provided his patients with anecdotes they could exchange at local cafes.

Some patients went to consult with Lacan in order to purchase entertaining stories. They weren't there to gain mental health.

Unlike most psychoanalysts Lacan did not pretend to be a proverbial (or preverbal) blank screen. Active, animated, in motion, he seemed more interested in putting on a show than in sitting quietly in a chair.

Sometimes Lacan received patients in pajamas and robe. Sometimes he was reading the newspaper or eating a meal. Sometimes he was counting and stapling stacks of banknotes. Sometimes he was tying or untying knots. Sometimes he seemed to be listening intently; occasionally, he seemed lost in his own thoughts. Sometimes he was personable; more often he was rude and dismissive.

Lacan made his sessions into drama. His patients did not have to project their own drama on his blankness. He enacted it in their presence.

Rather than chatter on about mental conflict, Lacan dramatized it. His in-session behavior seemed like living theatre. Or better, like pantomime.

Where most psychoanalysts offer platitudinous interpretations of dreams, symptoms and parapraxes, Lacan wanted his patients to interpret him. He seduced them into reading hidden meanings in his strangeness.

Patients played along because they believed that Lacan was trying to tell them something. In particular, they imagined that he was trying to tell them what they really, really wanted.

They took it as an article of faith that if Lacan did not speak to them, it meant that they could not handle the truth. They were convinced that the meaning of their dreams and symptoms was encrypted in his gestures, even his mannerisms.

On those rare occasions when Lacan did speak, he preferred oracular pronouncements to declarative statements. Good Freudian that he was he actively eschewed conversation.

Anyone can act strangely. Most people who do so elicit pity, concern or disinterest. Lacan was not like most people, so he provoked curiosity.

He did it by tempering his strangeness, turning it on and off, seemingly at will. Lacan was strange, but he was not always strange. People who are always strange appear to be abnormal. Since their behavior seems detached from any context, we do not believe that they are trying to tell us anything.

If normal people conform to society's rules and customs, supernormal people are chronic non-conformists. In principle they do so purposefully. If you can't conform because you are out of control, you are not a good candidate for supernormality.

Lacan did not want to imitate Freud or to inspire copycats. He did not want his followers to emulate him. He wanted each of them to be one of a kind.

And yet, a supernormal individual cannot be real. He must, ultimately, be a fictional being, a Zarathustra.

Roudinesco noted astutely that between 1932 when Lacan wrote his doctoral dissertation, and 1966 when he published a collection of his writings, he had redefined himself as a fictional being that would eventually be worthy of a cult following.

In his 1966 book, she explained:

...one no longer finds the Lacan of 1932, but a legendary character, the son of no man, without parents or family, having had as his sole master a solitary psychiatrist and as fellow travelers a famous painter and a poet who had committed suicide.

By making himself the son of no man Lacan was obviously identifying with the Son of Man. (As you know, mankind or "man" is not a man.)

Lacan recreated himself as *sui generis*, one of a kind. He seemed to want to be what Thomas Aquinas called a species unto himself, though not quite in the Thomist sense.

To do so, he manifested characteristics that belonged to him and him alone. Among the most obvious signs, evident to anyone who consulted with him or attended one of his lectures, were his shirts and his cigars.

When I was in Paris, Lacan conducted most sessions wearing a suit or a sports jacket... at least when he was not wearing pajamas and a robe. When he delivered lectures he was always appropriately attired.

But, he also wore collarless shirts that were closed in front by a three-inch tab. The shirts were uniquely his. No one else had the same shirts. They were evidently custom made.

Lacan seemed to have a stock of them, all in the same style, in a multitude of colors and fabrics. They were, at once, perfectly correct and utterly idiosyncratic.

To the untrained eye they bore an uncanny resemblance to shirts worn by priests. Perhaps it was Lacan's way of saying that he had missed his calling. Perhaps he saw himself as a high priest in a cult.

Lacking a collar these shirts could not be worn with a tie. Lacan refused to be tied up or tied down.

Also, Lacan always smoked twisted cigars. Shaped like oversized screws they were easily identified as *Culebras*. You can buy them from the Geneva tobacconist, Davidoff and Co.

In the world of French psychoanalysis only Lacan smoked these cigars in public. Devoted students sometimes smoked them in private but none dared appear in public holding a twisted cigar.

Why twisted cigars? Perhaps Lacan wanted to show that his was a peculiar warp of mind. Perhaps he was mocking those who thought he was twisted. Perhaps he believed that a cigar was never was just a cigar.

For the record, the French word for a screw—*une vis*—does not have the same vulgar connotation it has in English. As a consolation, the French *vis* is a homophone of the French *vice*, which means what you think it means.

Peculiar shirts and twisted cigars lay the groundwork, but did not suffice to make Lacan supernormal.

More significantly, Lacan proclaimed his uniqueness by refusing to conform to the standard fifty-minute hour. He departed from the Freudian norm by varying the duration of his sessions, usually by shortening them. Worse yet, he was prone to stop them abruptly, seemingly at whim.

By using short sessions, Lacan was showing that he did not feel bound by the rules that everyone else was following. He was setting himself apart from normal clinicians.

Before Lacan psychoanalytic sessions always had a fixed time limit. All analysts respected the rule and held sessions that lasted for an hour or fifty minutes. Many of them believed, rather quaintly, that the practice made their sessions resemble scientific experiments.

In time, Lacan's short sessions became a *cause célèbre* in the world of international psychoanalysis. Many psychoanalysts were scandalized by a practice that seemed to have been modeled on *coitus interruptus*.

When called upon to explain what he was doing, Lacan declared that he was punctuating his patients' verbal offerings in order to generate new meanings. Instead of interpreting, he was showing that another level of meaning was embedded in a patient's language.

In principle, patients would have more difficulty resisting a truth that was contained in their own words.

Some English examples will illustrate the point.

If a patient had intended to say: The man got off the subway, Lacan might have stopped him to make him say: The man got off....

If a patient had started to say: She wants to be taken seriously, Lacan could have made him say: She wants to be taken....

Obviously, believing that other meanings lay dormant in sentences was pure presumption.

It was also pure Heidegger. Writing in the *Stanford Encyclopedia of Philosophy* Michael Wheeler explained that Heidegger's peculiar use of language in *Being and Time* was a way to "reveal the hidden meanings and resonances of ordinary talk."

Cutting off patients in mid-sentence was unspeakably rude, but for those of us who wanted to access Lacan's aura, it was the price of admission.

Lacan was not the only rude psychoanalyst. He was just ruder than the rest. He differed from the others by never pretending to be other than rude.

Other psychoanalysts followed Freud's example and sat behind their patients. They did not converse with them or look them in the eye. They never answered direct questions.

In a normal conversation their behavior would have been grievously insulting.

Worse yet, psychoanalysts rarely took their patients at their word. They imagined that they knew their patients' minds better than their patients did. Surely, such an assumption was grossly disrespectful.

In everyday social interaction you would never tolerate such rudeness. In psychoanalysis you not only tolerate it; you assume that it's meaningful. How can it not be meaningful when you are paying for it?

Since Lacan's consultations did not have a fixed time limit, he did not need to respect temporal proprieties. A patient might have arrived for his 2:00 session, only to discover in the waiting rooms a half-dozen other people who also had 2:00 o'clock appointments.

At times Lacan would tell a patient to come by on a specific day, whenever he wished. Perhaps, he was teaching the importance of spontaneity and random encounters. Perhaps, he was making a fetish of rulelessness.

Many of Lacan's students followed his lead and varied the length of their sessions. Going back to the fifty-minute hour would have felt like a betrayal. Nearly none of them reduced their sessions to a few minutes or even seconds as Lacan did.

Sessions of variable length were basic to the Lacanian ritual.

One likes to think that he knew it, but even if he didn't, they also brought psychoanalysis closer to confession. The length of a penitent's confession is variable; it rarely lasts for an hour. Most often it does not even last for fifty minutes.

Lacan's short sessions were not just an innocent variation on a theme. They deserved an extended theoretical elaboration. Lacan never provided one.

By unilaterally modifying his practice and not explaining himself Lacan was saying that he could do as he wished because he was who he was. Some of his colleagues believed that he was enacting the Freudian truth. Others saw it as pure provocation. Surely, he meant it as a sign of supernormality.

At the least, Lacan was defying Anglo-American cultural norms. British culture, in particular, requires consistency and regularity, punctuality and decorum. It does not respect people who follow their whims. A culture where everyone queues up does not abide deviants gladly.

No one should have been surprised that the leaders of the International Psychoanalytic Association were appalled by Lacan. For nearly a dozen years Lacan's bizarre conduct—his supernormality—provoked an intense drama in the world of Parisian and international psychoanalysis.

The crisis began in the early 1950s when the leaders of Lacan's local society took offense at his deviations and insisted that he revert to the norm.

Having noticed that Lacan was accumulating an especially large number of candidates in training analysis, they refused to stand idly by while he took away their business.

Having been psychoanalyzed himself, Lacan took the rejection personally. He and his supporters resigned from the local society and founded a new institution. They quickly applied to the International Psychoanalytic Association for accreditation.

The IPA rejected the application. Like most of Lacan's former colleagues, its leaders refused to accept his short sessions.

Thus, Lacan became the central character in an international drama. His defenders saw him as a hero. His detractors saw him as an attention-seeking troublemaker. He saw himself as an intrepid defender of the Freudian faith.

When the first split occurred Lacan had not yet written very much. His colleagues knew that he was exceptionally intelligent and that he was a talented writer. But, he had not yet become the central character in the history of French psychoanalysis. In other words, he was not yet Lacan.

In the years that followed the 1953 rejection, representatives of Lacan's society and the IPA engaged in protracted negotiations over accreditation. These parleys dragged out for more than a decade.

Surely, Lacan did not help his cause by attacking the "ego psychology" championed by senior IPA officials like Heinz Hartmann and Rudolph Loewenstein.

Lacan did not just disagree with them. Contemptuously, he denounced them for having betrayed Freud. He declared that they had caused psychoanalysis to lose touch with the inner truth of Freudian theory.

So, he called for a crusade to recover the Freudian text. He called it a "return to Freud."

As concepts go, the "return to Freud" was brilliant. With a few backward-looking words Lacan seized the reactionary essence of Freudian theory.

After more than a decade the IPA offered to recognize the new French society, but only on the condition that Lacan not be allowed to teach or to train future psychoanalysts.

Lacan could never have accepted the restriction. How could he have sustained his Jesus complex if he had been forced to stop teaching?

To his mind he was being unjustly persecuted by a bunch of *faux* Freudians who resented him for being more Freudian than they were.

Immodestly, Lacan declared that he now knew how Spinoza felt have when he was excommunicated from the Amsterdam synagogue.

He could have said that he was being crucified and would soon rise from the dead, but he did not. I suspect that he was saving his best for last.

Faced with the IPA diktat, the French society split in two. Those who were willing to accept the restrictions on Lacan remained within the society. The others joined him when he founded the Freudian School of Paris.

For Lacan, having his own school turned out to be a mixed blessing. When you surround yourself with people who treat you like a god you no longer need to craft your language to connect with others. If they do not get it, it's their problem.

Lacan must have thrilled at the prospect of not having to answer to anyone. In his School, his word was law. He made it a place where everyone would obsess about disseminating what he called his "teaching."

His teaching always revolved around what he called his seminar.

Lacan had held his first private seminars in 1951. In truth, they were more lectures than seminars. Eventually, they became public spectacles.

Why did Lacan call public lectures, "seminars?" Apparently, he wanted to remind everyone that psychoanalytic institutions were like seminaries.

At first, Lacan limited his seminar to his students and colleagues. In the mid 1960s, at the time of his "excommunication," he moved it to the famed *Ecole Normale Supérieure* where he attracted a goodly number of philosophy students. Eventually, he held forth at an amphitheater in the *Faculté de Droit* on the *Place du Panthéon*.

By then Lacan's seminars had become important cultural events, attracting hundreds of listeners and almost as many tape recorders.

When he began his teaching Lacan said that he wanted to provide a close reading, an exegesis of Freud's sacred texts. After a time, he ceased his *explication de texte* mode and turned his lectures into public theatre. Thereby Lacan could better advertise his supernormality.

When Lacan lectured, he careened from one topic to another, in no special order. At times he seemed to be free associating about subjects that had captured his interest.

Eventually, his lectures became larded over with jargon, to the point where he no longer seemed to be speaking French. The lectures were a dance of signifiers and signifieds, of barred subjects and capital Otherness, of little objects and foreclosed names.

If the jargon wasn't bad enough, in his later years Lacan took up the Joycean practice of seeming to speak in tongues. He invented *portemanteau* words that embodied multiple meanings. Many of the faithful saw it as a sign that he was on intimate terms with the Holy Spirit.

Lacan's French versions were not as good as the ones that James Joyce used in *Finnegans Wake*. To spare you Lacan's inferior efforts—and to spare myself the trouble of translating them—I offer two memorable examples from Joyce: *awethorrority* and *gracehoper*.

In his writings Lacan had always cultivated the art of obfuscation. Where Freud had succeeded in simplifying—or perhaps oversimplifying—complexity, Lacan worked long and hard to complicate simplicity.

He got away with it because he convinced people that he was a mere vessel through which a higher power was expressing itself.

Why did so many people attend lectures that they could not understand? If it was not for the instruction, it must have been for the show.

Histrionic to a fault, Lacan manifested spontaneity, enthusiasm, surprise and misdirection. Such values are endemic to cultures that place a high value on romantic love and psychodrama.

From a Freudian perspective, less decorum meant more love. Less propriety meant better sex. True love required that you break the rules, defy convention and shatter routines.

By this reasoning, if you fall in love with someone your parents would have chosen for you, it cannot be true love. If you fall in love with someone who would be a suitable spouse, it cannot be true love. You can only fall madly in love, Lacan and the poets believed, with someone you are not allowed to love.

In fact, Lacan did not make true love the goal of psychoanalytic treatment. He was too sophisticated to traffic in adolescent banalities.

When it came time to define the goal of treatment, he shocked his audience by saying that he wanted his patients to become... saints.

What did he mean by sainthood? Your guess is as good as mine.

Like it or not, the word brings along a great deal of theological and even philosophical baggage. Neither you nor I nor Lacan can annul the word's usage.

Theology notwithstanding, Lacan could not have ignored the fact that Jean-Paul Sartre had previously canonized the writer Jean Genet as a saint.

If Lacan was influenced by Sartre's concept of sainthood, he never let on. Since he rarely acknowledged his debt to Sartre, it's not surprising.

Obviously, Sartre's Genet embodied the dark side of sainthood. If you understand that devils are angels, Genet was to sainthood as a devil was to an angel.

A career criminal, unholier than thou, Genet had sublimated his anguish in works that Sartre considered to be beautiful.

Sartre saw Genet as one of society's rejects, an abandoned child, an amoral being who embraced his status as pariah and redeemed his anomie in acts of creative sublimation.

Whatever his wishes, it would have been impolitic for Lacan to extol Jean Genet as the right kind of saint. Similarly, he could not have labeled Genet's "Our Lady of the Flowers" an exemplar of femininity.

On its face, Christian sainthood does not appear to embody the Freudian truth. Turning people into saints is not the same as producing master seducers. We do not normally associate sainthood with a higher level of sexual fulfillment.

If we look more closely, however, Lacan's point becomes germane. What, after all, could be more supernormal than a saint?

Saints do not live in the real world. As human manifestations of the sacred, they embody an otherworldly piety. In St. Catherine of Sienna's words, saints are "earthly angels." They do not compromise with the profane.

Saints do not follow society's rules or play society's games. It is almost too obvious to say, but you do not become a saint by having good table manners, conforming to sumptuary codes or sending thank you notes. You don't queue up to become a saint.

In the Catholic Church, a candidate for sainthood must have performed a certain number of miracle cures. If clinical psychoanalysis is a scam, and if its cures were, as Lacan said, accidental by-products of treatment, positive results had to be miracles.

By definition, miracle cures cannot be explained by science.

Saints do not necessarily indulge in psychodrama but they do live storied lives. The Catholic Church has produced many volumes recounting the lives of the saints. In its view such lives contain moral lessons.

If psychoanalysis aims at making its patients into true-believing Freudians, saints can serve as good role models. No one believes more completely and deeply than a saint.

By invoking sainthood Lacan shifted the frame of psychoanalytic reference from the profane to the sacred, from the clinic to the cathedral, from the empirical to the fictive.

When Lacan despaired of becoming a saint, he might have been thinking that he could not reach the goal while he was living like a voluptuary or profiting from a scam.

He knew from Augustine's example that indulging in lubricious pleasures is not disqualifying, but he must also have known that no one has ever fornicated his way to sainthood.

Even if Lacan despaired of becoming a saint, he did not necessarily abandon all hope.

He found his last best chance to become a human argument for the Freudian faith in martyrdom. Can you think of a better way to make a Freudian Passion the foundation of a new pseudo-religion?

As a Freudian, Lacan knew that he could only earn sainthood by going beyond the pleasure principle. That is, by suffering agonizing physical pain.

Spiritual anguish would not have sufficed for a man who saw himself as the Logos incarnate.

14

SHORTLY AFTER LACAN said that he despaired of becoming a saint, he contracted colon cancer. To the dismay of those near and dear to him, he rejected painkillers and refused surgery. He let the cancer consume him.

If any of us were suffering from this cancer, we would seek out the best medical care. We might not fight to the bitter end but we would surely accept some treatment.

When faced with the medical options, Lacan said No. Eventually, he underwent surgery, but by then he was comatose and had no say in the matter. After surgery, his kidneys failed and he died of the post-operative complication.

One understands that Lacan might have rejected painkillers because he wanted to emulate his spiritual father. When Freud contracted cancer of the jaw, he refused to take any opioid substances because he thought that they might cloud his thinking.

When Lacan's followers learned of his decision they offered a more sophisticated explanation. According to Roudinesco they diagnosed an unanalyzed needle phobia.

Even if this were true, there comes a time in every man's life when he has to put away the phobias of childhood. Why would any psychoanalyst suffer excruciating pain and precipitate his death in order to demonstrate that psychoanalysis cannot cure phobias?

It is more likely that Lacan was, with his death, living out his Jesus complex. He was martyring himself for the Freudian cause.

Lacan had long since turned away from God and had apparently rejected the Catholic Church. Still, he had been raised a Roman Catholic. His brother was a Benedictine monk.

Having been educated by Marist brothers, Lacan once said that he had been produced by priests. His ever-faithful son-in-law explained that Lacan had been a pious child and had known spiritual torments.

Whatever his personal beliefs, Lacan, like Freud lived in a Catholic culture. Nations that have been most receptive to his teaching—France, Argentina, Spain and Brazil—are predominantly Catholic.

Within that context, Lacan's way of dying can count as an act of penance. Isn't cancer a mortification of the flesh?

By the time he contracted cancer Lacan had become identified with French psychoanalysis. Thus, he was not just doing penance for his own sins; he was paying for the sins of psychoanalysis itself. Through his Passion he was offering his fellow scam artists a path to redemption.

If psychoanalysis had been founded on the original sin of pretending to be a scientific discipline offering a medical treatment, all analysts were burdened with a debt. With his Passion, Lacan was paying it off.

If someone pays off your debt by suffering your penalty, you become severely beholden to him. By martyring himself for the Freudian cause Lacan was purchasing the eternal love of his followers.

Or so he thought.

Many found it strange, but as his life drew to a close Lacan tormented himself with the question of how much his students loved him. Believing that they owed him everything, he insisted that they declare their love.

Undoubtedly, the love in question was closer to *agape*, Christian charity, than to Freudian *Eros*.

Those whose love was sufficient would show it by making psychoanalysis into a religious experience and proselytizing the true Freudian faith. In Lacan's name and through his Passion, they would become a secular priesthood and would minister to the disaffected.

The new Freudian Church would not imitate the Roman Catholic Church. It would be a Catholic Church in reverse.

Where the Christian Church worships the Virgin Mother of God, Lacan created a cult to the ultimate Non-Virgin, a mysterious figure he called Woman. In his French, she was *la femme*.

If Jesus is destined to be married to the Church, Lacan was looking for love in the arms of Woman. He wanted his Freudian Church to be Woman's representation on earth.

If the Virgin Mary was sexually impenetrable, Woman was the opposite: She was nothing but penetrable.

If the Virgin Mother was a model of chastity, Woman was the opposite. In Biblical terms Woman was the whore of Babylon.

If the Virgin Mother loves you, you feel blessed, as though you have received grace. If the whore of Babylon accepts your love you do not feel very special. You might even feel disgraced.

If the Virgin Mary was a pure source of light, Lacan's Woman was more like a black hole.

To my knowledge, Lacan never opined about black holes. Yet, he spent a great deal of time contemplating holes. While he understood the importance of holes in sexual experience, he was, in many ways more interested in the Idea of the hole. In his cogitations about holes, he ignored the astrophysics of black holes and the biology of bodily orifices.

When Lacan said that Woman did not exist, he meant that she lacked existence. By his logic she had to desire what she lacked: existence. Like a black hole, she would draw existence into her, destroying it.

As is well known, a black hole destroys light. What could be more anti-Biblical?

In the Bible, God created light by saying: Let there be light! If Lacan wanted to replace Judeo-Christianity with a pseudo-religion he was correct to organize it around a figure that destroys light.

If Lacan was Freud's only misbegotten son, he was saying that he, as the last psychoanalyst, had been born, not from a Virgin but from a black hole called Woman.

You might object that nothing is ever born of a black hole. It obliterates whatever approaches it.

But, that is the point. Under normal circumstances virgins do not give birth either.

Christian theologians have often wondered how God could have impregnated the Virgin Mary. After all, we are not talking about Leda and the Swan.

Many of them have accepted Augustine's explanation: God impregnated the Virgin Mary through her ear. If Christ was, in the beginning, the Word, he would naturally enter a human body through the ear.

But, how could Freud the Father have engendered a child through spiritual intercourse with a black hole?

What Word could Freud have tossed into a black hole to misconceive Lacan? Perhaps, he did it when he asked the only question that could have caused Woman to reverse her force field.

That question must have been: What does Woman want?

Freud's question reversed what happened when the sphinx asked Oedipus what walked on four legs in the morning, two legs in the afternoon and three legs in the evening. When Oedipus answered: Man... the sphinx self-deconstructed by throwing herself off a cliff.

Oedipus made Man the answer. Freud made Woman the question. When Woman heard the question, she misconceived Jacques Lacan.

Thus, Lacan fulfilled Freud's wish and went beyond the Oedipus complex.

It might sound strange, but true believing Lacanians take this as an article of faith.

I will grant that this sequence is chronologically disjointed. (If you like, you can tax me with poetic license.) I am aware that Freud did not ask what Woman wants in 1900, the year that Lacan was really conceived. Still, the first edition of his *Traumdeutung* was dated in that fateful year.

If we assume that the question of Woman's desire lay dormant in a book that asserted the importance of a mother's desire and its interpretation, the narrative makes more sense.

In any event, this fable also has a clinical application.

In Roman Catholicism the faithful do not pray directly to Jesus. They pray to his mother and ask her to intercede with him so that he will answer their prayers.

When patients begin psychoanalytic treatment, they usually try to converse with their analysts. Believing that their analysts know them better than they know themselves, they await the moment when their analysts will tell them what they really, really want.

When their analysts do not respond, they ought, in the best cases, to conclude that they were wrong to address their analysts directly. They should realize that they need someone to intercede on their behalf. That someone is Woman.

Imagine the scene. A patient undergoing Freudian psychoanalysis is lying on a couch talking. If he asks his analyst a direct question, his analyst might remain silent or might throw it back at him: Why are you asking me that? Or, more lamely: How does that make you feel?

At some point, the patient should conclude that he has gotten it wrong. He might be thinking that he is addressing his analyst, but his words are going elsewhere.

When he recognizes that he is not talking to the blank screen sitting behind him, he should see that he is really addressing the black hole that Lacan called Woman.

In psychoanalysis, a patient's words become most meaningful when they articulate Woman's desire. Since the patient's desire is elicited by her desire, he can only arrive at what he wants by solving the ultimate Freudian mystery: what does Woman want? If he succeeds she will intercede on his behalf with his analyst-confessor and the latter will forgive his sins.

Psychoanalysis began when Freud pretended to heal hysteria. It ended when Lacan founded a cult to a Lady.

Lacan was a man who loved Woman. Like the great mystic (and great crusader) Bernard de Clairvaux he craved Woman's desire. To prove his unconditional devotion, he offered her a sensual enjoyment that she could experience without a man.

No greater love hath any man than to save a woman from depending on him for her *jouissance*.

For all his talk about the phallus, Lacan did not want to found a patriarchal institution. He did not want his new Freudian Church to be a phallocracy.

When Lacan began theorizing about Woman, he was also trying to solve the greatest Freudian problem. It is so mysterious that most analysts do not even know that it exists.

As a combatant in the culture wars, Freud fought valiantly against modesty and shame. By promoting self-exposure he helped produce a culture where many people believe that they have a sacred duty to embarrass themselves, in front of friends, family and even strangers.

Most people understand intuitively how a man might expose his genitals. For the feminine sex, overcoming shame is more complicated. If, as Lacan theorized, the feminine sex is a hole, how can it be exposed?

How can a hole be laid bare? What does emptiness look like? How do you make present an absence or a lack or a void?

Conventional wisdom identifies the feminine sex with the flesh surrounding a hole, but Lacan disagreed. You might picture the vulva, but you cannot draw a picture of a hole.

Lacan understood the distinction well. After all, he was the proud owner of a famous painting of the exposed female sex, Gustave Courbet's: "The Origin of the World." It hung in the study of his country house, discreetly covered by a screen.

If Freud wanted, above all else, to defeat shame and modesty, he or his followers had to find out how women could expose their sex. Freud never really found the solution.

After agonizing over the problem, Lacan found the answer in a sculpture by Gian Lorenzo Bernini: "The Ecstasy of St. Teresa."

Gazing on it, Lacan realized that the truest visual representation of the feminine sex was the image of a woman in the throes of ecstasy. Having heard that feminine enjoyment feels like succumbing to the pull of gravity—another fortunate fall, perhaps—Lacan concluded that a woman can exhibit her sex by looking as though she is ecstatically falling through a hole.

If you are still wondering what drew le tout Paris to Charcot's presentation of his hysterical patients the answer is now clear. Everyone was entranced at the sight of women going into states that looked like ecstasy.

This explains why the Surrealists declared St. Teresa the patron saint of hysterics.

In St. Teresa of Avila Lacan found an exemplary instance of meta-phallic enjoyment. Only a celibate religious could have described her rapture so openly and immodestly.

Lacan fell to his metaphoric knees to worship the sculpted image of a saint who embodied Woman's ecstasy. Doubtless he joined Bernini in thrilling to the following passage from her Autobiography.

Describing her encounter with a cherub, St. Teresa wrote:

> I saw in his hand a long spear of gold, and at the point there
> seemed to be a little fire. He appeared to me to be thrusting it
> at times into my heart, and to pierce my very entrails; when
> he drew it out, he seemed to draw them out also, and to leave

me all on fire with a great love of God. The pain was so great, that it made me moan; and yet so surpassing was the sweetness of this excessive pain, that I could not wish to be rid of it...

In a mind-over-matter world of Freudian psychoanalysis the ecstasy of St. Teresa is as good as it gets.

Unless she was faking it.

Alas, that was a problem. When he commented on the Bernini sculpture Lacan declared that no one could doubt that St. Teresa was in ecstasy.

But, how did he know?

A man who thinks that he can know to an absolute certainty that a woman has experienced *jouissance* might well be a perfect dupe.

Yet, Lacan had to believe that she was not faking it. If there was any doubt about it, his pseudo-religion would have been yet another scam.

15

IN EARLY 1980, twenty months before he died, Lacan mounted his last institutional drama. He dissolved his Freudian School of Paris. Thereby, he produced a public spectacle, reminiscent of the old Parisian puppet show, the *Grand Guignol*.

For Lacan's most devoted students and colleagues it felt like an apocalypse.

In 1964 Lacan said that he could found a Freudian School by saying so. If God created light by saying: "Let there be light," why shouldn't Lacan found a School by saying that he was founding a School?

He would have saved everyone a lot of trouble in 1980 if he had declared the School to be "unfounded," but he did not.

It took more than Lacan's imperious word to destroy his Freudian School. Some of his followers, believing that his actions were extra-legal, decided to fight.

Lacan's *pronunciamento* set off what was called the work of dissolution. The process dragged on for months. New groups were formed and deformed. Alliances were forged and dissolved. Meetings were held and reported on. It was May '68 without the street theatre. Throughout it all, psychoanalysts peppered the French media with grandiose proclamations and histrionic denunciations.

Dour psychoanalysts became mini-celebrities. Many Parisian and even a goodly number of South American analysts seized the opportunity to exhibit their Freudian passion, openly, honestly and shamelessly.

They acted as though the "dissolution" had *enfin* given them a way to show the world that psychoanalysis had cured them of shame.

By choosing the word "dissolution" Lacan was saying that he was not trying to solve a problem, to resolve a conflict or to reform his School.

When he took as his motto the battle cry of Cato the Elder: *"Carthago delenda est."*—i.e., "Carthage must be destroyed."—he left little room for ambiguity.

But, why would Lacan destroy an institution whose success had vindicated him? Why would he punish his faithful students by depriving them their professional guild? Was he so narcissistically self-fulfilled that he did not understand how important it was to belong to a group?

It would have been more logical for him to announce that his School's success demonstrated his merit as a teacher and as a training analyst. He did not.

As his life drew to a close Lacan became alarmed that his School was becoming a respected training institution. He had not intended to make psychoanalysis a healing profession whose leading practitioners, acting in his name, would become wealthy bourgeois professionals.

He seemed especially offended that senior psychiatrists in the School were prospering. They owed him everything, but they were not showing him sufficient love.

While paying lip service to his brilliant theories they were expanding their ever-more-lucrative practices. They were acting more like money-changers than saints.

A dying Lacan also feared that, with his impending passing, his Freudian School would become afflicted with bureaucratic sclerosis. He would then be remembered as just another professional, not as a pseudo-god.

In the years leading up to the dissolution Lacan's School had become more like Plato's Academy than like a normal training institute. There was no admissions procedure, no curriculum and no graduation. People came and went, attending courses as they wished, unencumbered by academic requirements. Aspiring analysts pursued knowledge, not credentials.

Those who were adept at rattling on about complex philosophical concepts enjoyed the greatest prestige. Clinical work was an afterthought, if that.

Increasingly, the School attracted budding philosophers. Having discovered Lacan at the *Ecole Normale*, they had known him first as an intellectual. Later, they made his teaching the gateway to a career.

These students had no experience with neurotics or psychotics but they were well versed in Descartes and Hegel. As Lacan sought collaborators who knew philosophy and could work the theory, they gained prominence.

Many psychoanalytic institutions have had a few token non-physicians. Lacan's School was the only one that had a significant number of itinerant intellectuals in its midst.

In the "dissolution," in the final conflict between physicians and philosophers, Lacan sided with the philosophers. In practice, that meant that he promoted members of his own family. In his parting gesture he threw his most loyal, longstanding supporters to the winds.

Whatever his reasoning, Lacan had little use for the wisdom that came from experience. He seems not to have worried about the difficulty of building a new School with very, very few experienced clinicians.

Some of the rejected senior analysts denounced Lacan's philosophically-minded son-in-law for manipulating a dying man in order to deprive them of a privilege that they had earned. Others recognized the old French habit of keeping a business in the family.

When the work of dissolution ended, Lacan replaced his Freudian School with a new institution, the *Ecole de la Cause Freudienne*. Strictly, the phrase translates: The School of the Freudian Cause. Less strictly, it means: The Wholly Freudian Church.

If the dissolution was an apocalypse the Wholly Freudian Church was like the New Jerusalem, or, to be more precise, the New Babylon.

The School of the Freudian Cause was more frankly a cult. Clinical practice is not a cause. Fighting for a cause means taking sides in the culture wars.

By founding his Wholly Freudian Church, Lacan sacrificed the practice in order to save the theory.

But why did Lacan abandon his most devoted followers in favor of a bunch of *Jean*-come-latelies?

He might have been following Christ's precept: "the last shall be first and the first shall be last." In siding with the youngest members of his School, he was elevating those who had been last to arrive.

Or, he may have been thinking of another of Christ's precepts: "many are called, but few are chosen." Lacan's version was: "I don't need a lot of people and there are a lot of people I don't need."

Most of those who refused to join the Wholly Freudian Church had attended Lacan's lectures religiously for decades. They had been analyzed by him and had been supervised by him. In the dissolution he abandoned them.

When Lacan dismissed them he was effectively admitting that he was not a very good teaching and training analyst. If you are teaching the same students for nearly three decades, and if, at the end of that time, none of them knows what you were talking about, you are not a very good teacher.

Those who lost out in the dissolution had their reasons for doing as they did. Many of them insisted that they were following a principle that Lacan made the basis for a Freudian ethic: they were acting according to their desire.

Hadn't Lacan taught that you cannot be subservient to a master's authority and, at the same time, act on your desire? Besides, senior analysts were not going to kowtow to a callow young man who had no clinical experience. They had not been analyzed out of all their self-respect.

If you want to found a pseudo-religion you need to offer precepts and principles, rules to live by. And they have to be intelligible to people who did not attend the *Ecole Normale Supérieure*.

It might have felt unnatural, but Lacan had to overcome the habit of obscuring his thought behind veils of equivocation.

If no one can find guidance in your words, you are more a clown than a teacher, more an entertainer than a leader.

In one of his earlier seminars Lacan declared that people who wanted to live Freudian lives should follow one basic rule: they should bring their actions into accord with their desire.

In everyday language this translates: Do what you want!

Unfortunately, when someone tells you to do what you want—in English or in French—he is really saying that you should stop pestering him. "Do what you want" means: Get out of my face!

The principle is either very obvious or very obscure. Lacan called it an ethical principle, but it was more amoral than moral.

At the least, it differs starkly from the principle that tells you to keep your word. It stands opposed to the classical ethic that instructs you to do what you say and say what you do.

The psychoanalytic pseudo-ethic does not tell you to act honorably in all things great and small. It does not tell you to do unto others as you would have others do unto you. It does not tell you to love your neighbor as yourself.

If you follow it irreligiously, you will not improve your personal relationships. Then again, that is the point.

The Freudian ethic tells you to be true to your desire, even at the cost of your good name. It tells you to make your relationship with Woman your most meaningful connection. Evidently, it's not a higher calling. It's a lower calling.

Given a choice between your good character and your desire you should, by Lacan's ethic, choose your desire. If keeping your word forges bonds of trust between you and other people, yielding to the siren song of desire will probably damage your relationships.

Lacan showed what he meant by the way he conducted his professional life. When he was a candidate in the mid-1930s he promised his analyst, Rudolph Loewenstein that if he were admitted as a member of the local psychoanalytic society he would continue his training analysis.

Taking Lacan at his word, the society granted him the status of member. The next day he quit his training analysis.

In a 1953 letter to his former mistress, Princess Marie Bonaparte, Loewenstein assessed Lacan's character. He added an opinion of Lacan's short sessions:

> What you tell me of Lacan is depressing. He always constituted for me a source of conflict: on the one hand his lack of character, on the other, his intellectual value, which I prize highly, though not without violent disagreements. But the problem is that even though we had agreed that he would continue his analysis after his election, he did not come back. One does not cheat on so important a point without dire consequences (let this remain between us.) I hope that his trainees who have been analyzed in a rush, that is, not analyzed at all, will not be accepted.

Later, when his short sessions were being negotiated by the local society and the IPA, Lacan pledged to bring his sessions into closer conformity with accepted international standards. In reality, he did not.

Lacan occasionally paid lip service to the imperative to be good to your word, but when faced with a choice between being a man of his word and provoking a drama, Lacan chose the latter. Surely, it was a more Freudian choice.

As an ethical precept, Lacan's idea contains its own problems. Doesn't Freudian theory rest on the supposition that you never know what you really, really want? If so, how can you or anyone else know whether you are acting on your desire?

You might say that you only need to answer to Woman but how can you or anyone else know whether you have done so? You are not going to put in a call to Woman, are you?

If you follow an ethic that involves keeping your word, people can know for a fact whether you have fulfilled its terms. Giving your word is a public action. An objective observer can see whether your actions accord with your word.

But, how can anyone know whether you are acting in according with something as mysterious as your desire?

Lacan's ethic was not designed to facilitate human fellowship or companionship. It aimed at undermining social harmony, not producing it. Like a good Freudian he was setting people on the path toward a superhuman amorality.

As unpleasant as it is to say it, many of Lacan's followers were notorious for their bad manners. Most members of the Freudian School of Paris did not like each other, did not care for or about each other and did not bother to observe the minimal formalities that allow people to get along.

True religions create communities and congregations. People who follow their rules live in social harmony.

Lacan could never accept such a model for community life. After all, he had come to fulfill Freudian theory, not to abolish it.

Unfortunately, he had read Freud correctly.

Believing that society's rules of propriety and decorum denied the cold, hard truth about human nature, Freud rejected the rule that told him to "love thy neighbor as thyself."

In a world defined by the Oedipus complex, your neighbor can only be an obstacle to your ability to ravish his wife.

Distrustful of other people, whether neighbors or strangers, Freud dismissed the injunction to love your neighbor in these words:

> *Not merely is this stranger in general unworthy of my love; I must honestly confess that he has more claim to my hostility and even my hatred. He seems not to have the least trace of love for me and shows me not the slightest consideration. If it will do him any good he has no hesitation in injuring me, nor does he ask himself whether the amount of advantage he gains bears any proportion to the extent of the harm he does to me. Indeed, he need not even obtain an advantage; if he can satisfy any sort of desire by it, he thinks nothing of jeering at me, insulting me, slandering me and showing his superior power; and the more secure he feels and the more helpless I am, the more certainly I can expect him to behave like this to me.*

In Freud's dog-eat-dog, exploit-or-be-exploited world, anyone who loves his neighbor is denying a wish to aggress his neighbor.

Producing a community out of people who believe such things was always going to be a challenge. If true religions taught camaraderie and fellowship, a Freudian pseudo-religion was destined to produce conflict and psychodrama.

Witness the dissolution of the Freudian School of Paris.

16

BY NOW EVERYONE knows that psychoanalysis does not work. There is no need to belabor the point.

Over the decades many psychoanalysts, Freudian, post-Freudian, neo-Freudian and anti-Freudian have tried to make it into a more effective clinical practice.

They have rejiggered the theory, refocused the emphasis, worshipped new idols, created new sects, told new stories... and have kept on failing.

Jungians, Kleinians, Adlerians, Kernbergers, Horneys, Kohutites, Bionics, Sullivanians, ego psychologists, object relations theorists and self-psychologists have desperately tried to make psychoanalysis work. To no avail.

Some held fast to the Freudian credo; others broke with the Viennese neurologist. They all came up short.

Most of them merely introduced different narratives. Jung offered a smorgasbord of new narratives. Others preferred to focus on Electra or Hermes. French analysts saw the transgressive sexual desire of the Oedipus complex as a perfect foundation for decadence. American analysts wore out their little gray cells speculating about the nice young lad named Narcissus.

When a psychoanalyst offers an interpretation he is folding your experience into a narrative. In the narrative you can see yourself with your desire fulfilled.

Despite the evidence, many psychoanalysts continue to insist that their patients will be able to return to reality once the storytelling has ended.

If that is their goal, they would do better to dispense with the mystical journeys and guide their patients through reality from the onset of treatment.

Real life is not stationary. It does not stand still while you are trying to seize the Freudian truth about your unconventional toilet training.

By refusing to help their patients to manage their lives, psychoanalysts allow them to make unnecessary errors. The more a patient gets it wrong and the more he obsesses about what he and his loved ones have gotten wrong, the more difficult it will be for him to see himself as someone who can get it right.

Psychoanalysis will provide him with blinding insights and deep self-awareness but none of it will show him how to analyze a real world dilemma or to plan and implement a course of action.

If an analyst trivializes real experience in order to provide better access to a field of dreams, his patients will be wasting time and energy that they could have used to learn how better to conduct their lives.

Patients might feel consoled to imagine that their lives are structured like a story, but what if they take the next logical step and select friends who can best play out their appointed roles in their scripts. Serious people do not choose their friends for their entertainment value.

Normally, when you choose friends, colleagues and even spouses you want to be able to trust them. You want to know that they will keep their word, fulfill their responsibilities, do right by others and not yield to temptation.

When your spouse has to choose between picking up your child after school and having a mid-afternoon tryst with your neighbor's wife, you need to feel confident that he will not have to think very long or hard before making the right decision.

Funnily enough, if a man decides that having carnal knowledge of his neighbor's wife is more important than honoring his commitments, he will need to master the art of storytelling.

He might take a page from *Hamlet* criticism and explain that external obstacles prevented him from fulfilling his parental duty. Or he might excuse himself by saying that his unresolved mental conflicts made him stray.

People who systematically honor their commitments do not need to become great *raconteurs*. They do not even need to do psychoanalysis. Those who excel at narrating their lives are likely to be less reliable and less responsible. If they are that good at making excuses they have probably had many chances to hone their skill.

Psychoanalysis has always tried to transport people out of everyday life into a new fictional world. There, your libido will not be fettered by civilizing constraints. You can follow your desire, if not your bliss and do as you please, when you please, with whom you please.

Psychoanalysis does not transport people to this other world on the wings of angels and it does not book them passage on Charon's barque.

In Lacan's theory, the feat can only be accomplished through the magic of... metaphor.

The Greek root of the word metaphor means: to transfer, to carry over or to transport. When Homer talks of a "wine-dark sea" he is transporting you to a world where the sea is inviting you to limitless drunken debauchery. Metaphor might also move you into a world where pigs fly and horses talk. In such a world you see with a metaphoric organ: your "mind's eye."

By Lacan's lights, the best way to exit the social whirl and enter a new fictional world was to change the way you use language.

He believed that psychoanalysis had to grant metaphoric and poetic speech priority over declarative or descriptive statements. In a new Freudian world, words would not refer to reality; they would be subject to constant interpretation.

At their Freudian best, utterances never really mean what they say or say what they mean. They are mysteries waiting to be solved.

In such a world, you will not need to keep your word or to honor your obligations. If an 8 o'clock appointment can be interpreted in more than one way, you need not feel derelict when you do not show up.

You can say that you got waylaid while following your bliss. Be sure to make the narrative compelling.

The more you speak poetically, the more you will be working to seduce people, to entice them to leave their realities and to live in your fiction. Since poetic speech precludes any real connection with other people, seduction is the only recourse you have left.

Unfortunately, speaking predominantly in metaphors, like speaking in tongues, mutilates the language. Anyone who tries to make his way in the real world by using a mutilated language will be less effective and less functional.

Metaphors, like free associations, do not commit you to action. If they dominate your discourse, you will never be able to run a business, command an army, conduct a relationship, organize an outing or even make an appointment.

Freud began the work of mutilating language when he invented the rule of free association. By forcing his patients to think out loud he made their treatment into a training exercise in incoherent, obnoxious and trivial speech.

Following in the footsteps of his Surrealist friends Lacan saw free association as a necessary step toward activating your inner poet.

Surely, poetry is meaningful. It does not, however, gain meaning by referring to objects or situations in the real world.

Poetry wants to transport you into an alternative, possible world. There your histrionics can become a meaningful expression of your heart's desire.

Of course, the most important metaphor in Western civilization is a human metaphor, the Word that became flesh. In Christian teaching, only a human metaphor could transport souls to Paradise.

We all make occasional visits to fictional worlds. We regularly imagine what might be or what might have been. These fictional worlds tend to be inchoate and messy. They are not self-contained, but point away from themselves. We use them to orient ourselves in reality.

Moreover, our musings do not have a predetermined outcome. Like a good game plan they are subject to modification once conditions change.

Unless we are artists or philosophers we do not normally attempt to create a possible world that is coherent, consistent and complete, one that someone might be tricked into thinking he can inhabit.

This raises an important philosophical question. When a metaphor transports you from the real world into a possible world does it thereby make you into someone else? Are you the same person in a different world or do you become a different person in that other world?

In *Reference and Existence* Saul Kripke asked this question: When Tolstoy wrote a novel containing a character named Napoleon, was he attributing fictional attributes to the real Napoleon or was he writing about someone else?

Kripke answered that when Tolstoy used the name Napoleon he was referring to the real Napoleon. It did not matter whether the novelist described Napoleon accurately or inaccurately. Attaching the wrong descriptive predicates to the proper name, Napoleon does not turn him into someone else.

As I understand it, if you describe Napoleon incorrectly, in the sentence: Napoleon was the first president of the United States, you are making a mistake about Napoleon, not referring to George Washington. In Kripke's terminology, the proper name designates Napoleon rigidly.

Many psychologists, even non-Freudians, hold a different view. They believe that human beings change into different beings as circumstances or as the script requires.

In their theory there is no baseline human identity. We are all just a series of shifting personae. Behind each mask there is, effectively, just another mask.

Katherine Sharpe summarized some recent academic theories of personhood in *Coming of Age on Zoloft*:

> *For the last twenty years, the dominant academic theories of personhood have focused not on the idea of essence but on performance and changefulness, the sense that we don and doff identities at will as we move through our lives.*

By these theories human life is a dramatic performance in which we are all characters playing different roles at different times. If so, social norms are fictions and social roles are arbitrary constructs.

If you are just a series of different personae, when one of them does something wrong, you can evade responsibility by changing your mask. Call it an extreme makeover.

These theories pretend to show you how to escape from a repressive civilization, but they trap you in a script whose demands are far more inexorable. By making you a character in a story, they strip you of your freedom and your social being.

Since, in a Freudified world, we are merely reciting scripted lines and following cues, we are not acting freely. If the script says: "Exit, pursued by a bear" your character exits, pursued by a bear.

Freud and Lacan insisted that it's all interpretation. They were systematically ignoring the face behind the masks. Conveniently, this absolved them of any responsibility for helping anyone to save face.

Aristotle and Kripke would have disagreed. So would Homer.

Aristotle first proposed that nouns and names have meaning because they refer to essences. A noun, for example, refers to an essence that is contained in all objects belonging to the same class or species. The word "cow" is meaningful because it refers to an essential "cowness" in each cow.

In its turn, a proper name refers to a quality that belongs uniquely to the person or place that is being designated.

Proper names also differ from common nouns because they are never translated from one language to another. As Kripke said, they do something, they designate. They do not mean something.

In Chinese, the words Hong Kong mean "fragrant harbor." Yet, once the term becomes a proper name it loses its meaning. An English speaker can use the name Hong Kong correctly without knowing the meaning that the term would have if it were being used as a qualified noun.

If identity is the connection between your name and your essence, you maintain it by doing what you say and saying what you do. If your name establishes your identity by designating you rigidly, as Kripke has said, you should act as though your words and your actions are connected rigidly.

It makes sense that people who chronically go back on their word would persuade themselves, and others, that they possess many different personae.

When someone fails to keep his word, his entourage will want to know whether he is the person who said he would do this or the person who did that. Worse, he will not know the answer himself. In truth, there is no way of knowing.

With this in mind we can explore Freud's unspoken promise: if you rewrite your history and change the way you describe yourself or interpret your dreams, you will magically become a new You.

In this case Homer did not only disagree. He presented the ethical question in a form that would make it more intelligible.

In *The Odyssey* the greatest literary voyager traveled to many possible worlds. Between the reality of the Trojan War and the reality of Ithaka, Odysseus moved from one fantastical world to another.

Over the years his appearance changed so radically that, by the time he returned to Ithaka he no longer resembled himself.

And yet, he was always Odysseus. In one of the most famous scenes in literature, Homer showed Odysseus returning home to Ithaka. Having been absent for twenty years, and having undergone more than his share of strange experiences, he did not look like himself. Covered with soot, dressed in rags, unshaven and ill-kempt he looked like a beggar. Even his wife did not recognize him.

And yet, he was still Odysseus. His former nursemaid saw it first. As she was bathing the itinerant beggar, Eurykleia recognized the scar on his thigh. She remembered that the young Odysseus had acquired it while hunting a boar.

Throughout his voyages, the scar remained constant. Whether it was a presence or an absence or both, it told Eurykleia that the great warrior had returned home.

Being home was not enough. Odysseus knew that if he had identified himself he would have suffered martyrdom at the hands of Penelope's many suitors. Like the brothers in Freud's primal horde, they had been trying to supplant him in his wife's bed. Unlike the women in Freud's primal horde Penelope exercised her wits and kept them at bay.

By disguising himself, Odysseus rejected the role accorded him in Freud's myth—to be the father who had been murdered by his "sons."

He also did not draw attention to himself by putting on an "antic disposition." He put on a disguise that made him look harmless and inconsequential.

Still, he was Odysseus. Despite being twenty years older, he was the only man who could draw the great bow. After using it to eliminate the intruding suitors, he regained his rightful place as leader and husband.

Odysseus identified himself to his people by performing an action that he and only he could have performed. Without speculating about the aging process and muscle mass, we understand that Odysseus alone had the moral authority to do as he did.

As his story makes clear, it was not enough just to be Odysseus. Nor, Shakespeare made painfully clear, was it enough just to be Hamlet. As Hamlet discovered, what matters is what you do. To be or not to be is not the question.

Unless, of course, you aspire to be Hamlet.

All human beings bear proper names. Their names place them in families and communities. Having a place in a family or a community entails having certain duties and responsibilities.

As a husband, a father and a ruler Odysseus was responsible for the good order of Ithaka. He was responsible for protecting his wife. His moral responsibilities were built into his role. They were known to everyone. And everyone would have known whether or not he was fulfilling them.

By fulfilling duties that were uniquely his, Odysseus affirmed his moral being. Had he done otherwise he would have become yet another tragic hero.

If he had failed to act ethically, his scar would have become a tragic flaw, even a stigma.

Lacan wanted to draw people out of their world into the story of psychoanalysis. Odysseus, however, returned to his world and fulfilled his moral responsibilities. His actions compensated for his failures. He cured the problem of his absence by becoming present.

Like Odysseus, Oedipus possessed a uniquely identifying mark, his swollen feet. In Greek, his name means: swollen foot. Lest we forget, his feet were also scarred.

The swollen feet of Oedipus identified him as the abandoned son of Laios and Jocasta. When his identity was revealed he lost his fictional identity and fell out of the fictional world he had inhabited and ruled.

17

PSYCHOANALYSIS CANNOT SOLVE your problems because it has never solved its own. You see, it has what philosophers call a mind/body problem.

Psychoanalysts have always been frustrated to see that their dazzling insights and brilliant interpretations produce such meager results.

A psychoanalytic patient will unearth his past history, recover his forgotten traumas, learn his sordid motives, accept that he has an Oedipus complex, embrace his unconscious fantasies, overcome his control issues... and, most often, not get better.

Analysts have always found it puzzling—if not mysterious—that Freudian insights so rarely produce meaningful behavioral or attitudinal change. It's almost as though their precious insights had been tossed in a black hole.

Once they saw this, they might have concluded that their presuppositions were flawed. They might have grasped that the mind does not direct behavior, that psychological symptoms do not express unresolved mental conflicts and that human experience cannot be reduced to a story.

They did not. Being physicians most of them did not grasp the mind/body problem.

The problem dates to Descartes. Oxford philosopher Gilbert Ryle defined it well in *The Concept of Mind:*

> *How can a mental process, like willing, cause spatial movements like movements of the tongue? How can a physical*

change in the optic nerve have among its effects a mind's perception of a flash of light?

Ryle argued persuasively that philosophers invented the problem when they decided that they could best understand the human mind by seeing it as a fictional being, a ghost in the machine. The machine in question was a body separated from the mind.

In the philosopher's myth, a ghostly mind controls and directs our actions. Thus, you can only change the way you behave or feel by changing the ghostly mind. When psychoanalysts say that a patient who gets better without understanding his unconscious motives has only improved superficially, they are, however inadvertently, assuming the existence of a controlling ghost-like mind.

Psychoanalysts of all persuasions believe that, to help a patient achieve real change, you must change his mind. If a change of mind does not change mood, attitude or behavior, they do not feel responsible. If a patient makes bad use of his new mind, the fault lies entirely with him.

In Ryle's words:

> *According to the legend, whenever an agent does anything intelligibly, his act is preceded and steered by another internal act of considering a regulative proposition appropriate to his practical problem.*

Ryle did not solve the mind/body problem. He dismissed it. He declared that there is no separate, autonomous mind in the bodily machine.

This led him to observe that vanity, what psychoanalysts call narcissism does not express a mental conflict. It is merely a constellation of behaviors.

Curiously, Ryle's description of vanity seems to describe Freud and Lacan:

> *...on hearing that a man is vain we expect him, in the first instance, to behave in certain ways, namely to talk a lot about himself, to cleave to the society of the eminent, to reject criticisms, to seek the footlights and to disengage himself from conversations about the merits of others. We expect him to indulge in roseate daydreams of his own successes, to*

*avoid recalling past failures and to plan for his own advance-
ment.*

If vanity does not express a conflict between an unconscious mind
that is trying to say something and a conscious mind that does not want
to let it do so, vain behaviors are bad habits.

Of course, other people know whether you manifest vain or confident or humble behaviors. They treat you accordingly. They might want
to know whether you mean it or not, but they can only know that by
observing other behaviors. They cannot divine it by reading your mind.

You may try to fill your bad habits with meaning, but that will not
change them. The history of psychoanalytic treatment demonstrates the
point.

If Ryle was right, one can overcome vanity by identifying each bad
habit and doing what Aristotle suggested: replacing it with a good habit.

If a man behaves slothfully, he can overcome his character flaw by
behaving industriously. Amazingly, he can do so without unearthing an
infantile trauma or a repressed fantasy. He does not need to understand
what made him the way he is. He can effect real change by disciplining
himself and doing the right thing, repeatedly.

After a time, and after others accept him as such, he will become his
good character. At first, it will feel strange. After a time, it will become
familiar... to him and to others.

Obviously, it is easier to do so if you live in a culture that values
discipline and perseverance. If your culture tells you that you can only
overcome a bad habit by discovering a root cause, you will believe that
you should not even try to change it.

Thus a psychoanalytically-inspired culture nourishes and sustains
bad habits.

If a man holds on to his bad habits while he is sleuthing out the
ghost's motives, he will be allowing them to persist, unmolested. The
more ingrained they become the more natural they will feel. The more
natural they feel the more difficult it will be to overcome them.

If psychological symptoms, aka bad habits, do not express mental
conflicts, where do they come from?

You can acquire them by imitation, emulation, peer group pressure,
climate change or accident, but they do not express a mind's intentions

or conflicts. You can also acquire a bad habit—like the habit of expressing emotion intemperately—by following a culturally defined rule.

The philosophical mind/body problem began when Descartes decided that he wanted to find out what he could know with absolute certainty. The notion that we can or need to know something with absolute certainty is the MacGuffin of Cartesianism.

Descartes began his quest by casting a net of doubt. First, he doubted the evidence of his senses. Then he doubted his emotions, his perceptions and his experience. He doubted any knowledge that had been filtered through a bodily intermediary. He believed that if he allowed his body to have a say, he would never attain epistemological certainty.

Perceptions lie; so do sensations and feelings. Experience deceives us. Therefore, we should not base our knowledge on feelings, perceptions, sensations or experience.

To our modern way of thinking, Descartes was recognizing that the mind can play tricks on us. Living in the early seventeenth century he justified his systematic doubt by imagining that a crafty genie, a trickster, might have been fooling him. It might have been making him believe that the objects he was observing were real. For all he knew the world as he sensed it was nothing but a mirage.

In his *Meditations*, Descartes wrote:

> I will suppose that the sky, the air, the earth, colors, figures, sounds, and all external things are nothing better than the illusions of dreams, by means of which this being [this crafty genie] has laid snares for my credulity.

After he cast doubt on everything he thought he knew Descartes had an epiphany. He saw that there was one thing he could not doubt: he could not doubt that he was doubting.

Since doubting is a cognitive activity, someone who doubts is necessarily thinking. Descartes discovered that he knew only one thing with certainty: that he was thinking. He concluded: I think, therefore I am. *Cogito ergo sum.*

At that moment Descartes believed that he had found himself. He affirmed his existence as a thinking being, that is, as a metaphysical subject, a mind.

To which one might reply that when I say that I am thinking, the first person pronoun does not refer to my mind. "I am thinking" does not mean: "My mind is thinking."

When he arrived at what he took to be certainty, Descartes had to face a new, more intractable problem. If you detach your mind from your body in order to find yourself as a metaphysical subject, how can you get back into your body and back in touch with reality? And, why would you want to?

Once you have disembodied your mind it's very difficult to re-embody it. It's almost like raising the dead. If you have benefited from distrusting your emotions, your sensations, your perceptions and your experience, how can you restore that trust? Why would you want to?

The problem manifests itself in psychoanalysis. If treatment makes you get into your mind, what makes you think that you will easily get out of it?

If you master the habit of introspection, why do you believe that you will easily redirect your gaze at the external world? If you have explored every nook and cranny of your mind, why do you think that you will be able to use the same skill set to observe and negotiate with reality? Why would you want to?

If you are a pure mind, not the face you present to the world or the way you conduct yourself in it, how can you navigate a world where other people are not in on the joke?

The philosophical mind/body problem offers a different perspective on Freudian theory. Freud began by supposing that his patients did not know their own minds. He assumed that once they solved the murder mystery that had been haunting them the victim's ghost would be sent packing to a better place.

To Freud, someone who does not know his own mind does not know what he wants. If he doesn't know what he wants, he will be acting on the wrong desires and will always be neurotically unsatisfied.

But, if our sensations and perceptions and even appetites are not telling us what we want, how can we find the Freudian truth? Can we do it by taking a voyage of self-discovery? Should we launch an investigation, to solve the crime and to find our desire?

Sometimes neurotics confuse sensations or appetites with desire. Sometimes they misunderstand desire by believing that a mere object will satisfy it. At times they mistake others' expectations for what they really, really want.

In Freudian theory, if you try to fulfill other people's expectations— to be the good son, the perfect husband, the best ad man or the best lover —you are not acting on your desire. If you feel that you must possess certain objects because they signify status, you are out of touch with your desire.

To facilitate the mind's quest to find itself, thus, to know its desire, Freud wanted his patients to disconnect from their bodies, from their communities, and, as much as possible, from other people.

By lying on a couch out of Freud's line of sight they could pretend to be disembodied minds engaged in introspective voyages of self-discovery.

People who felt alone, isolated and disconnected thought that Freud's demands made good sense. People who had poor relationships were happy to find in psychoanalysis a practice that made a virtue of their anomie.

Of course, it could not work. Anomie is impervious to insight.

When you are thrown into an unfamiliar community and have trouble adapting, your problems derive from the circumstances, not your upbringing.

If you were brought up in a home where your parents fought all the time, it will feel strangely disconcerting to be in a harmonious relation- ship. First, you will not recognize yourself. Second, you will discover that you never acquired good relationships habits.

The skills you used to deal with past family conflict will not serve you in the present. No one gives up skills easily or willingly. Even if they are not needed in your current situation, they did once serve a useful purpose. Worse yet, you probably had to work to acquire them. Hanging on to them does not bespeak a death wish.

If you grew up surrounded by drama and conflict you are likely to provoke drama and conflict. If you can engineer more familiar situations, you will feel competent to deal with them.

You might also suffer anomie because a parent sexually abused you. Incest confuses roles and relationships, scrambles generations, and vio- lates the rules of family and social life.

Having been molested, you will be confused about who you are, how old you are, who you can trust, who loves you and who wants to hurt you.

If you try to understand the problem with psychoanalysis you will eventually learn that you wanted it to happen. Your ghostly mind directed you into a situation that would fulfill its wishes. The insight will not change anything in the constellation of behaviors that constitute your anomie.

Understanding why you feel alone and isolated does not make you feel less alone and isolated. It will make you feel that you deserve to be alone. By instructing people to get out of their lives and into their minds, psychoanalysis was doubling down on anomie.

Lacan understood this better than Freud. He still wanted to transform the ghost in the machine, but he tried to do so by following the example of religious mystics. He decided that psychoanalytic patients, like mystics should set out on mental voyages of discovery.

It was a clever, even a crafty ploy. If psychoanalysis is a mystical journey it does not have to promise better socialization. It does not have to get you back into your life.

It will try to make your social isolation a saving grace, a step toward a better relationship with God, that is, with Freud.

Like detectives, mystics seek out mysteries. They are not crime fighters, but they are seeking to know the unknown.

Why would a mystic take an introspective voyage? He might do so to resolve his doubts about God. If he is a religious and he begins to doubt God, he will feel alienated from a community whose embrace he can no longer accept.

If a mystic finds God, his anomie will be assuaged, not because he understands why he feels as he feels, but because he will reconnect with his religious community.

Similarly, a psychoanalytic patient who abandons all else to travel into his mind will, if he finds Freud, be able to join a community of true believers.

Lacan understood that if you are providing something that resembles a religious experience you must also provide something that resembles a religion.

If psychoanalysis could cure by allowing the unconscious to speak, it would not have had to become a pseudo-religion.

After all, people who privilege mind over body and who believe that they can change themselves by changing their minds will never be able to function within a real community. For them, a pseudo-religion will be the best they can do.

Yet, a simulation is not the real thing. A community of true believing Freudians differs significantly from a true religious community.

In the most obvious sense, communities that are based on Freudian principles never claim to be religions. In fact, they can never really become communities in the sense that we understand the term. Since they idolize charismatic individuals like Freud or a Lacan they are really personality cults.

Lacan, in particular, tried to create a community comprised of individuals who had been taught to ignore rules of decorum and propriety in favor of a relationship with Woman. It has proved to be a daunting challenge. Some might even call it impossible.

The differences between a real religion and the Freudian pseudo-religion are very clear.

Judeo-Christian religions encourage humility. Psychoanalysis produces hubris.

Religions want people to follow the rules and respect the law. Psychoanalysis allows people to violate both with impunity.

Religions show how to palliate guilt, but they also use shame to deter future sin. Psychoanalysis wants people to overcome shame in order to act on their desires.

Psychoanalysis writes human psychology into a narrative involving prohibition, transgression, guilt, penance, and absolution. Religions have their fair share of taboos, to say nothing of atonement and penance, but they also prescribe proper conduct.

Psychoanalysis emphasizes what you must not do. Religions also tell you what you should do.

Religions offer rules that will, if followed, produce harmonious communities. Wanting people to get along with each other, they facilitate the process by providing common rituals and ceremonies.

A community based on Freud's mistrust of his neighbors will have no rules showing people how to get along. If you are merely following a script, you do not have to learn ethics. Better yet, you do not have to learn how and when to apply ethical principles.

Like psychoanalysis, Judeo-Christianity recognizes sins of transgression. But, it adds sins of intemperance.

To take an obvious example, the seven deadly sins take normal behaviors to intemperate extremes. They do not involve law-breaking or transgression.

Each of the seven deadly sins refers to a quality that is good when practiced in moderation but bad when indulged excessively.

When religion declares gluttony a sin it does not mean that appetite is intrinsically sinful. Saying that avarice is a sin does not tell you to avoid thrift. If a day of rest is a good thing, sloth takes repose to an extreme. Confidence is a good thing, but arrogance, the sin of pride is not.

Psychoanalysis has no real use for temperance. It does not value your ability to control your appetite or to moderate your craving for filthy lucre.

Within the strict confines of Freudian theory there are no ethical precepts promoting good behavior or good character.

Freud believed that ethical systems were designed to deprive people of instinctual satisfaction. He did not believe in the positive virtue of doing the right thing.

Freud defined a fictional world in terms of an inexorable conflict between libido and civilization or between life and death. It was a compelling fiction, possibly a good home for a fictional character, but it will never be fully realized. For his part, Lacan was not deterred by the impossibility. He thought that it would leave people hungry and thirsty for more.

Given their druthers most people just want to get along. And they want to know what they need to do in order to get along. Only in extreme circumstances will they even imagine that changing their minds will automatically show them how better to conduct their relationships.

18

NEARLY ALL ENGLISH speakers understand the word "desire." Since Romance languages have words that are roughly equivalent to the English, their native speakers have no problem with the words for "desire."

When Freud wrote his *Interpretation of Dreams*, he used the German word *Wunsch* for desire. The word can mean desire but it is usually translated into English as "wish."

In everyday speech we say that we want or desire many things: a warm bath, a new job, a deep-dish pizza or our neighbor's wife.

Wishing is slightly squishier, but we normally know our wishes. When we make a wish we do not ordinarily ask ourselves whether we really want what we are wishing for.

Normally, we are conscious of our desires. It does not make much sense to say that we do not know what we really, really want. If we want something that badly, we probably know what it is.

As the term is used in English, and not just in English, we mostly desire objects and situations that are morally acceptable. All cultures add a few depraved desires for taste, but most of our desires are well within our comfort zone.

For his part, Freud believed that our true desire was always in our discomfort zone. For that reason, he posited, we do not know what we want and do not even want to know what we want.

Defying common sense and language usage, Freud argued that what you think you want is never what you really want.

If you think that you want to learn Latin, you are disguising your desire to copulate with your mother.

Almost by Freudian definition, if you think that you want this, you really want that.

If you happily tell your friends that you want to vacation in Nepal, the trip cannot, Freud theorized, be what you want. If you are thrilled to announce that you are going to fulfill your fondest wish and marry Phoebe, you do not really want to marry Phoebe.

For Freud, desire is a mystery that can only be solved by using your, or more likely, your psychoanalyst's powers of detection and deduction.

As obscure as it seems, the notion is reasonably familiar. Many a young man has believed that a woman loves him but does not know it. Many a woman has insisted that a man really wants her, even while he is lusting after her best friend.

If you think that desire is a stirring in the loins or a hunger running up your digestive tract you are where Descartes was before he began his introspective journey. You are confusing desire with sensation. If you persist, you will never know, with certainty, what you really want.

Once psychoanalysis convinces you that you do not know what you want, it will help you solve a problem that it itself has created.

It will teach you how to find your repressed desire by deciphering the clues that appear in your dreams, fantasies, symptoms and slips of the tongue.

In other words, Freud was not using the term "desire" as it is normally used. But why would he have introduced an idiosyncratic meaning? Perhaps he believed that attaching special meanings to words could draw people into his cult. Surely, Lacan did.

Others may believe that the word "desire" means what it means, but if you are a true believing Freudian, you and your fellow cultists will think that only you possess its private meaning. Joining a cult means unlearning what you thought you knew and embracing the new meanings that are only known to cult followers.

True enough, sometimes we are not sure what we want. We might not know whether we want the chocolate chip cookie or the blueberry muffin. Such is life.

To understand Freud we do not need to get lost in a textual maze. We can see what he meant by examining what happened to the patients he treated. Freud's theory generated a practice. Lacan notwithstanding, the results of that practice are its meaning and its truth.

To read Freud's case studies correctly we need to recognize that they teach moral, or better, amoral lessons. By now everyone knows that they were highly fictionalized, but they are a special kind of fiction. They are parables.

Jesus told the parable of the Good Samaritan, the parable of the prodigal son and the parable of the workers in the field.

Freud gave us, among others, the parable of the unworthy patient and the parable of the man who dreamt of wolves. Those were Dora and the Wolf Man.

We have already examined the parable of the man who may or may not have wanted to be eaten by rats. Less well known is the parable of the married analyst who fell in love with his married patient.

A brief look at two of these parables will show how Freud conceptualized desire.

In his parable of the unworthy patient Freud recounted his treatment of an eighteen year-old adolescent named Ida Bauer. Freud dubbed her Dora.

Analyzing Dora's dreams and associations, Freud concluded that she had fallen ill because she refused to accept that she was lusting after a man he called Herr K—the husband of her father's mistress.

Dora had known Herr K for several years. He had made his first but not his last romantic overture to her when she was fourteen. She had no feelings for him. She felt no concupiscent longings for him. Once, when he made an amorous entreaty, she slapped his face.

Herr K denied that it had happened and Dora's father sided with Herr K.

She may have been a mere adolescent, but Dora knew her mind well enough to know that she did not desire Herr K in any sense of the word.

She found the prospect even more repulsive because she suspected that her father had made her the object of an ignoble exchange with Herr K. Apparently, Herr K was willing to ignore his wife's dalliance with Dora's father because he believed that he would be rewarded with Dora's maidenhead.

Dora assumed, plausibly, that her father was trying to pimp her out. Why else would Herr K have willingly accepted the role of cuckold?

One understands why she fell ill.

Since the idea of a love affair between Dora and Herr K was especially sordid Freud decided that Dora really wanted it. When he told her, she demurred. Amazingly, Dora rejected Freud's brilliant interpretation.

Freud was unmoved. He did not care what Dora thought. Believing that he knew her mind better than she did, he tried to convince her that she really wanted what she insisted she did not want.

Undoubtedly, Freud was offended that a mere adolescent could know her mind better than he did. He set out to convince her that her dreams were expressing a baser truth.

His presentation was impressive. It was a model of good storytelling. Freud could have taken his case to a jury.

If treatment were really structured like a detective story, it would have ended with Dora recognizing the truth of Freud's narrative.

Freud knew that he was at least as brilliant as Sherlock Holmes, so he refused to believe that anyone, no less a slip of a girl, could doubt him. How could she reject her proper role in his fiction?

And yet, resist she did. Dora refused to be talked out of her identity. Eventually, she found Freud's persistence insufferable and walked out of treatment. The great psychoanalyst was left to nurse his narcissistic injury.

Freud may have thought that his interpretations were scientific fact. He may have believed that he was presenting objective evidence. In truth, his treatment was a failed seduction.

When a man tells a woman that he knows her mind better than she does, he is using a seducer's ploy. If she bites, he will take it a step further and tell her that she really wants him but does not know it.

Ask yourself this: if Dora had accepted Freud's interpretation, what should she have done with it? Should she have yielded to Herr K's lascivious yearnings? Should she have repressed her desire? Should she have transferred it to another lover, to be haunted by the knowledge that he could never be more than a surrogate? Should Dora have engaged in a mental struggle to keep this desire under control? Should she have sublimated it by painting landscapes?

Surely, you don't believe that once she had embraced the desire it would have magically disappeared.

If Freud had convinced her that she really desired Herr K, and if she had become part of a degrading exchange between the two men, he would have talked her out of her identity. He would have persuaded her to behave as though she were not really her father's daughter and were not worthy of his protection and care.

Having failed to seduce Dora with the power of his argument, Freud took his case to a larger jury. In an effort to convince the world that he was right, he wrote up the case.

It must have seemed like the dishonorable thing to do.

Obviously, Freud was defending his reputation as a healer. He felt a burning need to tell the world that if Dora did not get better, it was her fault. He did not fail Dora; she failed him. Worse yet, she failed psychoanalysis... in both senses of the phrase.

Why did Freud feel compelled to write up a failed case? Perhaps, he had been racking up so many failed treatments that he felt a need to rationalize the fact that his "dangerous method" did not work. An effective treatment would not have qualified as dangerous.

Being a disreputable professional Freud was also issuing a threat to his patients. If you do not get better I can expose your case in public. If patients thought that they could avoid becoming case studies by not getting better, they were overestimating Freud's integrity.

In his study of Dora's case Freud was not showing how well psychoanalysis worked. He was saying that he was not responsible for failure. He was saying that he had done nothing wrong and that he did not need to change his technique or his theory.

As you know, Freud closed his case parable with an ostentatious display of false humility. He admitted that he might have made a mistake.

Swallowing his false pride he declared that if he had followed his logical train to its ultimate *terminus* he would have seen that Dora did not really desire Herr K. She was lusting after Frau K.

Freud was willing to admit to failure, but only on the grounds that he had not been sufficiently Freudian. He had erred by failing to see Dora's Oedipal desire for the mother surrogate, Frau K.

Freud did not like it, but Dora left his office with her integrity intact. Three years later she married. She had one son, who eventually became the director of the San Francisco Opera.

As a sidelight, Dora also became an excellent bridge player. Her preferred partner was a woman named Peppina Zellenka. You know her by the name that Freud gave her: Frau K.

Freud failed to transmogrify Dora, but psychoanalysis was not finished with her. When Freud's student, Dr. Felix Deutsch had the chance, he slandered her. No woman could be allowed to defy the great Freud.

Two decades after she left Freud's office, Dora was suffering from an inner ear condition, known as Ménière's disease. Her physician asked Deutsch to consult on the case.

Dora had been hearing loud noises in her ears; she had been having bouts of dizziness and had not been able to sleep. Since medical science did not understand the illness, Deutsch concluded that she was suffering from hysteria.

During her consultation with Deutsch, Dora ranted and raved. One might forgive her the bad behavior. Tormented by severe tinnitus and vertigo, she had not been sleeping.

Besides, being psychoanalyzed by the great Freud had not helped her. One doubts that she harbored warm feelings toward either Freud or psychoanalysis. If she knew that her case had been published, she might have felt that Freud had betrayed her confidence.

In an effort to salvage Freud's tattered reputation as a clinician, Deutsch later wrote a paper about treating Ida Bauer.

Believing that her good name was less important than the Freudian cause, Deutsch denounced Dora as a "repulsive" human being. One feels that a medical professional could have shown more sympathy for a suffering patient.

By slandering Dora, Deutsch was telling the world that she had not been cured because she had refused to accept Freud's interpretation. Future patients beware: believe what your analyst says or you will be exposed as a repulsive human being.

Freud believed that he was always right. It did not matter whether his patients profited from treatment. For reasons that defy reason, he was very proud of the work he did with a Ukrainian patient we know as the Wolf Man.

When young Sergei Pankieff told Freud that he was chronically constipated Freud quickly understood that the man was repudiating his Oedipus complex.

Like an archeologist of the mind, Freud set out to unearth evidence that would prove his interpretation correct. After years of excavating, he found it in a traumatic event that he believed had occurred during the Wolf Man's childhood.

The patient could not remember the event, but Freud did not care. He declared it to be a fact.

Freud took his patient's childhood dream of wolves, mixed it with some recollections that had arisen during analysis and fabricated a story. Insisting that the story referred to a real event, he called it a primal scene. He then convinced himself that it explained all of his patient's symptoms.

Pankieff did not believe a word of it. Decades after his treatment had ended he told journalist Karin Obholzer that it was bizarre to see Freud get so lathered up over something that could not possibly have occurred.

What had not happened in the primal scene?

One summer afternoon, Freud mused, the eighteen-month old Wolf Baby was napping in his parents' bedroom. Thinking the boy safely asleep, the Wolf Parents started to indulge a coital interlude. Apparently, they were going at it like hungry wolves. Their grunts and groans awoke their child.

Glancing in the direction of his parents, not knowing what was happening, the child became so excited—or fearful—that he had a spontaneous bowel movement.

When he cried out he interrupted his parents before they could complete their act. From there on the Wolf Man was burdened with guilt for having deprived his parents of some sorely needed *jouissance*. He became chronically constipated in order to atone for his sins.

Why on that fateful afternoon did the Wolf Baby's bowels go into spasm? Freud answered that the reason lay hidden in his Oedipus complex. When young Sergei saw his mother being penetrated wolf style, he was seeing his desire realized: he too wanted to be buggered by his father. He was constipated because he could not embrace his wish to be penetrated.

As always, Freud was proud of his brilliant analysis.

It did not cure the Wolf Man. Upon finishing analysis the man had a nervous breakdown. He was later granted many more years of psychoanalysis with Freud and several of his students.

These psychoanalysts did nothing for the Wolf Man's depression, but they kept him out of public view. They also succeeded in covering up Freud's clinical failure. Ultimately, the Wolf Man became a ward of the psychoanalytic movement.

As for the amoral teaching contained in the case parable, consider this: regardless of whether the primal scene really happened, Freud was inviting his patient to visualize his parents having carnal relations. He was inducing the Wolf Man to violate the Fifth Commandment.

Had he embraced Freud's fictional primal scene the Wolf Man would have dishonored his father and his mother. He would have become a monster of filial impiety. How much more shameless can anyone get?

People who have a sense of shame do not merely keep their pants on. They also look away when confronted by someone who has inadvertently exposed himself.

We know that the Wolf Man's constipation was not cured by Freud's analysis. In truth, the problem seems to have had a physiological, not a psychological cause. Freud's fable did not alleviate his patient's depression, either.

Besides, if the Wolf Man had accepted that he wanted to be buggered by his father, what should he have done about it? Should he have become a homosexual? Should he have gotten involved in pegging?

Be that as it may, there is another, less convoluted way to understand why young Sergei dreamt of wolves.

The Wolf Man told Freud that, in his dream, the wolves in the tree looked like foxes or sheep dogs. He added that they were white, thus suggesting that they were more sheep-like than wolf-like.

Since wolves eat sheep, the dream may have been connecting them metonymically.

When the Wolf Man was a child, the 250,000 sheep on his father's estate were threatened with a disease. His father hired experts from the Pasteur Institute to inoculate them. Something went wrong with the inoculations and the sheep all died.

It makes sense that the child was trying to wrap his mind around the ovine holocaust. He might have thought that it was the work of a ferocious band of wolves. When he dreamt of treed animals he might have been asking himself where the sheep had gone. He might have been picturing an idea that had been communicated by a parent. And he might have been asking what would become of his father's estate without its sheep.

The Wolf Man ended his treatment with Freud in 1914. In 1919, he returned to 19 Berggasse. He did not want to do more psychoanalysis; he wanted to ask Freud's advice about an important life decision.

The Wolf Man was the scion of an important Ukrainian family. His father had been one of the richest landholders in the country.

When the Russian Revolution broke out Pankieff was living in Vienna. He feared that, in his absence, the Bolsheviks would steal the possessions he had left in his ancestral home. He wanted to return to Odessa in order to recover what he could while he could. So he went to ask Freud whether he should act on his plan.

Freud believed that the question was a ruse. Interpreting it as a wish to undergo more psychoanalysis—what else could it have been?—he invited his former patient to return to the couch. Or, as Lacan might have said, to return to Freud.

Unfortunately, the Wolf Man did not have the strength of character to say No. He yielded to Freud's entreaties and acted on a desire that Freud said was his. He remained in Vienna and lost everything. Thereby, he dishonored his parents by allowing their possessions to fall into the hands of the Bolsheviks. In the end he became a martyr for the psychoanalytic cause.

If Freud had failed to transform Ida Bauer into someone other than who she was, he seems to have succeeded with Sergei Pankieff.

Using his "rough magic" he transformed the son of one of the richest men in the Ukraine into a low-level Austrian functionary, a man whose life gained its greatest meaning when he became an important character in the story of psychoanalysis.

If any of his patients ever got better it was despite, not because of Freud.

19

HAPPILY FOR THEIR patients, psychoanalysts rarely give advice.

Wanting to convince you that you are destiny's plaything, they refuse to suggest that you have or can set the course of your life by exercising free will. They do not want you to suspect that things could have turned out differently. They do not want you to imagine that you can do otherwise than follow the script.

If your life is theatre, you can play your role well or poorly. You can embrace the inevitable or fight it. In Freud's world you have no other options.

Freud being Freud, he did not always follow this rule. Occasionally he told his patients what to do. He did not, however, present his advice as something they were free to accept or reject. He preferred to impose his views with threats and intimidation.

He was not offering counsel; he was acting like a play's director.

It was not very pretty.

Witness the case of Horace Frink. Less well known than the parables that Freud wrote himself, it is still instructive.

With Dr. Frink, Freud showed us that he was in close touch with his dark side. He behaved like a charismatic cult leader, not as a responsible professional.

Freud did well by not writing up the case. Had he done so he would have had to admit, not only that he had not helped his patient, but that he had, by indulging his venal instincts, tried to exploit him.

Sometimes the Freudian truth, that is the truth about Freud, is hard to bear.

The case of Dr. Frink is well known in psychoanalytic circles. Rational people consider it an ineffaceable blot on Freud's reputation. True Freudians dismiss it as an aberration. (Apparently, they missed the chapter where Freud explained that lapses reveal repressed truths.)

Lavinia Edmunds presented a well-researched account in an article ironically entitled "The Marriage Counselor." It appeared in the book, *Unauthorized Freud: Doubters Confront a Legend*, ed. Frederick Crews.

In 1921 a brilliant New York psychiatrist named Horace Frink traveled to Vienna to undergo a training analysis with Freud. His treatment lasted for four months.

Freud was happy to receive the American because, Edmunds notes, Frink was: "a gentile among Jews."

Freud observed that his Christian patient had shown: "...signs of deep understanding...." He added that Frink: "...learned so much by his neurosis that I have a high opinion of his chances as a healer."

Apparently, Freud believed that self-knowledge would make Frink a great clinician.

During his analysis with Freud, Frink confessed that he had been having an affair with a former patient, an heiress named Angelika Bijur. Both Frink and Bijur were married. Each had two children.

When Freud learned of the affair, he concluded that Frink was suffering because he refused to admit that he loved Bijur. Freud wrote: "I thought it the right of every human being to strive for sexual gratification and tender love...."

But, what did Freud mean? Frink and Bijur were having a love affair at the time. Was Freud saying that "sexual gratification" and "tender love" could only exist in marriage?

We might wonder where he got that idea. We know where he didn't get it.

Trying to help his patient to deal with his problem, Freud told Frink to divorce his wife. He also instructed Frink to tell Bijur to divorce her husband. In Freud's vision, the two would marry and live happily ever after.

Curiously, it sounds more like the ending of a romance novel than the *dénouement* of a Greek tragedy. It doesn't even recall the myth of

Narcissus. There's nothing very Freudian about it, so we have reason to be suspicious.

Perhaps Freud imagined that Frink had to choose between marrying Bijur and ending the affair. Clearly, he saw adultery as more of a problem than a solution.

What was Freud thinking? Strangely, he seems to have believed that if Frink had ended the affair, he would have been consigned to terminal sexlessness, or worse.

Freud did not consider the possibility that either or both lovers might re-invest libido in their respective marriages. He did not imagine that either or both lovers might find tender love and sexual gratification with other people.

Apparently, he believed that Frink and Bijur had each found what young people today call "the One." Or better, that destiny had brought them together for a reason.

To his discredit, Freud did not care that two divorces would traumatize all of those involved or that the aftershocks might dampen Horace and Angelika's ardor. He showed no consideration for the effect that the disruptive events would have on the children.

Again, Freud ignored real human experience. He seems to have believed that a marriage without love should be terminated. Surely, he was naïve. It is far from self-evident that the trauma of divorce is easily redeemed by a new love marriage.

But, Freud was not thinking in real world terms. In his fictional world patients were actors who were being called upon to play the roles that Freud had consigned them. That explains why the great doctor refused to allow either Frink or Bijur to consider other alternatives. He wanted to force them to follow his script.

Freud also ignored the consequences this marriage might produce in the world of New York psychoanalysis. Wouldn't the marriage of an analyst and a former patient have thrown psychoanalysis itself into disrepute? In later years, faced with similar cases, New York analysts chose to protect their reputations.

Were we to offer an alternative explanation, perhaps Freud calculated that since Frink and Bijur were violating so many taboos, only marriage could temper their intense desire.

It is also worth noting that the great psychoanalyst did not see his patient's slightly sordid love affair as the product of an unresolved neurosis. He did not believe that Frink had a problem that could be solved by an injection of insight.

After six weeks of analysis Freud convinced Frink to do the honorable thing—to propose to Bijur. All that remained was to convince her to accept.

To advance his scheme, Freud told Frink to invite Bijur to come to Vienna. There the two men would persuade her to divorce her husband and marry Frink.

Bijur agreed to the trip. She arrived in Vienna in July. To her chagrin, she found Frink depressed. When she asked Freud about it, he told her that she could cure her lover by marrying him.

He added that her new love marriage would also benefit her. If she did not marry Frink, he explained, her "existence" would be "incomplete."

Unwilling to grant Bijur a free choice in the matter Freud issued an ominous threat. If she rejected Frink, she would render him terminally neurotic or make him into a homosexual.

Bijur reported that Freud said: "...if I threw Dr. F over now, he would never again try to come back to normality and probably develop into a homosexual, though in a highly disguised way...."

Since Frink and Bijur both worshiped Freud as a god, they were easily persuaded.

The unhappy couple next traveled to Paris to meet with Bijur's husband. There Angelika told Abraham Bijur that she wanted to divorce him in order to marry her former psychoanalyst. For good measure, she added that Freud himself had blessed her new marriage. During the sojourn, she later said, Frink was "dazed" and "ineffectual."

Abraham Bijur reacted badly. Furious and confused, he did not understand why, a few days before, his wife had made love to him and had offered him a gift of expensive pearl studs. He objected strenuously to the divorce and denounced the Viennese "charlatan" who was directing the drama.

He decided that he would defend his marriage by buying a page in a New York newspaper, there to expose the truth about Freud. Unfortunately, he died before he could implement his plan.

I think it fair to say that Angelika Bijur's behavior suggests something less than undying love for Horace Frink.

When Frink returned to New York he told his wife that he wanted a divorce. She was more compliant than Abraham Bijur and easily acquiesced.

Having cleared the path to a new marriage, Frink and Bijur started questioning their decision. They began to doubt their compatibility and even started thinking that they were making a grievous error.

It makes sense. Freudians believe that prohibited lust is the best kind. Or better, that it is the only kind. Once a desire becomes prescribed, it must, for true believing Freudians, dissipate.

In the meantime Frink continued to suffer from depression. Bijur was worried, so she sent Freud what he called a "long and desperate cable" asking for counsel. Freud tried to comfort and manipulate her. He wrote back to explain that marrying Frink was not a mistake. She should, he added, be "kind and patient."

Freud then wrote to Frink: "Mrs. B is a treasure of a heart. Tell her she is not to blame analysis for the complication of human feelings which is only exposed, not created, by analysis.... I don't think continued analysis can be of any use for you, your case is complete."

True to his own mania, Freud quickly shifted the blame away from himself and away from psychoanalysis.

He did not seem to know that depression dampens sexual desire.

Obviously, psychoanalysis had not cured Horace Frink.

Now, Freud redirected his interpretations toward the transference. If Frink was depressed, it must have been a sign of his unanalyzed transference to his analyst.

Freud told his sometime patient that his depression manifested an unconscious wish to prove his psychoanalyst wrong: "It is true you are taking all possible pains to put me in the wrong. Yet I know I am right."

As always, Freud was impervious to any reality that would prove him wrong.

Since Frink and Bijur worshipped Freud, they acted like cult followers who felt privileged to abandon their free will to their cult leader.

A year or so after he had first started analysis with Freud Frink developed a new problem: he stopped desiring Bijur. Apparently, his depression had gotten worse. In a letter to Freud he explained that when he looked at her she looked: "queer, like a man, like a pig."

Freud replied with an interpretation that honed in on Frink's transference:

Your idea that Mrs. B had lost part of her beauty may be turned into her having lost part of her money [.] Your complaint that you cannot grasp your homosexuality implies that you are not yet aware of your fantasy of making me a rich man.... Let us change this imaginary gift into a real contribution to the Psychoanalytic Funds.

True love notwithstanding, Freud believed that Frink could best demonstrate that he had overcome his resistance by making Freud rich. Evidently, this is what Freud meant when he suggested that patients should bring their actions into accord with their complexes.

Freud's cupidity easily overwhelmed his concern for his patient's well-being. Lacking an ethic that proscribed greed or an ethic that prescribed benevolence, Freud indulged his venality freely.

You do not need to explore Freud's unconscious mind to see that his true goal was to use Angelika Bijur's fortune to enhance his fame and glory.

If the couple had owed their conjugal bliss to Freud, they would have felt indebted to the Viennese charlatan. It would have been easy to induce them to show their gratitude by funneling extra funds to the Freudian cause.

It was not to be.

In December, 1922 Frink fell into another depression. Screwing up his genius Freud told Frink that he had completed analysis and should marry Bijur. Apparently, he thought it was the therapeutic thing to do.

The unhappy couple complied. On December 27, 1922 Frink and Bijur married in Paris. Where else?

They did not live happily ever after.

Frink began to abuse and beat his new wife. Both he and the new Mrs. Frink saw that they had been victimized by Freud.

When Angelika wrote to Freud to ask for his counsel, he dismissed her concerns. Unsurprisingly, he suggested that she was unworthy of his genius: "Extremely sorry. The point where you failed was money."

Was he saying that things would have been better if she had contributed more money to the psychoanalytic cause? For Freud the fault was never his. And, of course, psychoanalysis never did anything wrong, either. If she had not gotten better, that could only have meant that she had failed.

Later, Bijur came to see that Freud's sole interest was to use her as: "a source of funds for his movement in the U.S."

With his new marriage falling apart, Frink had another nervous breakdown. After committing himself to Johns Hopkins psychiatric hospital, he learned that Bijur had decided to divorce him. Distraught, he made two suicide attempts. One time, he took an overdose of medication. Another time, he cut open an artery.

Frink barely survived. After he recovered, he returned to New York and attempted to practice psychoanalysis. When he tried to re-establish himself within the New York Psychoanalytic Society, its leader A. A. Brill wrote to Freud to ask his opinion. Freud replied that Frink was mentally ill. (By Freud's own judgment, psychoanalysis had not helped Horace Frink.)

With his position in New York compromised, Frink moved with his children to North Carolina. He died there of heart disease at age 53.

Before his death, Frink told his daughter that he wanted her to say this to Freud: "Tell him he was a great man, even if he did invent psychoanalysis."

When Frink was at Hopkins Angelika Bijur wrote to his physician, Dr. Adolph Meyer: "I have so far not met any analist (sic) who does not appear to me an obvious neurotic, lost in their theory and unable to deal with life...."

Presumably, that would have included Freud himself.

Faced with a choice between the good of his patient and the good of psychoanalysis Freud chose the latter. Having himself given up on "tender love" and sexual gratification he had sublimated his libido into the work of gaining immortality by founding a pseudo-religion.

For that he needed funds, especially for the American branch of the cult. Wanting desperately to advance his own cause, he did what he had to do to achieve his goal.

One question remains: was Freud's treatment of Horace Frink an exception or the rule?

In 1990 Daniel Goleman answered it in *The New York Times*.

After remarking that recent studies of Freud's clinical practice had shown the great psychoanalyst to be an ineffective clinician, Goleman added that Freud was also not an ethical individual:

New revelations depict a Freud who seems at times mercen-
ary and manipulative, who sometimes claimed cures where
there were none, and who on occasion distorted the facts of
his cases to prove his theoretical points.

Perhaps, Freud thought he was helping Frink and Bijur. The evidence tells us that he was willing to destroy eight individuals in order to gain access to Angelika Bijur's money.

Incapable of helping people to construct good lives, Freud had reached a point where he could only exercise his power by deconstructing the lives that they had created for themselves.

Calling Freud's treatment of Horace Frink a failure is too generous. It was a debacle, produced by a zealot who cared more for his fame than for his patients.

20

DESPITE ITS CLINICAL failings Freud's brainchild has succeeded in transforming cultures.

In communities where it has taken root, psychoanalysis has introduced new customs, new values and new mores. It has influenced the way people conduct their lives, the way they choose their careers, the way they raise their children, the way they date and mate.

It was neither unintended nor inadvertent.

Freud and his followers talked a good game about science, but, in their secret meetings they acknowledged that they were founding a new religion.

Peter Gay collected the evidence but flinched when it came to seeing the truth. Concluding that Freud was speaking in metaphors, he dismissed the idea that Freud's "darker purpose" was to found a new religion. Apparently, Gay did not see that metaphors could found religions.

Gay wrote:

> But Freud was trapped by his gift for vivid metaphor. He appealed to his "god logos" and scattered other terms borrowed from theology through his voluminous writings. As a medical student, he glorified "our modern saints, like Darwin, Haeckel, etc. In the early 1880s, in a letter to his fiancée, he called Helmholtz, that Renaissance man of modern science, "one of my idols." More damaging still, in 1899, he spoke to his friend Fliess about "the religion of science—Wissenschaftsreligion—which is supposed to have

superseded the old religion." Freud's most ardent supporters imitated him faithfully in this as in so much else. They would refer to analytic candidates as novices, think of Jung as a schismatic, detect in the meetings of the Vienna Psychoanalytic Society the pious atmosphere of a religious fraternity.

Gay's demurral notwithstanding, the truth was hiding in plain sight.

In his best known later works, *Totem and Taboo, Civilization and its Discontents* and *Moses and Monotheism* Freud analyzed the origin of human communities.

Some might say that Freud was offering an objective analysis of human culture. It is equally plausible to believe that he was laying down a blueprint for the creation of a new pseudo-religion.

Obviously, he couldn't say so explicitly. Freud had attracted adherents by pretending that his musings were scientific fact. Telling people who prided themselves on having overcome vulgar superstition that he was peddling an even more vulgar superstition would not have advanced his cause.

Thus, Freud never offered a vision of the utopia that would emerge once people learned to live by his theories.

Since he left the question open, other thinkers have rushed in to fill gap. Often they have done so by marrying Freudian theory with radical politics.

Some, especially the French, forced psychoanalysis into an arranged marriage with Marxism. Philosophers were happy to join in. Jean-Paul Sartre and Herbert Marcuse, among others believed that Freudian theory could help incite the revolution.

Psychoanalysts in Great Britain and America showed little interest in this side of Freudian theory. Believing themselves to be scientists and physicians they have mostly ignored the theory's political and cultural implications.

In France, however, many psychoanalysts happily proclaimed their allegiance to one or another version of Marxist thought. Some were more public about it than others, but French psychoanalysis has always been associated with the radical political left.

Lacan never declared himself a Marxist, but he treated Marx's philosophy with respect. His theory of the *plus-de-jouir,* whose intricacies I will spare you, derives in part from Marx's theory of surplus value.

And in one seminar Lacan declared: "Freud doesn't bullshit. Neither does Marx." To the faithful the implication and the connection were clear.

Lacan referred to Marx only rarely, but he often invoked the name and the theories of the great Nazi philosopher, Martin Heidegger. Apparently, he believed that Heidegger's thought could illuminate Freud's theory. I suspect that he also wanted to provide Freud with the prestige that would come from being connected to a recognized genius like Heidegger.

Lacan believed that psychoanalysis had more in common with cultural politics than with medical science.

But, Heidegger is a problem. He did not see his philosophy as a mere academic exercise. He wanted to use it to reform the German university system. When he became Rector of the University of Freiberg in 1933 he had to power to do so.

The problem was: Heidegger converted to the Nazi cause in 1933. Since he was a highly respected, with something like a cult following, his conversion was a propaganda victory for Hitler's National Socialism.

After a time, Heidegger became disillusioned with some Nazi practices, but he always believed that his philosophy was consistent with what he called "the inner truth and greatness" of National Socialism. After the war ended and after the full extent of Nazi horrors was known, Heidegger refused to recant his Nazi views.

Since his followers consider Heidegger a genius they have happily absolved him of responsibility for his political actions and beliefs. His most prominent defenders lived in France.

In post-war Paris, everyone knew of Heidegger's past. They knew that he had been banned from teaching. And yet, serious French thinkers declared that Heidegger's great ideas had nothing to do with his commitment to the Nazi cause. Obviously, they had learned their Descartes well.

To their minds, ideas were just ideas. Whatever ensued when they were put into practice was irrelevant. It did not reflect on the great mind that had thought them up.

When called on to justify their infatuation with Heidegger, French psychoanalysts joined with philosophers in declaring that Heidegger, like Freud and Marx, was a genius. To them, genius transcended politics.

To found a religion, even a pseudo-religion, you need a god, or a reasonable facsimile. At the very least, you need a genius. It's even better when you can have an unholy trinity of geniuses: Freud, Marx and Heidegger.

One can easily imagine that Lacan saw Freud as someone who could be connected with Marx and Heidegger in a structure that looked like a Borromean knot.

Since Lacan had overcome the pretense that psychoanalysis was a science, he had no use for the trinity of Darwin, Copernicus and Freud.

For Lacan, the linkage of Freud, Marx and Heidegger would found a new culture.

Freud's theories would be used to manipulate the human psyche. Marx's ideas would show how to change political economy. And, Heidegger's thought would promote a more aesthetic and more authentic way of life.

Joined together the three would help conceive a new and better version of human being. They would also create the cultural conditions in which it could flourish.

People flocked to these men, because... what else was there to worship? If you cannot rely on God to give you your moral bearings, you are left with the authority of genius.

When, during the Enlightenment, serious intellectuals ceased believing in God, they began to worship genius. Apparently, it's not just nature that abhors a vacuum.

The original Latin word *genius* refers to a being that we would call a genie. Like a guardian angel, a *genius* was originally a tutelary spirit.

In *Divine Fury: the History of Genius* historian Darrin McMahon showed that early Christians transferred the functions associated with Roman geniuses to angels. They also transformed cults to pagan gods into cults to saints.

Centuries later, during the Reformation and the Enlightenment people began to worship human genius.

Strangely, while believing that they had thrown off the superstitions that attached to saints they were collecting the body parts of dead geniuses. They treated them as relics and have preserved to this day: Galileo's finger, Napoleon's penis and Einstein's eyeballs.

The French Revolution continued the process of redefining the proper function of human genius. The revolutionaries expected that great minds could produce a vision that would guide those who wanted to change the world.

McMahon explained the new cult:

> *And in their repeated insistence that exceptional individuals were the true motors of history, who had ushered in the glorious dawn of 1789, the revolutionaries worked to drown out the doubts of skeptics like Adams. Consolidating a myth of the genius's political power that even their opponents would come to share, the revolutionaries elaborated a belief that would long outlive them. The genius could be a maker of revolutions, a leader of the people, a revolutionary man.*
>
> *By linking geniuses emphatically to politics and political change, the revolutionaries highlighted the capacity of extraordinary individuals not just to understand the world, but to change it. Only with the Revolution could a myth of revolutionary genius emerge, and with the propagation of that myth was born a possibility, still fledgling, but soon to be fulfilled: that genius might be used as the basis of political power, celebrated not only in death but in life, employed to justify an extraordinary privilege and license.*

Freud, Marx and Heidegger boldly took the next step. They did not merely want to change human cultures. They wanted to recreate human being.

They may not have used the term, but they saw themselves as demiurges, creative spirits whose work could produce a better version of human being, one that would be in closer accord with their ideas.

Many people still see Freud as a genius, but not as a scientific genius. They have granted him an exalted status for his philosophical mythmaking. His theories were beautifully constructed and artfully expressed. They might not have had anything to do with human psychology, but they were consistent, coherent, cogent and complete. Besides, they told a great story.

More demiurge than scientist, Freud was not describing human beings as they were. He was trying to create a new form of being, one that would overcome the limitations that inhered in being civilized.

It made sense for Freud to name Goethe, Schiller, Shakespeare, Sophocles and Dostoevsky as his forebears. After all, they created characters and placed them in new worlds.

Freud believed that these new characters and their new worlds embodied a truth that surpassed normal human experience. This truth was more poetical than empirical.

By undergoing psychoanalytic treatment people would deconstruct their prior being and recreate themselves as characters that embodied the Freudian truth.

These new creatures would no longer need to connect with human beings. They would overcome their impulse to follow the rules that sustained a harmonious community.

No longer would they need to compete in the arena. No longer would they be involved in actions that were best described as games. They would henceforth do as the narrative commanded. And they would like it.

In Marx's world human beings were not social beings who affirmed themselves by competing in the marketplace. In place of the Biblical injunction, "to every man according to his deeds," Marx substituted: "to each according to his needs."

The Biblical statement, from both Old and New Testaments can be the basis for a work ethic. When Marx rejected the connection between work and reward, he eliminated the concept of earned achievement. And, he was saying that people should not be allowed to enjoy the fruits of their labor.

Marx and his followers believed that with the advent of the New Socialist Man people would flourish within a Workers' Paradise. Evidently, they suspected that the Workers' Paradise was unfit for human habitation.

Leon Trotsky's New Socialist Man sounded like the bastard spawn produced by coupling Freud and Nietzsche:

> *Man will make it his purpose to master his own feelings, to raise his instincts to the heights of consciousness, to make them transparent, to extend the wires of his will into hidden recesses, and thereby to raise himself to a new plane, to create a higher social biologic type, or, if you please, a superman.*

Because his thought is so obscure, the case of Martin Heidegger is less obvious. The great philosopher first gained fame by conceptualizing a humanoid creature out of the verbal copula and its attendant adverbs.

He believed that he could thereby help recover a purer form of human being, one that had last been seen in pre-Socratic Greece. Heidegger was reactionary to the roots of his *Dasein*.

In his kingdom of the Verb, Heidegger reduced an action where a carpenter was hammering a nail into a floorboard to "hammering." By eliminating any indication of an agent, he could argue that no one should be held responsible for good or bad hammering.

Like Freud before him Heidegger found a way to absolve people of responsibility. And he did it long before he forgave himself for his Nazi past.

All three of these great modern geniuses held, if I may put it this way, that God had made a grievous mistake when he endowed human beings with free will. Wanting to subvert free enterprise, the Industrial Revolution and liberal democracy they knew that they had to attack its cornerstone, free will.

But, you will be thinking, Marx, Freud and Heidegger promised liberation. Freud promised to free people from civilized sexual repression. Marx promised to free the proletariat from capitalist oppression. Heidegger promised to free the human spirit from nihilism... through the intermediary of the German *Volk*.

Paradoxically, the three geniuses wanted to free people from freedom. They were offering to free people from moral responsibility. To do so, they attacked its metaphysical basis in free will.

Given his dialectical materialism, Marx had no use for metaphysics. Freud rejected free will because he believed it to be an illusion based on religious superstition. Heidegger laid the groundwork for an assault on metaphysics that gullible graduate students still suffer today.

By rejecting free will the three could refuse to take responsibility for what happened when their theoretical lucubrations were applied to real world problems.

In many ways that was their genius.

It is almost unnecessary to say it, but Communist governments never took responsibility for the horrors they unleashed on their own populations. They preferred to scapegoat capitalist roaders and counter-revolutionaries.

In Heidegger's case his followers and acolytes have used his great ideas to absolve him of responsibility for his Nazi past.

Among those who were willing to overlook Heidegger's Nazism was Lacan. Believing that Heidegger's thought was consonant with Freud's, Lacan even tried to befriend him.

Roudinesco reported that Lacan was so "transfixed" with Heidegger that in 1950 he traveled to the Black Forest to meet with the great philosopher. At the time, Heidegger was banned from teaching.

According to Roudinesco, Heidegger had no interest in Freud or psychoanalysis. He barely read any psychoanalytic writings and refused to engage any discussions on the topic. One suspects that he did not want to risk having his mind contaminated with Jewish thought.

In 1955, Lacan received Heidegger and his wife at his country house in Guitrancourt. Several other philosophers were present, but Sartre and Maurice Merleau-Ponty boycotted the meeting to protest Heidegger's political activities.

Morally, Sartre and Merleau-Ponty were correct. Who could say with confidence that making Heidegger respectable would not also make his politics respectable?

Heidegger believed that his thought was consistent with Nazism. Who can say that he did not understand his own philosophy? Why risk propagating a philosophical pestilence?

In 1945, when the occupying French authorities were deciding whether to allow Heidegger to teach, they solicited the opinion of famed philosopher Karl Jaspers.

Jaspers understood well that Heidegger's thought left no place for freedom:

> *Heidegger's mode of thinking, which seems to me to be fundamentally unfree, dictatorial and uncommunicative, would have a very damaging effect on students at the present time. And the mode of thinking itself seems to me more important than the actual content of political judgments, whose aggressiveness can easily be channeled in other directions. Until such time as a genuine rebirth takes place within him, and is seen to be at work within him, I think it would be quite wrong to turn such a teacher loose on the young people of today, who are psychologically extremely vulnerable.*

Lacan occasionally quoted Heidegger, but he was not a Heideg-gerian. That honor belongs to the practitioners of deconstruction.

If anything, deconstruction demonstrates that Jaspers was correct. The ill-effects of Heidegger's thought can easily be channeled in more politically correct directions.

For his part, Lacan identified points of convergence between Heidegger and Freud. More importantly, he treated Heidegger as a friend. Since we choose our friends freely, we bear responsibility for the choices we make.

Like many Parisian intellectuals, Lacan believed in great ideas more than he believed in choosing his friends by the "content of their character." Would you, given the opportunity, befriend an unrepentant Nazi? Would you be "transfixed" by him?

Roudinesco was unfazed by the fact that Lacan had befriended Heidegger. She wrote that: "...friendships and relations are one thing and conceptual borrowings another."

One appreciates her application of Cartesian dualism, but another adage expresses a more important truth: "You are known by the company you keep."

How did Heidegger convince people that he was not responsible for his own behavior? How did he persuade them that he did not need to recant his views or offer an apology for the work he had done on behalf of the Nazi Party?

When called on to defend himself he offered a bevy of legalistic excuses. Apparently, he saw no evil, heard no evil and spoke no evil.

He had never worked in the camps and claimed not to have known what was going on. Thus, he did not feel responsible for what had been done in the name of National Socialism.

He even suggested that he wanted to reform National Socialism from within. Think of how much worse Nazism would have been without Heidegger's efforts to change it!

Of course, Heidegger's excuses were fraudulent.

When he joined the Nazi cause in 1933 he had had ample time to read the virulently anti-Semitic *Mein Kampf*. It is inconceivable that someone who had made a career out of reading arcane philosophical texts did not know what was in that book. To say, as Heidegger's apolo-gists do, that no one took the book seriously does not relieve him of responsibility for what ensued. Ignorance is not an excuse.

Heidegger had to know about the pogroms and the book burnings that were occurring in 1933. If he was unconcerned, perhaps he saw them as manifestations of the cultural *Destruktion* that he himself had promoted. He might have thought that the activities of the Storm Troopers were street theatre.

Heidegger once explained that he referred to the "inner truth and greatness" of National Socialism in 1935 in his *Introduction to Metaphysics* because he feared not conforming to contemporary mores. Besides, he said, everyone knew that he didn't mean it.

And yet, when he republished the book in 1953 he retained the offending phrase.

Some of his apologists have argued that Heidegger's Nazi beliefs were founded on aesthetics, not on the ideology of racial purity.

They would do well to read Modris Eksteins' great book, *Rites of Spring*. In it, Eksteins demonstrated a point that others have noted. Nazi genocide was in large part motivated by aesthetic considerations. Hitler and his henchmen saw Germany, and eventually the world, as their canvas. On it they wanted to create something beautiful. Thus, they felt compelled to exterminate people they saw as aesthetically flawed.

As Darrin McMahon noted, Joseph Goebbels saw Hitler as a genius and a demiurge:

> Joseph Goebbels claimed to have known from his first encounter with Hitler that he was a "genius," "a natural, creative instrument of divine fate," who would shape the German *Volk* into a political-artistic masterpiece. "The people are for the statesman what stone is for the sculptor," Goebbels observed in his novel Michael, *first published in the 1920s.*

Many psychoanalysts find it difficult to associate Freud, a man they consider a great liberator with thinkers who have promoted despotism and tyranny.

And yet, Freud's work aimed directly at shifting blame and avoiding responsibility. Defining psychological motivation in deterministic terms, he also dismissed free will as an illusion.

In *The Psychopathology of Everyday Life* Freud stated that we trick ourselves into thinking that we have free will. He said that sometimes we examine unimportant choices and imagine that we might have acted differently. From that we conclude that we were exercising free will.

When faced with the choice between Tide and Wisk or between scrambled and poached eggs we believe, Freud was suggesting, that we are exercising a free choice.

Then, we extrapolate and conclude that we exercise free choice in all of our actions.

In Freud's words:

> ...it is precisely with regard to the unimportant, indifferent decisions that we would like to claim that we could just as well have acted otherwise: that we have acted of our free and unmotivated will.

It is worth mentioning, if only in passing, that Freud was wrong to dismiss minor everyday decisions as trivial. If you live in a country where you are not allowed to choose your detergent or your candy bar you will have lost a portion of your freedom.

If the supermarket shelves only contain People's Soap and People's Chocolate you are being robbed of your freedom. It is not a trivial matter.

Tyranny does not merely deprive you of a say in the way you are governed. A pervasive tyranny will deprive you even of the most banal choices, the better to demoralize you and teach you to submit.

Freud theorized that major life decisions—the ones that he told his patients not to take while in analysis—were never made freely.

He discovered this by introspecting. When he himself had made momentous decisions in his life, he felt like he was being compelled to do as he did.

Unfortunately, this is off the point. Regardless of what you think was going on in your ghostly mind you are responsible for your decisions. Shifting the blame to the unconscious or the devil does not obviate your responsibility.

Besides, if life is a game, and not a Greek tragedy, the outcome is not predetermined. If a free choice produced your current state of affairs a free choice can modify or correct it.

In his essay on "The Uncanny" Freud said that people clung to the illusion of free will because they were nostalgic for missed opportunities.

An individual who could have done otherwise than he did becomes responsible for his action.

In Freud's view, people who believed in freedom and responsibility were resisting the unconscious and refusing to give it pride of mental place. More precisely, they were refusing to join his cult.

Freud wrote:

> There are also all the unfulfilled but possible futures to which we still like to cling in fantasy, all the strivings of the ego which adverse external circumstances have crushed, and all the suppressed acts of volition which nourish the illusion of Free Will.

Of course, Freud did not grant his patients free will. He did not allow Horace Frink and Angelika Bijur the freedom to choose whether they would divorce their respective spouses and marry.

Doubtless, he felt compelled to get his hands on Bijur's money, but does that relieve him of responsibility for his appalling intervention?

Clinically, a psychoanalytic patient does not have the freedom to accept or reject his Oedipus complex. He might not accept his analyst's application of the concept, but he is not free to believe that Freud was wrong about such an essential point. If he refuses to accept it, he will, according to Freud, be punished with inhibitions, symptoms and anxiety.

Of course, some misguided analysts believe that the practice of free association involves the exercise of free will. Lacan was much closer to the truth when he asserted that its true purpose was to persuade patients that their associations were not free.

By Lacan's reasoning, anyone who believes that free association is consistent with liberal democratic values has been poorly analyzed.

As you can imagine, many psychoanalysts will not find these arguments persuasive. Their confusion, if I may call it that, derives from a failure to distinguish between two freedoms.

Recall Tocqueville's remark that when women gained the freedom to choose their husbands they also gained the freedom to be held responsible for their choices. Being free to assume a responsibility, Isaiah Berlin later explained, is not the same as being freed from responsibility.

Surely, human beings can be tempted. They can be influenced. The concept of free will says that, as tempted as you are (or as Eve and Adam were), you are responsible for your actions because you could have done otherwise.

You might not have felt that you could do otherwise. You might even have felt compelled to do as you did. That only serves to shift the blame and relieve you of responsibility. It is an intellectually sophisticated way to cover your shame.

Free will says that your choices are yours even if the lure is irresistible. If you know that you will be powerless to resist temptation, you should do what Odysseus did when he prepared to encounter the Sirens. You should instruct your men to tie you to the mast.

Homer's hero did not say that temptation was too powerful or that he could not control his instincts. He did not allow himself to yield to temptation, and later try to escape responsibility.

Unlike the unholy trinity of Marx, Freud and Heidegger the great Homeric hero knew that he was responsible for his actions and for their consequences.

He knew that his truth did not lie in the depths of his soul. It lay in the way he conducted himself and in the way he fulfilled the duties that inhered in his position as leader.

What he felt didn't matter. What he really, really wanted didn't matter. What was happening in his mind while he was making his decision didn't matter either.

What mattered was the way he looked to others. In a world where people have a sense of shame, it's all about face.

As reality would have it, you are the only person who can never see your face directly. In this and only in this sense you are unique, one of a kind. You might see your face's reflection in a limpid pool or even in a mirror, but you will never look yourself in the eye.

Since you have a better chance of seeing God's face than looking directly at your own, you might follow the philosophers and compensate by convincing yourself that you possess an inner truth that you alone know.

If you believe that you are that inner truth, you will be immunizing yourself against the shame that you should feel when you fail to uphold your moral responsibilities.

Those who defend Heidegger, Marx and Freud declare that their inner truth and greatness cannot be judged by what happened when their ideas were put into practice.

Poor results, even calamitous results only show that reality must be changed. If it does not affirm their ideas, it needs to be modified. One does so by changing the culture and changing human beings.

The great geniuses did not believe that people were social beings who aspire to follow rules of good conduct. They saw people as raw material that could be shaped, thus, recreated, to conform to the requirements of a grand philosophy.

For our purposes, Freud's efforts are the most relevant.

After absolving himself of responsibility for what happened to his patients, he also relieved them of responsibility for the way they were conducting their lives. Mental health aside, the process had an appeal. Doesn't everyone want to be permitted to sin with impunity?

By Freud's teaching, when people acted on their desire they could disregard the results. If they had overcome shame they did not need to worry about how they looked to others.

He must have known that it is easier to ignore how others see you than to change the way you are conducting your life. Through psychoanalysis you can become like the ostrich that buries his head in the sand and believes that no one can see him.

Freud sold his idea by employing a brilliant rhetorical ploy. He could not offer scientific proof that free will did not exist. Instead, he trotted out a literary character, Oedipus, that apparently had no free will. And he declared that we are all just like Oedipus, only we don't know it.

Freud did not choose the Oedipus of legend, of course. He chose a literary creation, a character produced by an artistic genius.

And yet, the hubbub over whether we are all just like Oedipus obscures a more important question. Did Freud read the Sophoclean tragedy correctly? Did he see the play as it is or did he distort it to serve his purpose?

I would argue that Freud, wanting to recreate human being began by recreating the tragedy of Oedipus.

He did not much care about the play itself. He wanted to use it as a vehicle to promote and propagate his ideas, and, of course, to aggrandize himself.

Wanting to create a humanoid creature that lacked free will and a sense of shame, Freud tried to make his project plausible by suggesting that the characters in *Oedipus Tyrannos* could be understood without any reference to free will or shame.

If Sophocles could portray a set of characters interacting only in terms of guilt, it makes sense to say that you too can live your life without shame. And that you can do so without going completely mad.

The tragedy of Oedipus looks like a detective story in which a city was saved from its malaise when a criminal was brought to justice. By this reading it's all about guilt.

Unfortunately, the play does not support Freud's reading. Art has an integrity that ideology lacks. Great artists do not have absolute freedom to do as they wish with their raw material. Propagandists do; demagogues do; artists do not.

If an artist warps his material to fulfill the terms of an ideology he will eventually lose his audience. No one can respond emotionally to a play that tells him what to think.

Freud believed that the Sophoclean play was all about guilt. He was wrong. The tragedy did not eliminate shame and responsibility.

At the play's climax, Oedipus did not just discover that he was the criminal he was seeking. More importantly, he learned who he was. His new identity changed the nature of his crime.

However much guilt he felt for murdering the old man on the road —Oedipus had always known that he had killed someone—it was nothing compared to the shame he felt when he discovered that the man he killed was his father and that his wife was his mother.

Once he learned who he was, Oedipus had to face the inescapable fact that he had dishonored his parents and had consigned his children to irredeemable anomie.

When Oedipus gouged out his eyes, he was punishing himself for his crime. But he was also manifesting shame for the disrespect he had shown his parents.

Good Freudians believe that Oedipus was performing an act of auto-castration. But, wasn't he also saying that he could no longer bear to be looked at?

If guilt had been as important as Freud believed, Oedipus would have been indicted and put on trial. He would have been imprisoned or executed for his crimes.

Freud might have believed that Oedipus could not have done otherwise, but the implications of the story do not sustain that opinion.

When Oedipus first learned of the curse that had been placed on him, he was living in Corinth. Believing himself to be the son of the king and queen of Corinth he tried to avoid it by fleeing. Thereupon, he met his fate.

To be slightly fanciful, if you should ever discover that you are cursed to murder your father and marry your mother, the better part of caution would tell you not to murder any man who is old enough to be your father and not to marry any woman who is old enough to be your mother.

Lacan once suggested, astutely, that it was difficult to believe that Jocasta did not know with whom she was sharing her conjugal bed. If so, she was morally responsible for a choice that was freer than we have been led to believe.

As a tragedy of anomie, *Oedipus Tyrannos* does not tell us that all human beings are fundamentally corrupt. It tells us that some are corruptible.

Freud must have known that Aristotle had granted the Sophoclean tragedy a special place in his *Poetics*. When the philosopher wrote that spectators at a tragedy experience an emotional catharsis he was suggesting that watching it could be therapeutic.

According to Aristotle, the audience at a tragedy will feel pity and terror, or, as he put it, *pathos* and *phobos*.

The terror you feel as you imagine that you might be a budding Oedipus is annulled by the pity you register when you see that you are not. This produces an emotional cleanse, a catharsis, a sense of relief.

Unfortunately, psychoanalysis cannot produce the same effect. When Freud insisted that his patients be fully convinced that they are just like Oedipus, he was saying that treatment should provoke terror without pity.

If a spectator watches a Sophoclean tragedy and does not distance himself from the hero by feeling pity, there will be no catharsis. Left alone with his guilt, he might calm himself with moral self-flagellation but that is a poor excuse for a cure.

21

WHEN FREUD SET out on his intellectual journey he saw himself as a new Oedipus, a son replacing a father.

By the end of his life he had written himself into a new role—the founding father of a pseudo-religion. The budding Oedipus had metamorphosed into a modern Moses.

Since his primary role models were Oedipus and Moses, Freud was less a founding father than a "foundling" father.

As a young insurgent, Freud believed that he was fighting the Viennese medical establishment and civilized morality. If he could rescue hysterics from sexual repression they and their paramours would be forever grateful. Fame and glory would be his.

Later, having lost confidence in his "dangerous method," he began to lay the groundwork for a new culture. He might not have known what that new culture would look like, but he did know that, in order to achieve his goal, he had to replace the story of Adam and Eve with a new myth of the culture's origin.

Freud saw the Bible as a cover-up. He believed that it was peddling a false narrative to hide the dire truth about the origin of human community. To his mind Western civilization had invented the story of Adam and Eve in order to propagate the illusion of free will and burden people with a sense of shame.

In crafting a replacement story, Freud became a mythmaker. Thereby, he sought to undermine the Biblical foundation of Western civilization and to liberate people from sexual repression.

It was better than curing a few flighty, histrionic young women.

Freud did not see his new myth as a product of his imagination. He believed that it depicted a forgotten series of events.

Just as he insisted that his patients discover their truth by regressing to infantile states, Freud believed that the truth of human culture could only be found in its most primitive form.

He had no difficulty convincing enlightened minds that the story of Adam and Eve was an empty fable. Constructing a new myth that harmonized with the tragedy of Oedipus was a more daunting task.

Freud was up to the challenge. Basing his story loosely on Darwin, he posited an original or primal horde led by a patriarch who had arrogated all of the horde's women for his personal sexual use.

At some point, this man's alienated and sexually repressed sons banded together and murdered him. Drunk with a realization of what they had done, they consumed their father's remains.

From that point forward, human beings had, Freud believed, been living in denial. Western civilization, in particular, had been founded on a willful forgetting of the action that had founded it. Westerners were not tough enough to accept that their culture had originated in two horrendous crimes.

Unable to prove that there had ever been such a horde or that the first crimes had really happened, Freud insisted that they must have happened.

His argument had a clinical correlate. Didn't Freud try to convince the Wolf Man that his primal scene had really happened because it must have happened?

Freud's primal horde was systematically oppressive. A tyrannical first father oppressed his sons by refusing them sexual access to their mothers and sisters. He consigned them to chronic sexual deprivation.

Freud did not seem to care, but the horde's women, forced to produce children with a man they could not refuse, were also severely repressed.

Evidently, Freud did not hold a very positive view of fatherhood.

Most of the time, Freud had focused on a child's criminal intentions toward his parents. He placed the story of Oedipus within the context of childhood development. He had not used it to ponder paternal vice or virtue.

Freud had little to say about the crimes of King Laios. He ignored the fact that these crimes had provoked the curse that the gods had placed on Oedipus.

With the story of the primal horde, Freud offered a decidedly unflattering picture of fatherhood.

By making the first father the first tyrant, Freud was implying that all fathers are incipient tyrants. They might be more or less successful in controlling their malevolent urges, but they want nothing good for their sons or daughters. In their unconscious minds they want to own and abuse their wives and daughters and to oppress, if not castrate, their sons.

Given the structure of Freud's primal horde, the sons had no other option but to murder their psychopathic progenitor. Compelled to do as they did, the sons did not exercise free will.

The first father did not have free will either. He did not have the choice between holding on to power and stepping aside in favor of his sons. As conceived by Freud, the first father's retirement would have spelled death.

The founder of psychoanalysis could not conceive of a father who passed the torch to his sons. If asked about how George Washington could have given up power willingly, Freud might have declared it to be a self-serving deception, one that would lead America to become a failed experiment.

But, what compelled the sons to cannibalize their father's dead body?

Perhaps, they felt a need to absorb his charisma. Since the father was the only man who had had carnal knowledge of women, he must have possessed an aura. His naïve sons might have believed that they could access his potency by ingesting his remains. If this is true, the first cannibal meal was caused by sexual performance anxiety.

In *Totem and Taboo* Freud wrote that the brothers cannibalized their father's corpse because they wanted to "identify" with his strength. Obviously, he was using the word "strength" euphemistically.

But, the first father did not merely have charisma. He was also a psychopath. However justified the murder of a psychopath, the sons, by Freud's reading also shared guilt over what they had done. Their cannibal meal affirmed their shared responsibility for his crime, but it must also have allowed them to absorb their father's psychopathic tendencies.

To Freud, human communities were criminal conspiracies. They were all about guilt.

In *Totem and Taboo* he wrote:

> *Society was now based on complicity in the common crime; religion was based on a sense of guilt and the remorse attaching to it; while morality was based partly on the exigencies of society and partly on the penance demanded by the sense of guilt.*

Even though many psychoanalysts have distanced themselves from the myth of the primal horde, true Freudians understood that the actions and the characters contained therein were the basis for Freud's effort to recreate human being.

Unfortunately, Freud's theory contains a flaw. He posited that the guilt from the first crime had been transmitted from generation to generation. Yet, he failed to see that guilt is not transferable. When a man commits a crime, he alone suffers the penalty. Other members of his family are neither prosecuted nor punished.

Guilt attaches only to the individuals who committed the crime. Shame is shared. It belongs to the group.

If a sin, even a crime, provokes both shame and guilt, only the shame is inherited. When a father's criminal activities tarnish his good name, his children will suffer the stigma. He alone will suffer the punishment that attends his guilt.

Just as Freud had misinterpreted *Oedipus Tyrannos* by erasing shame, he misread his myth of the primal horde by rendering it only in terms of guilt.

In the myth's terms, the brothers were compelled to do as they did. But, did their act really bespeak an absence of free will? Were there no other alternatives and no other possible outcomes?

Even if there was an initial murder, it was not, by the terms of the narrative, merely a crime. It was overkill. Freud saw it in terms of compulsion, but the brothers did have a choice. They could have expelled their father from the horde. Numerically and physically, they outmanned him.

Perhaps the brothers feared the return of the expelled, but neither of Freud's role models, Oedipus and Moses were murdered. They both disappeared, without leaving a trace.

True, their deaths were mysterious. This might mean that a crime was being repressed, but, then again, it need not.

Effectively, Freud mistook shame for guilt. If anything had been transmitted from the supposed initial crime, it was the sense of shame. The guilt feelings, such as they were, died with the first co-conspirators.

Being obsessed with guilt, Freud neglected to provide any sense of how the brothers or their progeny could have dealt with their shame.

In Freud's story, the first band of brothers, after committing murder and cannibalizing their father's corpse, were so overwhelmed with guilt that they did penance. They renounced the spoils that they had won—their mothers and sisters—and became ascetics.

We might also say that since the first father had imposed laws by the force of his charisma, the sons, once they got over the thrill of having killed him, realized that they were facing a lawless future.

At some point, Freud imagined the brothers holding a meeting where they invented the institution of marriage. They decided that they would divide up the horde's women. Each brother would have one, or maybe two or three wives. No one would have all the women, and no one would be excluded from the marital exchange.

Freud never really explained how the brothers, having only known oppression, suddenly discovered how to negotiate a compromise. They didn't acquire it by gorging themselves on their dead father's flesh.

Having articulated the myth of the primal horde in *Totem and Taboo* Freud later applied it to the founding of the Jewish religion. He might have thought that Biblical history would show how right he was. Or, he might have thought that, by attacking Moses, he could subvert a major foundation of Judeo-Christian civilization.

As unpleasant as it is to say, Freud was undermining Judaism at a time when German-speaking Europe was indulging an especially virulent form of anti-Semitism.

In *Moses and Monotheism* Freud argued that Jews had built their religion on denial. They had refused to accept that their ancestors, the founders of their faith had murdered Moses.

Being in constant denial Jews had never been able to repent the founding crime. In Freud's imagination, their unatoned-for guilt had remained active and was transmitted from generation to generation, unconsciously.

In order to sustain their selective and collective amnesia Jews had repressed all thoughts that might have provoked an awareness of the first parricide. They insisted that they loved Moses, because, had they admitted to hating Moses they might have started thinking that their forefathers had killed him.

It was guilt, guilt and more guilt. In Freud's words:

> *There was no place in the framework of the religion of Moses for a direct expression of the murderous hatred of the father. All that could come to light was a mighty reaction against it —a sense of guilt on account of that hostility, a bad conscience for having sinned against God and for not ceasing to sin. The sense of guilt... was uninterruptedly kept awake by the Prophets, and soon formed an essential part of their religious system....*

Freud had to solve a conundrum. If the Jewish religion had been founded on a crime whose purpose was to allow everyone a fair share of sexual delight, why did it enforce such a repressive attitude toward all things erotic?

He answered that Jewish "instinctual renunciation" was another way to deny a criminal past. When a man is accused of murdering his father in order to gain sexual access to his mother and sisters he might defend himself by showing that he has not enjoyed the fruits of the crime. Asceticism can serve as a defense against an indictment. An accused criminal might say that his asceticism shows that he had no motive to commit the crime.

By choosing to live sexlessly, Moses's followers were also claiming that they had not bridled under his tyranny. In fact, they loved him so much that they continued to live as the first band of brothers had lived. What possible reason would they have had to kill him?

Next, Freud took a turn toward the unsavory. Believing that Jews were unconsciously yearning to be punished for their crime, he declared that they had adopted negative character traits in order to incite people to persecute them. In that way, they could allay their guilt without accepting that they had murdered Moses.

How did they do it? First, they acted like self-important narcissists. Freud could barely suppress his disdain for his fellow Jews:

> ...there is no doubt that they have a particularly high opinion of themselves, that they regard themselves as more distinguished, of higher standing, as superior to other peoples...

> ...[the Jewish people have] developed special character-traits and incidentally [have] earned the hearty dislike of every other people.

Note well, Freud believed that Jews "earned" the hatred of "every other people." Just as he said that hysterics were suffering because they refused to admit that they wanted to be abused, Freud saw anti-Semitism as the realization of a repressed Jewish wish.

They earned the most hatred, Freud argued, by arrogantly claiming that they were God's chosen people.

They were wrong, Freud said. Judaism began when a group of Semitic tribesmen was selected by a monomaniacal Egyptian potentate named Moses to be his following. Only in that sense could they be "the chosen people."

Freud also denounced his sometime co-religionists for being especially stubborn. Being habituated to finding a dark side to every positive character trait, Freud refused to respect Jews even for persevering in the face of persecution.

Here his attitude verges on contempt:

> The poor Jewish people, who with their habitual stubbornness continued to disavow the father's murder, atoned heavily for it in the course of time.

Freud might have thought that he could help Jews to put an end to persecution by teaching them to overcome their pig-headedness.

Yet, failing to distinguish between pride and arrogance, he attacked the pride that Jews had earned through their achievements. In so doing he was using his "dangerous method" to demoralize a social group.

In the opening sentence of Moses and Monotheism, Freud announced his intention: "To deprive a people of the man whom they take pride in as the greatest of their sons...."

Yes, Freud recognized that Jews excelled in intellectual pursuits, but, he added it was merely a symptom of their sexual deficiencies.

In his words:

All such advances in intellectuality have as their consequence that the individual's self-esteem is increased, that he is made proud—so that he feels superior to other people who have remained under the spell of sensuality.

Since psychoanalysis only treated individuals, Freud did not know how Jews could be cured of their "collective" guilt. If cure required avowal (and penance) how could Jews, as a group, do so? Did Freud want them to accept Christ as a Savior who had sacrificed himself for their crime?

Strangely, Freud saw the advent of Christ as proof that his theory was correct. He believed that Christ sacrificed himself to atone for the crime committed by the first band of murderous sons.

By assuming the role of leader of the band of murderous brothers and accepting punishment, Christ had paid off everyone's guilt.

Christ appeared to be guiltless, but he was really, Freud wrote: "the most guilty person, the ring leader of the company of brothers." Thus, Christ's crucifixion was less about redemption and salvation, and more about proving that Freud was right.

In *Totem and Taboo* he wrote:

If Christ redeemed mankind of the burden of original sin by the sacrifice of his own life, we are driven to conclude that the sin was a murder. The law of the talion... lays it down that a murder can only be expiated by the sacrifice of another life: self-sacrifice points back to blood guilt.

His idea makes good narrative sense, but Freud was making an unwarranted assumption. He was taking the law of the talion to be a fundamental truth, one that always pertained, even when it didn't.

Freud imagined that since the law of the talion preceded Judeo-Christian laws, it was more primal. He was unwilling to accept that a revision might have been better suited to the interests of human community and thus, closer to the truth.

Again, Freud had no use for progress. He believed that the truth lay in the first draft and that subsequent revisions denied it.

The law of the talion says: do unto others as others have done unto you. Judeo-Christianity replaced it with a new rule: do unto others as you would have others do unto you.

If you believe in progress or believe that human beings can improve their principles or even try out different cultural principles, you should reject Freud's attempt to ground human justice in the law of the talion.

To sustain his theory, Freud had to reduce the story of Christ to a blood sacrifice whose purpose was to atone for an act of parricide. Thus, he ignored the fact that Christ was not only punished, as one would be for a crime, but was also subjected to public humiliation.

When Pontius Pilate declared to those who were witnessing Christ's humiliation: "*Ecce Homo*," "Behold the Man," he was diminishing a man who claimed to be the Son of God by calling him a mere human being.

Just as a stigma against adultery is less a threat and more an encouragement to love one's spouse, Christ's humiliation is meant to inspire people to act generously toward others.

Thus, Christian love involves doing the right thing because it is the right thing to do. It assumes that human beings are instinctively primed to do right by others.

Obviously, Freud disagreed. He did not believe that humans had a moral impulse to do good for the sake of doing good. As Lacan was at pains to emphasize, Freud's theory was based on prohibitions, transgressions and threats.

In Freud's fiction, good deeds, such as they were, could only be elicited by fear of the consequences of behaving badly. Freud rejected the idea that good behavior was natural or satisfying.

If human beings obeyed laws that imposed abstinence, it could only have been because they feared castration.

Note the way Freud describes Jewish rules of good conduct in *Moses and Monotheism*:

> ...the Prophets believed that God required 'nothing' other from his people than a just and virtuous conduct of life—that is, abstinence from every instinctual satisfaction which is still condemned as vicious by our morality today.

Of course, Freud was misreading the Hebrew Bible. Had he thought more deeply about, for example, the Ten Commandments he would have found laws that did not involve condemnation or prohibition. He would have found an imperative to remember the Sabbath and keep it holy. And he would also have seen a principle that defined filial piety: *Honor thy father and thy mother.*

Like Judaism, Christianity is based on a love that is not elicited by fear.

In 1 John 4, 18, we read:

> *There is no fear in love; but perfect love casteth out fear: because fear hath torment. He that feareth is not made perfect in love.*

Augustine declared that it is a sin to abstain (to renounce instinct) only because one fears punishment. He elaborated the point in *The City of God*:

> *For it must be a sin to desire what the Law of God forbids and to abstain merely from fear of punishment and not for love of righteousness.*

Those who do the right thing because they love righteousness are doing it for the right reason.

Here we see the most significant failing of Freud's theory. By writing human psychology into a dialectical struggle between impulse and threat, Freud was ignoring the possibility that people might be inclined to do the right thing in order to fulfill themselves as moral and social beings.

He could not imagine that people could love their neighbors because they enjoyed having harmonious social relations. By his theory, people got along with their neighbors because they were afraid of what their neighbors would do to them if they found out their true intentions.

At the risk of sounding repetitious, Freud was not talking about human beings as they were. He was talking about characters that functioned within a myth that he had created himself.

Freud thought that he had found an ultimate truth in his narrative of the primal horde. But, he was also proposing a systematic, and perhaps deliberate, misreading of the moral foundation of Western civilization.

In the final analysis, it's not about whether Freud's myth is true to past facts. It makes more sense to see it as a prophecy about the future of psychoanalysis. I suspect that the founding father of psychoanalysis was showing his followers how to transform a clinical practice into a cult.

If Judaism began with the assassination of Moses, Freud's pseudo-religion would be founded by an act that resembled a homicide. If Freud was to be the new Moses, the tyrannical founding father, he was destined to be murdered by his intellectual heirs.

Then, his sons would consume his body and form a community by sharing his substance.

If, as was perhaps inevitable, those who murdered Freud denied their complicity, they would have had to await salvation through the intermediary of a martyred Messiah.

Obviously, Freud was not murdered by his sons, his students or his followers. He died of an overdose of morphine, administered at his request by his physician and fellow analyst, Max Schur.

But, there are other kinds of murder. Lacan, for one, implied that Freud's heirs in the International Psychoanalytic Association had "murdered" him by systematically misreading his texts.

The analogy seems farfetched, but Freud said as much himself. In *Moses and Monotheism* he wrote:

> *In its implications the distortion of a text resembles a murder. The difficulty is not in perpetuating the deed but in getting rid of its traces.*

However intriguing the analogy, Freud was incorrect to see misreading as a homicidal act. Right reason tells us that he skipped a stage. Distorting a text feels more like cannibalizing the dead author's body... of work. It is not the same as murdering an author, unless, of course, you should choose to eat him alive.

But, what does it mean to murder an author? Better yet, since Freud did not see himself as just any author, what does it mean to murder an author who is a genius? How do you murder an author who possesses superhuman powers or is channeling divinity?

If the value of Freud's writings rests on the fact that they were written by someone of extraordinary intelligence, killing him would involve finding fault in his works. A genius is never wrong; he can only be misunderstood, especially by inferior minds.

By Lacan's reading, Freud was, for all intents and purposes, never wrong. I cannot recall a single occasion where Lacan declared flatly that Freud had made a mistake. When he discovered inconsistencies in Freud's writings Lacan declared that they required further explication.

When other psychoanalysts attempted to improve on Freud or even to redefine concepts, Lacan denounced them as heretics and renegades. By his reading they had betrayed the sacred truth of Freud's text.

Of course, Lacan's attitude to the Freudian text might also have been self-serving. He might have been reading Freud as he wanted others to read his writings.

In fact, that is what happened. Within the Wholly Freudian Church it is strictly forbidden even to suggest that Lacan was ever wrong.

This creates a difficult problem. To be the psychoanalytic Jesus, the incarnate Logos whose death would redeem Freudian theory Lacan had to assume the role of first brother, the man who led the murderous assault on Freud, the first father.

But, this implies that Lacan himself was distorting the meaning of Freud's sacred texts.

Obviously, the mere suggestion that Lacan misread Freud will send his minions into paroxysms of righteous fury. Out of concern for their emotional well-being, I will qualify the statement.

Lacan's reading was a distortion in only one sense: he revealed truths that were so deeply hidden that Freud himself did not know they were there.

I'm sure that they all feel better already.

Lacan often intimated that Freud, like a man who was letting a divine being speak through him, did not fully grasp his own truth.

For those who gained access to Freud through him, the French analyst's texts embodied the Freudian truth, at times even more than Freud's own writings.

If so, then Freud's Logos was embodied, first in Lacan himself and, after he died, in his writings.

As strange as it seems, especially for those who cling to the notion that psychoanalysis is science, this hypothesis sheds light on a peculiar and hitherto unintelligible practice.

Within the Wholly Freudian Church Lacan's words have become the object of a sacred ritual—a kind of communion—where priestly authorities recite them out as though they were the body and blood (or is it the paper and ink) of Lacan.

When they take this communion Lacan's followers are atoning for the original sin of psychoanalysis and accepting responsibility for having killed Freud.

Not literally, of course... but still.

Consider this. If you ever attend a meeting led by the high priests of the Lacanian movement—I don't wish it on you—you will hear speeches filled to overflowing with Lacan's words. All sentences either begin with: "Lacan said," or with: "But Lacan said."

Anyone who disobeys this rule will be denounced for failing to show sufficient reverence for Lacan.

Why do they do it? I suspect that, haunted by the memory of what happened to the Freudian School of Paris, the movement's priests believe that without this ritual communion their Church would dissolve into warring factions.

Worse yet, it might suffer a Reformation.

22

NORMALLY, HUMAN BEINGS connect by finding common ground. They follow the same rules, participate in the same rituals, refer to the same facts and forge agreements that are mutually beneficial.

Whether they are having a family dinner, playing tennis, negotiating a deal or talking about peaches, humans connect by sharing an experience or by referring to the same reality.

Effectively, people connect when they are playing the same game according to the same rules on the same playing field.

They do not connect if they are playing roles in a drama.

Characters in a play simulate a human connection. For some people, of course, a simulated connection is better than nothing.

Certainly, it is better than what happens when two therapy patients, each living out his own personal drama, try to connect. They soon discover the downside of pretending that human life is a narrative.

Freud seems to have understood the problem. He attempted to solve it by saying that all individuals were living different versions of the same story, the myth of Oedipus.

When the time came to help all of those Oedipuses to form a social group, he had to find a single narrative that would connect them all as partners in crime. Thus, he invented the story of the primal horde.

When we use language to connect, reference matters more than interpretation. If we are not referring to the same reality we remain alone and isolated. Insisting that all designations are subject to interpretation puts you on the road to anomie.

Naming and saying are not the same. Grammatical subjects are not the same as predicates. In principle, names designate objects and predicates say something about whatever the names designate. Two people might have different opinions about a typhoon, but they cannot connect unless they are talking about the same thing.

As the old saying goes, you can have your own opinions but you can't have your own facts.

As a true Freudian, Lacan wanted interpretation to prevail over designation. Didn't Freud become Freud by saying that desire lay in the interpretation, not in the facts?

Thus, Lacan reduced words to their meanings and suggested that meanings refer to meanings that refer to meanings. If you try this yourself you will end up scatterbrained. Lacan once wrote an essay about it, entitled: "*L'étourdit*."

Confucius famously emphasized the importance of reference. With his concept of the "rectification of names" the sage argued that a human community cannot function if people attach different meanings to the same nouns. And he added that people can only be good to their word if their word has a precise reference.

Confucius believed that the proper use of language could produce social harmony. Sensibly, he preferred harmony to perpetual psycho-drama:

> *If names be not correct, language is not in accordance with the truth of things. If language be not in accordance with the truth of things, affairs cannot be carried on to success. When affairs cannot be carried on to success, proprieties and music do not flourish.... Therefore a superior man considers it necessary that the names he uses may be spoken appropriately, and also that what he speaks may be carried out appropriately.*

For his part, Freud had little interest in showing his patients how to connect by finding common ground. He must have seen formal rituals and negotiated agreements as efforts to avoid the unbearable truth of depraved unconscious wishes.

And yet, if humans are fundamentally social beings, they can only connect by affirming their social being. If they are inchoate bundles of raw instincts or even raw feelings, they will never really connect.

When you participate in a family dinner or a wedding feast you are connecting with other people by following the rules of civil conversation, working to harmonize with others and practicing good table manners.

You are present because of your formal relations with the other members of a constituted group, because of your place in a family or your position as colleague, friend or neighbor.

The same applies to the erotic realm. Human beings most often seek sexual pleasure within defined relationships. Among them are marriage, courtship and adultery. All of them define roles and impose rules. Relationships are more durable when these are fulfilled.

Most people find sex more satisfying within a socially defined relationship. Only then can they own the experience. Random, anonymous sexual encounters are not as much fun because you do not feel that you are really there.

The question is not so much whether you are enjoying the experience, but whether the enjoyment is really yours. To own your enjoyment you must have face.

Since Freud did not see people as social beings, he defined human attachments in more visceral terms. In his mythic world people related to each other by sharing a common homicidal impulse and common appetites.

He believed that humans invented religions and ethics, good manners and objective references in order to repress this dire truth.

Perhaps Freud was trying to show people how to simulate a connection once they had lost face. Having no face means trying to connect without doing right by oneself or by others. Without face, you have nothing but raw impulses. Since Freud believed that these impulses were striving to express themselves without mediation, he was right to believe that for the humanoid creatures he was trying to create, such efforts would always end badly.

Freud believed that this was humanity's truth; in fact, it's an aberration produced when people pretend that humans are not primarily social beings.

In the culture that Freud created social connections were impossible and visceral connections were fraught with danger. People would have no choice but to live a permanent lie, thus a permanent drama. (Those who attain supernormality will be living a larger, world historical myth.) Having no face Freud's humanoid creatures could not function positively by fulfilling the duties inherent in socially defined roles. They were reduced to adopting personae and following scripts.

If you want to live a drama you need to adopt a persona. As you know, the word "persona" is Latin for theatrical mask.

If it's all just masks and we are all living out a script, you can forget about table manners, harmony and decorum. You can forget about following rules.

But then, in Freud's world, no one can ever really connect. Since this can only produce an unbearable anomie, Freud was obliged to conjure a way for these characters to feel that they were connecting. He solved it by suggesting that they should indulge in something resembling an orgiastic feast.

If you gorge yourself in a manner that resembles the primal cannibal feast, you will feel connected... even though you are not.

Civilized society will frown on your bad manners, but a Freudian will still recommend that you eat lustily. It's better than participating politely in a family dinner. *La grande bouffe* may be less appropriate, but it's much more authentic.

The difference is not between structured and unstructured consumption. A cannibalistic feast might feel like a free-for-all, but when people follow their instincts, impulses and appetites they are, Freud theorized, living an unconscious script.

In the largest sense they are re-enacting the myth of the primal horde. Residing in the unconscious minds of all humans, the myth, Freud believed, directs their actions. It also gives their actions a semblance of meaning.

They will not really connect, but they will feel like they have because they will have ingested what Freud called a "common substance."

In *Totem and Taboo* Freud related kinship to a common substance:

> *Thus kinship implies participation in a common substance.*

Later, he expanded the idea:

> *We have heard how in later times, whenever food is eaten in common, the participation in the same substance establishes a sacred bond between those who consume it when it has entered their bodies.*

Precious few, if any psychoanalysts have spent time pondering Freud's idea of "common substance."

Had they done so, they would have understood that when the first homicidal brothers were consuming a common substance they were also sharing a common emotion or passion.

By all appearances, the Eucharist proves Freud's point. Doesn't the Catholic Church hold that the Eucharist is, in reality, the body and blood of Christ? Moreover, when Christians take communion they are also sharing Christ's Passion. What could be more Freudian?

If Freud took this as proof that Christians connect by sharing a common substance, he would have been mistaken.

Since communicants are participating in a prescribed liturgy, they are following rules. They are referring to the same real object and having the same experience. When the experience becomes socially mediated, common substance becomes common ground.

Psychoanalysis notwithstanding, communion is an orderly, not an orgiastic rite.

As opposed to religion, psychoanalysis wants to show people how to form unmediated connections. It has always tried to serve up its passions raw. It has even suggested that raw passion is more authentic than the other kind.

When Lacan tried to diminish the mediating function of language in favor of its use as an instrument of seduction, he was being perfectly Freudian. By subverting language Lacan wanted to show people how to use it to inflame passions, often at the expense of social harmony.

In everyday language we say that people can be consumed by their passions. Surely, the first brothers were carried away by passion when they consumed their father's remains.

Inveterate Trinitarian that he was, Lacan listed three great passions: love, hate and ignorance. Having founded his Church on strictly Freudian principles, he would have been happy to see that its members have allowed themselves to be consumed by all three.

You may not think it's very enlightened, but the members of the Wholly Freudian Church love Lacan beyond reason. Having come together in response to Lacan's imperious demand for love, they are happy to belong to a group where everyone feels the same passion.

At the same time, sad to say, they often despise each other. Since members compete for status by showing the depth and intensity of their love, they lord it over those who have not given themselves over as fully to the cause.

In permanent denial about their hatred for each other they displace it onto heretics, apostates and assorted collaborators. Their fury against those who have abandoned their cause is unmediated.

Finally, it is worth re-emphasizing, nearly no one in the Wholly Freudian Church really understands Lacan's teaching. Thus, ignorance is one of the glues that makes, of many, one.

Most Church members are capable of mouthing a few empty formulae and quotations, but, by and large they are and always have been ignorant of what Lacan was trying to teach them.

They are joined by their passion, not by their reason. Many South American Lacanians have so little confidence in their powers of ratiocination that they allow their Parisian masters to tell them what they should and should not think. If you do not see the pathos in that, remove your blinders.

None of it would have shocked Lacan. He knew that most of his followers did not understand his ideas. Had he wished, he could have recalibrated his teaching so that people could grasp it. He did not. He did not seem to care. He preferred to ignore the problem.

If ignorance is bliss, Lacan's followers have found in his writings a mind-altering substance that produces, when ingested, all manner of *jouissance*.

Paris has not had a monopoly on Freudian passion. In their early years psychoanalytic societies in Vienna, London and New York were often riven by splits and secessions. By all appearances, the first generations of Freudians were in close touch with some very powerful passions.

New York psychoanalysts eventually overcame their Freudian passions and even their Freudian desires. They diluted them and turned them into feeling and emotion. When they finished the process they arrived at empathy. What could be more Freudian than an unmediated soulful connection?

Freud only mentioned empathy a few times. It does not play a role in his theories. Lacan had no real interest in empathy. To my knowledge, he never really discussed it.

Among American analysts, however, empathy has become a defining concept. Since anything that is "Made in America" has weight and influence around the world, the concept has infiltrated the minds of analysts in other parts of the globe.

One understands why American analysts fell in love with empathy. They must have felt an urge to circumvent the Freudian taboo against connecting with their patients. Even those who accepted the Freudian model of an out-of-body, mind-to-mind communication were forced to change their ways when many of their American patients refused to put up with their Freudian rudeness.

Lacanians believed that the new emphasis on empathy was yet another sign that their sometime colleagues had abandoned the Freudian truth.

Yet, the Americans had not deviated as much as the French believed. What could be more asocial than to have patient and analyst share a common feeling? What could be more visceral than sharing an unmediated emotion? It may not have felt sufficiently violent or depraved to be truly Freudian, but empathy is a form of *pathos* and *pathos* is Greek for passion.

And since no two people can feel the same feeling, the recourse to empathy retains a delusional quality. How much more Freudian can you get?

American analysts never understood what Lacan called the dialectics of desire, but their empathy kept them within the Freudian field. They were simply assuming that when Freud said that his patients did not know their own minds, he meant that they did not know their true feelings.

With the ascendance of empathy, many analysts and therapists came to believe that they could feel their patients' feelings, even when their patients weren't feeling them themselves. It doesn't make very much sense to tell someone who feels angry that he is angry.

If your analyst can feel your feelings even when you do not know you are feeling them, this implies that you are suffering because you do not know your feelings. If you do not know your feelings, you cannot very well express them.

If such is your case your empathetic analyst—isn't there something pathetic in the word, empathetic?—will take it upon himself to tell you what you really, really feel. Then he will teach you how to express those feelings openly, honestly and shamelessly.

In America, analysts and therapists took their theorizing to the next level and invented a new mantra. They would help their patients to get in touch with their feelings.

Of course, this raised an ancillary question: If you want to get in touch with your feelings, where do you put your hands?

No one has ever offered a satisfactory answer.

The new emphasis on pathos produced an unintended consequence. If analysts could conduct treatment by feeling their patients' inarticulate feelings, they no longer needed to produce anything resembling the brilliant deductions that made Freud famous.

After a time, analysts began to sound fatuous. It's difficult to pretend to possess expertise when your practice is based on your ability to feel someone else's pain.

When called on to explain their descent into apparent mindlessness, some analysts felt a need to borrow a few ideas. Glomming on to the theories of existential philosophers, Romantic poets and method acting coaches, they declared that strong emotions, expressed openly, are more authentic and therefore more truthful.

Many of them still believe that people who connect by feeling the same passions—by hating the same politicians, for example—are living more honestly than are those who are trying to find common ground by politely discussing the bond market.

Analysts who believe that people can do no better than to connect by consuming a common substance or feeling a common feeling believe that those who seek common ground are living an inauthentic and "factitious" existence.

Believing, as they do, in "the spontaneous overflow of powerful feelings" they encourage their patients to replace their inauthentic "factitious" existence with a more authentic fictitious existence.

Despite their obsession with inner emotional states and orgiastic rites, very few analysts of any stripe have analyzed Freud's notion of common substance. And yet, it is hardly a theoretical bagatelle.

Consider this: even before their cannibal feast, the half-brothers of the primal horde shared a common paternal substance. If there was only one father, all of the children had a paternal, but not a maternal substance in common.

This means that Freud's myth brilliantly conjured the only social organization where a child knew who his father was with as much certainty as he knew who his mother was.

By extension, the first father never doubted whether his wife's children were really his. In principle, the question did not arise. Oppression eliminated it... or better, was designed to do so.

The original cannibal feast served a dual purpose. Beyond joining the band of brothers together, it also enacted the substantive connection between father and son.

But, Freud's theory of common ingested substance is not the only way to understand group coherence.

Under normal, not mythic circumstances communities are formed through a series of alliances between unrelated families. In principle, two individuals can be joined as husband and wife because they do not share a common genetic substance.

When these two people consummate their marriage they are fulfilling a responsibility to their community. They are not becoming partners in crime.

If they conceive a child, he combines their genetic substances in his flesh. As a living symbol of their connection the child effectively unites the two families. His one flesh produces the oneness of community.

The child does not, however, represent a common substance. Since he unites two substances in one being, he is a common reference, a blood relative to both families.

Of course, this means that the community must know that the child contains his father's substance with as much certainty as it knows that he contains his mother's.

If the father's identity, as Lacan often said, is only known when his mother designates a man as such, social unity depends on a mother's virtue and her good word.

Freud and Lacan notwithstanding, social harmony never hinges on what the mother really, really wants. It does not even depend on her *jouissance*.

The community has a vested interest, not in her desire or her ecstasy, but in her being good to her word. It needs to know that when she names a man her child's father, the name designates one man rigidly. It needs to know that the name has an objective reference and is not subject to interpretation.

But, it is one thing for a woman to name a father; it is quite another for a community to accept that she is telling the truth.

I speculate that communities must affirm that the man the mother names as the child's father is really the child's progenitor. They do so through a public ritual, perhaps, but not necessarily, through a ritualized meal. This meal enacts the transmission of substance from father to son.

Also, when a social ritual places a woman's word beyond interpretation, it does more than just affirm that one man is the father. It charges that man with the responsibility to raise the child, to make him a functioning member of the community.

With such a ritual, the community accords a man a responsibility to protect and provide for his child. It tells him that it will hold him accountable for the child's growth and development.

Once paternity is affirmed publicly, a man no longer has the right to abandon his child, regardless of his doubts.

He is responsible for the child's care, no matter his suspicions. This ought not to feel unnatural. By this theory, men are normally inclined to protect and provide for their offspring. Their moral obligation corresponds to a natural inclination.

As might be expected, psychoanalysis has emphasized being a progenitor more than being a father. In so doing it has found yet another way to detach sexual behavior from any social context.

When psychoanalysts obsess about orgasms, they are privileging the act of engendering over the duty to be a parent. When they focus on a woman's desire and her enjoyment, they are saying that a woman's good word and her virtue matter less than how much she wanted to copulate and how good her orgasm felt.

Shifting the emphasis from ethical behavior to the varieties of spasmodic *jouissance* obscures the issue.

Ensuring that a child will grow up to become a responsible adult member of a community is of vital importance, both to a man and his community. Who did or did not feel what while engaging in coitus is best left to the people involved.

Given the moral basis for fatherhood, a man who fulfills that duty, even though he cannot know with absolute certainty that his child is really his, should be revered, respected and honored... like a totem animal. He is not an incipient or repressed tyrant. He is the model of benevolence.

Freud rejected the ethic of paternal benevolence. Refusing to believe that fathers were inclined to protect and provide for their children, he disrespected them.

When he tried to explain why anyone would revere a totem animal, he asserted in *Totem and Taboo* that it was a way to deny guilt.

Freud addressed the value of benevolence by channeling the thinking of the first half-brothers. To his mind they invented benevolence to shift the blame from themselves to their father:

> *If our father had treated us in the way the totem does, we should never have felt tempted to kill him.*

"Tempted?" Freud chose a strange word here. By the terms of his myth the brothers must have risen up as one man, impulsively. Being tempted involves giving the matter some thought. It does not fulfill Freud's wish that all major life decisions feel compulsive.

I suspect that Freud chose the word "tempted" to suggest that his myth exposed the truth that lay hidden behind Eve's temptation in the Garden of Eden.

Before modern minds were gender-bent out of shape everyone knew that mothers nurtured children and that fathers protected and provided for them.

Beyond the traditional duty to earn a living, fathers are also responsible for providing moral guidance, for pointing their children outside of the home and into the world. They instill good character—often by setting an example—and teach the rules and principles that will allow their children to function outside of the family.

Such wisdom should pertain to the conduct of life. A father should teach his children how to live in the world. His instruction should be clear, concise, intelligible... and open to discussion.

Among the best examples of such a teaching is Aristotle's Nicomachean Ethics. Apparently, the book was dedicated to the philosopher's son, Nicomachus.

A father who is living according to Freud's myth will not be giving his son advice. He will be too afraid that his son will use that advice to supplant him. To him a son is a competitor, not a successor.

But, doesn't a psychoanalyst function as a teacher? Doesn't he communicate his superior knowledge of unconscious mental processes and Freudian theory to his patients?

Lacan saw things differently. By his theory analysts are more like Socrates. They know their desire, but that is all they know. Beyond showing patients how to discover what they really, really want, analysts have no knowledge to communicate.

Patients who expect their analysts to tell them what they want are wrong. Patients who expect their analysts to explain human psychology are also wrong.

A psychoanalytic patient should devote himself to a single task: seeking his own desire within his unconscious mind. A psychoanalyst, Lacan said, can only facilitate the retrieval process.

At best, patients who have completed the process successfully will be left with the unenviable task of making their way in the world with only their desire to guide them.

No one should be surprised that psychoanalysts themselves, being exemplars of what treatment can do for you, should have trouble getting along with other people, especially with their fellow analysts.

Look more closely at what Lacan was saying and you discover why he thought psychoanalysis was a scam.

If you invest with an investment manager and he gives you a return on your investment, you naturally assume that your capital is earning a return. It's like buying a bond and receiving regular interest payments. When the bond comes due, you recover your initial investment.

A Ponzi schemer takes your money, does whatever he wants with it, and gives back just enough of it—as pseudo-interest—to ensure that you will not be tempted to ask for it all back. At worst, he will make you feel that you should give him more of your money. Or better, that you want to invite your friends to invest with him also.

In a successful Ponzi scheme new investments are used to pay high rates of pseudo-interest, the better to attract more investments.

The Ponzi schemer uses any money that is left over for his own *jouissance*.

Strangely enough, the same principle defines a placebo cure. At first, you believe that you are receiving a therapeutic substance. At some point, however, you will discover that the substance you thought was therapeutic was a sugar or even a bitter pill... of no value whatever.

If a patient learns about his own mind through psychoanalysis he will eventually discover that such knowledge has no real use. It will not show him how to navigate the world, conduct a relationship or negotiate a deal.

In a sense, it was never intended to be useful. If the analyst is playing the role of first father, he might feel good about seeing his underlings absorb themselves in an exercise that is neutralizing the threat they might pose to his authority. Sons who learn the habit of introspecting are not going to threaten anyone.

Only within a Freudian pseudo-religion do psychoanalytic theories have a value. They have an exchange value. You might see it as a saving disgrace.

Normally, both mothers and fathers give to their children. Even though mothers also protect and provide for their children, they are initially responsible for nurture. The less they need to nurture, the more they become moral teachers.

Most people understand that mothers possess a maternal instinct. Clearly, that instinct is consistent with a moral duty to nurture children. Since mothers offer unconditional love, they are sometimes not credited with providing moral guidance.

Freud would have contested this naïve view of motherhood. If drive theory and the Oedipus complex mean anything, they mean that maternal nurturance is overlaid with lubricious cravings.

A mother might look like she is nurturing her child, but within the confines of Freudian theory, she is dreaming of the day when he will share her bed.

In Freud's myth, fathers are not moral individuals who want to do the right thing by their wives or children. They are tyrants who dread the moment when their sons will rise up and destroy them.

On this among other scores Freud lost touch with the real world. He might have believed that no father would ever relinquish his authority voluntarily, but nature thinks differently.

Since the aging process causes fathers to grow old, their sons will eventually replace them. Even for tyrannical fathers, time is a more certain threat than their sons.

Social customs that promote filial piety and paternal benevolence are in closer harmony with the natural order. They encourage fathers to give constructive and useful advice to their children and they encourage the children to follow the advice.

Why would a father not do so? Does he not have a stake in the future of his community and the survival of his genes?

In a culture based on filial piety, a father is assumed to be benevolent unless proven otherwise.

If you want to decide for yourself whether Freud's primal horde or the culture of filial piety offers a more accurate version of human psychology, ask yourself this: which is more traumatic, losing your father or burying your child?

Freud believed that a father's death is the worst trauma because it evokes unprocessed parricidal urges and produces a wave of guilt. Recall his interpretation of *Hamlet*.

In other cultures, the worst trauma is to bury your child. If your child dies before you do, it reverses the natural order. A parent who loses a child will also suffer extreme anguish for feeling that he has failed as a protector.

People can reasonably feel confused by Freud's myth of the primal horde. After all, the man Freud called the first father was more progenitor than father.

A man who produces large numbers of children with many different women will rarely be able to provide for all of them. Even if he can provide food and shelter, he cannot possibly guide each child in building character.

To become a father a man must first constrain his instinct to impregnate multiple sexual partners.

If he does, he will be sacrificing a part of his *jouissance* in order to play an active role in the lives of his children. It is the only way he can leave them with something more than genetic material.

Freud would have called this repression, but it is more reasonable to think that the man in question is accepting a compromise. He is giving up one form of *jouissance* and gaining another satisfaction.

Assuming that he understands biology, he will know that he can father far more children than a woman can mother. He might conclude that he would be wise to accommodate the difference. After all, if he decides to spread his seed far and wide, his wife might conclude that she has no need to be faithful to him.

This is another way of saying that life is a negotiated compromise, not a permanent psychodrama.

In the Bible, the concept of father, as distinct from progenitor, was not fixed in the beginning. The Bible does not simply posit paternal benevolence. It teaches the concept through a developing narrative. As the story unfolds you learn what it means to be good father.

When the first humans arrived on the scene, they were described as man and wife. Adam called Eve the mother of all the living, but she did not call him the father of all the living. Adam was the first progenitor, but he was not designated as the first father.

To understand how the Bible develops the concept of fatherhood, I will add a new element to the Genesis narrative. Freud suggested that the text was hiding evidence of a great crime. He overlooked the possibility that the text might simply be incomplete. Isn't the prophecy of a Messiah a sign that the story, or the ethic, needs something more, one more element, to reach completion or fulfillment?

I introduce it to answer this question: was there more to the original sin than eating the forbidden fruit? Did something else happen? Was something else hidden behind the question of disobedience? If so, was it something other than a crime?

Some will feel that it is wrong to add a new character to the story, but there is no great virtue in being enslaved by the letter of the text. If my invention elucidates a point that the text itself makes in other ways, it is, at the least, doing no harm.

Let us imagine that Adam and Eve had had a child while they were in Eden. If so, this first, possible child would have preceded their three post-lapsarian offspring: Cain, Abel and Seth.

If Augustine was correct to say—we have no reason to doubt him—that the first couple might have engaged in carnal relations before the Fall, they might have conceived a child. Assuming, again with Augustine, that prelapsarian coitus did not involve concupiscence, it would have been purpose-driven. The purpose would have been procreation.

Evidence for this hypothesis is slim, but not non-existent.

Examine the following. The first line in Chapter 4 of Genesis reads, in most translations: And Adam knew Eve his wife and she conceived and bore Cain. And yet, the famed medieval Jewish exegete, Rashi noted that the first verb in the sentence is in the pluperfect tense. The line should read: And Adam had known Eve....

This implies that Eve was pregnant when she was expelled from Eden. If Eve was pregnant with Cain while she was in Eden, he might not have been her first child.

Obviously, if Adam and Eve had a first son while they were in Eden, we know nothing about him. He disappeared, without a trace.

(Similarly, Moses disappeared without a trace. For that matter, so did Oedipus.)

Since human beings were not subject to death until after the Fall, the child could not have died. He must have disappeared. Did God remove the child because Adam and Eve were neglecting him?

A lost child might have wandered off. He might have been taken away. And, by the doctrine of assumption, he might have gone to Heaven without having died.

A lost child might still be found. A child's absence does not mean that his parents will never see him again.

And yet, this first possible child was lost, never to return.

When God condemned Adam and Eve to a lifetime of hard labor, followed by the death penalty, he was, the Bible tells us, punishing them for having transgressed. He was holding them accountable for having yielded to temptation.

We might also say that, by introducing the concept of death, God was telling the first couple that their child was never going to return to them.

Everyone believes that the story of the forbidden fruit is implausible, to the point of being dramatically unsatisfying. But, if we reverse subject and object the issue becomes what Eve did or did not feed to her child.

Perhaps the Bible is saying that Eve, distracted by a smooth-talking serpent, neglected her child. Perhaps she was absorbed in more amusing pursuits. Perhaps she did not nurture her child. Perhaps, she left him exposed to the elements.

If so, Adam also failed to protect his offspring. The failure was mutual.

Were Adam and Eve therefore disobedient? If God had told them to care for their child, they would have been ignoring his advice. They might have been inattentive; they might have been distracted; they might have needed more explicit instructions.

If the first couple lost their first child, one doubts that either of them harmed him intentionally. Still, they would have been responsible for his mysterious disappearance. By the standards prevalent at the time their inaction would not have constituted a crime. Theirs would have been a sin of omission, not a crime of commission.

If such was their original sin, Augustine had reason to associate it with a bodily organ that escapes the active control of the will.

When Adam and Eve discovered that they were naked they might have learned that they had failed to protect a child that they had produced by a generative act. By covering their shame they were avoiding a potent reminder of their failing.

The first couple's shame would have been a first step toward responsible parenting.

Once expelled from Eden, Adam and Eve had two sons, Cain and Abel. After a time, Cain murdered Abel, presumably because he envied his brother for making a sacrifice that God found more pleasing.

God noticed that Cain was being consumed by envy. Playing the therapist, God warned Cain against acting on his passion. To little avail.

When Cain murdered his brother, the first parents were apparently not paying attention. Nor, for that matter, was God. An unsupervised Cain acted with homicidal impunity. Yet, he did feel guilty for his crime. He buried his brother's body in order to hide the evidence.

When God heard about what had happened, he stigmatized and banished Cain. It is worth noting that God was more interested in ostracizing the first murderer than in assigning a punishment that would befit guilt.

The first Biblical father was Noah. Being the first to establish a covenant with God, he was the first protector, of his family and of other living beings.

Yet, Abraham was the first patriarch. His story presents a profoundly moving, and somewhat puzzling version of an ethic of fatherhood.

When God told Abraham to kill his son Isaac, He was presumably testing the incipient patriarch's faith. He needed to know whether He could trust Abraham to be a father.

But, why did God demand that Abraham deprive himself of his progeny? Why would the ability to murder one's heir be an indubitable sign of faith? Was God asking Abraham to become a criminal? If

Abraham had done as God commanded would he have committed a crime?

In a barely scrutable way, God might have been raising an important question: was Isaac really Abraham's son? Or better, how could Abraham know for certain that Isaac was his son?

The text hints at this point. If Sarah gave birth to Isaac long after she had entered menopause, was it possible for her to have been impregnated by her husband or by any man? Did Abraham ask himself how he, a human being, could have engendered a child with a woman who was infertile?

Surely, Abraham might have suspected that something strange was going on. Might he not have wondered whether a superhuman being had engendered Isaac?

What was God really demanding of Abraham? Did He want to know what Abraham would have done if he had discovered that Isaac was not his son? Would Abraham have abandoned the child? Would he have allowed the child to die? Would he have killed him?

For all we know, the question might be reversed. God may have been trying to see whether Abraham would protect and provide for a child that might not be his.

God's intervention did not merely rescue Isaac from his homicidal father. It affirmed that both father and son were God's children, His legitimate heirs, the founders of a dynasty.

When Isaac was rescued at the last minute, the Bible seemed to be saying that a man must treat his wife's child as his even though the child might not be his.

Within the story of the aborted sacrifice of Isaac, God was transformed from a deity who ordered the murder of a child into a deity that acted to save a child. By showing benevolence God was setting an example for the man he would choose as first patriarch.

Abraham was said to be the father of faith. Wasn't God also testing Abraham's willingness to take his wife's word... on faith? In the absence of definitive proof, faith was all there was.

This does not mean that the truth of the matter was unknowable. The fact that it could not be known to a certainty did not mean that it was subject to interpretation.

If Abraham was showing that he trusted his wife, it implies that Sarah, like Eve before her, was endowed with free will. She conceived a child with her husband but she could have done otherwise.

If my reading seems less than persuasive, consider that Abraham had two sons. The first, Ishmael was born of Sarah's servant, Hagar. The second, Isaac, was born of Sarah. In Galatians the apostle Paul declared her to be a freewoman.

Note well the centrality of a woman's free will in these stories. Surely, Freud's myth of the primal horde was far more oppressive, to both men and women than were the stories that founded Western civilization.

By the letter of the text, Hagar conceived naturally, but Sarah could only conceive through a supernatural intervention. This suggests, if I may, that the kinship of father and son contains a sociocultural component. In Genesis 21.1-2 we read:

> *And the Lord visited Sarah as he had said, and the Lord did unto Sarah as he had spoken. For Sarah conceived, and bare Abraham a son in his old age, at the set time of which God had spoken to him.*

Since God's covenant only pertained to the children of the freewoman, it makes sense that the developing concept of fatherhood entails, to some extent, a woman's exercise of freedom.

Freud notwithstanding, in Jewish culture patrilineal descent is not established through a totem meal, but through ritual circumcision. When the scar of circumcision is transmitted from father to son, it denotes both the biological and social connection. It is fair to call it a common reference. Surely, it is not a common substance.

In the second book of the Bible we encounter the man Freud took to be the true first father of the Jewish faith. Rather than see Moses as the victim of the first parricide, we will read his story within the Bible's development of an ethic of paternity.

In the Bible, Moses barely survived his first days. Being a Jewish child, he was subject to a pharaonic edict demanding that all Jewish children be drowned. To prevent it from happening, his mother hid him in the bulrushes.

Craftily, she did so at a moment when the Pharaoh's daughter was bathing. The latter saved the infant and brought him up in the royal household. Unwittingly, she hired Moses's real mother, Jochebed, to nurture the boy.

Where the possible first child of Adam and Eve disappeared, Moses, like Isaac, was *saved*. Ironically, Moses was protected by a father-tyrant who would have killed him if he had known who he was.

Eventually, Moses freed his people from Egyptian tyranny and directed them to a place where they would be protected and provided for. And, of course, the greatest gift that Moses gave to his people was his teaching.

As a lawgiver and teacher Moses also wrote down a vast number of rules for good conduct. By following these rules Jewish people have constituted a community on common ground.

When we arrive at the New Testament we see God showing his greatest act of benevolence—sending his only begotten son to the earth. Through Christ, God offered believers a path to salvation and eternal life.

In this way, God allowed humans to overcome one consequence of the sin of the first parents. A God who sent a Savior to the earth was neither vindictive nor jealous nor punishing. He was allowing his own son to be sacrificed in order to provide all other children a chance at eternal life.

It is worth noting that Jesus was said to be "the seed of David." In his flesh Jesus descended from David, through his mother. He also belonged to the line of David, by adoption through her husband Joseph.

Perhaps God knew to a certainty that male genes had been transmitted in an unbroken line from David on down, but everyone else was taking it on faith.

Of course, Mary's husband Joseph knew one thing with certainty. He knew that he had not fathered his wife's child. Joseph showed benevolence to a child that he knew was not his.

Similarly, no Christian is a direct descendant of Jesus.

John, 3, 16-17 articulates God's benevolence:

> For God so loved the world that he gave his only begotten
> Son, that whosoever believeth in him shall have eternal life.

For God sent not his Son into the world to condemn the world, but that the world might through him be saved.

God had saved Isaac from a premature death, but He did not intervene to save Jesus from crucifixion. He did not cause it to happen, but He allowed it to happen. He did so to allow human beings, through Christ, to pay off the debt contracted by original sin.

But, which debt was being paid off? Was it guilt for having committed an act of parricide, as Freud would have had it, or was it the shame for having abandoned a child? After all, God did not only allow Jesus to be crucified; He stood by while His son was being humiliated.

By my reading, in Jesus the lost first child returned. The crucifixion enacted what would have happened to the first son if God had not intervened to shield him from the consequences of his parents' action.

If the stigmata of Christ represent the wounds suffered by the lost or abandoned first son, they are a permanent mark (and recollection) of parental shame. They tell Christian parents that they are duty-bound to protect and provide for their children.

Parents will comply, not because they fear the consequences of disobedience, but because their benevolent instinct tells them to do so.

Interestingly, Christ, like the first possible son, disappeared. After he was crucified and buried, his remains disappeared from his tomb. Each of the four gospels presents this story, with variations.

In all of them, the empty tomb is a sign that Christ was resurrected. Witnesses felt a sense of loss when they discovered that Christ's tomb was empty. Their loss was redeemed when they learned that Christ had risen.

The evidence for identifying Christ with the possible first child may be slight, but it is not non-existent.

According to Matthew and Mark, Christ's last words on the cross were: "Father, why hast thou forsaken me?" A neglected or abandoned first son might well have spoken or thought these words.

Among other theological curiosities, consider this: if Eve had given birth before the Fall, her child would have gestated in a womb that was untainted by sin.

In Catholic theology, only one other child had the same experience. According to the dogma of the Immaculate Conception, the womb that carried Jesus had been cleansed of sin.

Thus, the Bible teaches an ethic of parental responsibility and connects it integrally with an ethic of free will.

Parents are henceforth held to be responsible for raising their children because they could have done otherwise. They are responsible, regardless of their doubts and regardless of the temptations they confront.

Upon this ethic a culture, even a civilization was built. It makes sense to judge that civilization by how well it has protected and provided for its children.

How well has it done?

Freud thought that it had done a poor job. He believed that paternal, even parental benevolence was constructed to cover up a crime. And he believed that repressed libido was too high a price to pay for security and prosperity.

The truth lies elsewhere. However much Freud maligned it, the civilization founded on Judeo-Christian principles has done far better than most others.

Its history contains both good and bad. It contains trade-offs and compromises. But, if we balance the good and bad and compare it to other civilizations, its practitioners have a right to feel proud.

Freud was not the only modern thinker who was trying to reform or even destroy Western civilization. Some tried to replace it with a neo-pagan death cult, one that practiced human sacrifice.

Others have promoted a revolution that would create a new atheist culture. When put into practice, all attempts at producing an atheist culture have failed miserably.

Those who trumpet the truth of atheism should overcome the temptation to ridicule Judeo-Christian civilization. They will have enough to do defending the record of those societies that have tried to create a culture of atheism.

If Western civilization is judged on whether it protected and provided for its children, thus whether it worked in practical terms, one is obliged to say that it has.

Does this mean that it embodies the truth? It depends on what you mean by the truth. If William James was right to say that the truth is what works, then Judeo-Christianity has as good a claim as any other culture.

Of course, Freud invented psychoanalysis to liberate people from this civilization. He believed that its great successes, especially the modern Industrial Revolution and liberal democracy, had been purchased with libido.

Where the Biblical God prescribed benevolent parenting, Freud was more interested in taking than in giving.

When he was treating Horace Frink, he was primarily concerned with what Frink and his eventual wife, Angelika Bijur, could do for him. As for what he could give to them, it was, at best, an afterthought.

Through the intermediary of Freud's only misbegotten son, Jacques Lacan, true believers are now offered the chance, not to save themselves, but to save Freud. They are invited to rescue Freud from ignominy by covering up his failures and blinding people to his errors.

The Freudian truth, Lacan implied, was never about what psychoanalysis could do for you. It was always about what you could do for Freud.

Lacan understood that in Freud's pseudo-religion, people are called on to sacrifice themselves for the cause, thus, to become like saints. While Catholic saints supposedly gain access to Heaven and eternal life, Freudian saints only receive permission to sin with impunity.

You may decide for yourself whether it is a good or a bad bargain, but bargain it is.

Lacan believed that anyone who wanted to save Freud had to join the Wholly Freudian Church.

But, will the Wholly Freudian Church really save Freud? Will it grant him something resembling eternal life on earth? Will it allow him to fulfill another of his most important wishes: to be unforgettable?

Sad to say, but Lacan decided that it was highly unlikely.

One day when Lacan was in Rome he had an epiphany. He saw that the Catholic Church would outlive psychoanalysis.

He must have concluded that the real will always triumph over the pseudo.

23

LACAN COULD ACCEPT that psychoanalysis was a scam, but he refused to see it as a failure. After all, he had come to fulfill psychoanalysis, not to abolish it.

To his mind, psychoanalysis had never really been about cure. As a true Freudian, he lacked the benevolence that would have obliged him to do everything in his power to help his patients. Believing that he had been put on earth to embody the theory, he cared more for ideas than for people.

Whatever Lacan thought he was doing with his short sessions, those who suffered them felt like they were being tossed out of his office, even discarded, often unceremoniously.

A caring professional does not make the gesture of throwing people out of his office the signature of his clinical practice.

An honorable clinician who discovers that the treatment he is offering cannot work does not dismiss his patients as unworthy of him. He changes his practice. Aaron Beck did.

Having trained in psychoanalysis, Beck abandoned it to invent a cognitive therapy for depression. In so doing he was correcting Freud's most flagrant clinical failure.

With the exception of one essay and a few occasional comments, Freud ignored depression. He built his theory around a guilt/punishment/penance narrative where the primary affect was anxiety.

When it came to Freud's own depression, the best he could do was to medicate it with nicotine. Other psychoanalysts did as he did. When I was in Paris in the mid-1970s most psychoanalysts consumed tobacco products voraciously. I imagine that they saw it as a common substance.

When he theorized about depression, Freud said that it was misdirected anger. He saw depression as hostility that, having missed its mark, had boomeranged on the self.

In so saying, Freud implied that analysts could treat depression by placing it within a narrative context and transforming it into anxiety. Isn't that what he tried to do with the chronically depressed patient we know as the Wolf Man?

Some analysts have concluded that depressed patients need to transfer their anger to a substitute father-figure. Other, less sophisticated therapists have instructed their depressed patients to express their hostility, willy nilly.

Obviously, this technique never cured depression. Patients who mastered the art of venting came away feeling like fools. They ended up more depressed, only now they did not know what to do about it.

Beck saw things differently. He observed that depressed individuals were beset with hopelessness. They were not terrified that they would be castrated, but were stuck in a state of anomie. The least of their problems was finding out what it meant or pretending that it really meant something.

Beck understood that making depression meaningful produced no therapeutic benefit.

Depressed individuals are disconnected and disaffected. They do not have bad or neurotic relationships; most often, they have no relationships.

Many depressed patients, like Hamlet, try to overcome their condition by engaging in psychodrama. They produce artificial relationships and do not care how destructive or stressful they become. To their minds, it's better than nothing. They did not need Freud to figure out how not to treat depression.

Freud invented negative psychology by obsessing about the dark side of the human mind. He privileged bad dreams, horrific traumas and depraved motives. He assumed that the conscious mind was ill-disposed to face the horrors that threatened to invade it.

Aaron Beck wanted to help his depressed patients, so he set out in another direction. Rather than seek out the meaning of depression, he tried to mitigate the influence of the mental tics that were producing it.

In place of enhanced insight or awareness, Beck prescribed home-work exercises.

Beck did not treat psychic symptoms as meaningful expressions of anything. He did not believe that they could be eliminated by modifying the ghost-like mind that Freud believed was directing them.

To a cognitive therapist like Beck, psychological symptoms were habits. Depression, he believed, was produced by the bad mental habit of allowing self-deprecating, semi-automatic thoughts to go unchallenged.

So, Beck invented a technique whereby patients could neutralize their negative thoughts by performing homework exercises.

It wasn't as sexy as recovered memories. It wasn't as erotic as swooning hysterics. It did not lend itself to cinematic representation. It was more about work than about drama. It required mental discipline, not free association.

Beck told his patients to write down their depressive thoughts, thoughts like: "I never get anything right," "I am useless," and to make two short lists: the one containing evidence that might validate the thought; the other containing evidence that would invalidate it.

By showing his patients how to submit their thoughts to a reality test, Beck was teaching them to treat these thoughts as though they were someone else's.

Where Freudian psychoanalysis sees psychological symptoms as individualized expressions of unconscious motives, Beck saw that most people use the same wording in their depressive thoughts. These thoughts are not stylized. They are not even poetic. They are banal self-deprecating judgments.

If you thought that Freudian therapy taught people how to conduct reality tests, you have misunderstood it. Freudians never allowed their interpretations to be tested against reality. No reality test can affirm or deny that you want to copulate with your mother.

In truth, a renegade named Aaron Beck taught his patients how to test their ideas against reality. And he did it while ignoring the provenance of their harsh self-judgments.

Naturally, cognitive therapy has provoked a certain amount of criticism, especially from within the Freudian field. Many analysts believe that it provokes a naïve, rose-colored view of the world, one that ignores the dark side of human nature.

Since Freudians only see the dark side, the least glimmer of optimism sends them rushing back into Plato's cave.

In truth, cognitive exercises do not teach anyone to look at life through rose-colored glasses. They allow people to see a depressing thought as something that might or might not be true. They allow people to step back and judge the thought.

The differences between Freud's psychoanalysis and Beck's cognitive therapy are stark.

Psychoanalysis asks why; cognitive therapy asks how.

Psychoanalysis wants you to discover why you went wrong. It will induce you to believe that you wanted things to go wrong. In time, it will help you to cobble together a narrative that explains why you wanted to end up in the ditch. At its purest, it will never show you how to get out of the ditch.

Cognitive and behavioral treatments focus on getting you out of the ditch... as quickly as possible.

Freud wanted his patients to embrace the base instincts that manifested themselves through their symptoms. He did not believe that psychoanalysis would eliminate bad intentions.

Cognitive therapy rejects the idea that your complexes will or should always direct your actions in the world. It offers a choice and teaches moral responsibility.

Freud believed that human beings were trapped in unconscious dramas. Beck saw them as free individuals who could change the course of their lives through their own efforts.

Freudians see desire as the meaning of life. They want their patients to find out what they really, really want. Cognitive therapists want their patients to get along with other people.

Psychoanalysts have tended not to care whether their treatment was effective. Beck insisted on developing a therapy whose benefits could be measured.

Freud never offered instructions for how to conduct psychoanalytic treatment. Instead, he offered fictionalized accounts of his cases, most of which were failures. Lacan did not even do that.

Beck and other cognitivists have offered specific instructions for how to conduct their therapy.

Psychoanalysis can easily become endless. Cognitive therapy usually lasts for a matter of weeks.

Freud and his followers want their patients to become Freudians. Beck and his followers want their depressed patients to get better.

Freudian treatment is known for its iconic couch. Beck's cognitive therapy is known for its homework exercises.

Psychoanalysis creates new problems to add to your old problems. Cognitive treatment guides you toward solutions.

Where Freud focused on desire, Beck sought to cultivate habits that could be used to achieve negotiated compromise. A cognitive view of mental health emphasizes character building, not mystical rapture.

In the Freudian treatment script people are presumed to have forgotten painful traumas or elided degenerate fantasies. Psychoanalysis tries to help them to recover the desires that are embedded therein, the better to integrate them into a new life story.

Freud began his work by postulating that people were suffering from forgotten traumas. He seemed to believe that recalling them would put his patients on the road to cure.

But, he also knew that some trauma victims could not forget their traumas. When his treatment was shown to be ineffective against unforgettable traumas, Freud declared that they were evidence of a will to self-destruct.

Cognitive therapists never made a fetish of total recall. When faced with unforgettable traumas they invented a way for patients to neutralize them.

They instruct their patients to tell about the traumatic events on command, over and over and over again. They want to reduce sensitivity to the trauma, to drain it of affect, not to fill it with meaning.

This technique resembles the way that behavioral therapists treat phobias. When someone is suffering from a phobia, these therapists work to neutralize it by exposure.

It is well known that psychoanalysis is powerless to deal with phobia. No analyst has ever pretended otherwise.

Psychoanalysis has had no success with phobics, that is, with patients who are on far too intimate terms with their feelings.

Psychoanalysis has fostered a culture where people believe that they must express their emotions, no matter when, no matter where, no matter with whom. Cognitive therapy wants patients to see that they have a choice: to express or not to express.

Today, in America and in most of the world Beck's cognitive therapy is supplanting psychoanalysis. Thus, pseudo-science is being replaced by science.

In America, fewer and fewer psychoanalysts still practice psycho-analysis. Some continue to call themselves psychoanalysts, but they spend more time writing prescriptions and coaching their clients than they do practicing Freud's "dangerous method."

In America, psychoanalysis has gone the way of alchemy. However much it survives as a cultural force, it is no longer a clinical option.

Following America, much of the therapy world is transitioning away from psychoanalysis into cognitive treatment.

Yet, Lacan's French conquistadors march on. They have had con-siderable success in Argentina and other Latin American nations. And, they are fighting the good culture war against cognitive-behavioral therapy and Anglo-American hegemony.

To this day, they hold meetings where a high priest stands before a room, shuffles over to a white board, picks up a magic marker and writes a sign that looks something like this: $. Then, he solemnly intones: *In hoc signo vinces.*

Hope dies hard.

24

LACAN'S DEATH BROUGHT a new beginning, but it also produced a dramatic reversal, a *peripeteia*.

Aristotle used the term *peripeteia* to describe the moment in a play when an action changes into its opposite. We see it in the drama of Oedipus. When Oedipus, the man who was leading the investigation into the murder of King Laios, learned that he was the criminal he had been seeking, the play's action reversed itself.

Lacan gave the keys to the Wholly Freudian Church to the most philosophically minded of his followers. He did not want to repeat Freud's mistake and pass them to physicians who did not know how to do theoretical work.

While the International Psychoanalytic Association has been largely comprised of physicians who mistake themselves for philosophers, the Lacanian movement has now been overrun by philosophers who see themselves as healers.

Today, French Lacanians have gotten so wrapped up in their godlike powers that they believe that they need not limit themselves to treating mental illness. They claim that they can explain and even treat neurological conditions, like autism. And, no, that isn't a joke.

Of course, the analysts do not recognize autism as a neurological condition. They see it as an infantile psychosis.

Call me deluded, but I cannot imagine that Lacan, were he alive today, would have joined them.

Lacan was very good at playing the fool, but he was not a fool. He would never have wagered the future of his pseudo-religion on its ability to treat a neurological problem. He knew, as his followers do not, that the Freudian enterprise would not survive a reality test.

Psychoanalysts who insist that they can treat autism sound like witch doctors. More so since they believe that autism is caused by witch-like mothers.

Their argument would have had some persuasive force if psychoanalysis had ever been shown to be an effective treatment for psychosis. It never has. No one thinks it has.

Psychologically speaking, the Lacanian attitude toward autism bespeaks a thinly disguised reactionary impulse. Lacanians are still clinging desperately to ideas that were disproved decades ago.

In the 1950s and 1960s psychiatrists around the world believed that autism was an infantile psychosis. Today's science has shown it to be a neurological condition that can be treated somewhat effectively with cognitive and behavioral therapies.

Where psychoanalysis failed, cognitive-behavioral therapy has produced a measure of success. Outside of France psychiatrists and psychologists now offer autistic children a treatment that, in many cases, helps. Inside France, not so much.

So, what's wrong with France?

In 2011 Sophie Robert answered the question in her documentary film *Le Mur*, or *The Wall*. In it she blamed the situation in France on the reactionaries of the French psychoanalytic establishment. She could have entitled her film: *"J'accuse...."*

As she saw it, psychoanalysts had cowed French mental health professionals into rejecting cognitive-behavioral treatment methods. With the connivance of government authorities, they had stigmatized these "American" treatments to the point where young psychiatrists and psychologists feared that if they trained in them they would be shunned by their colleagues.

The result: if the parents of an autistic French child today want him to have the best available treatment they have to take him to Belgium. Imagine the indignity!

Inspired by Freud, French psychoanalysts still suggest, delicately, that the mother of an autistic child is responsible for her child's condition.

If this mother consults a French psychoanalyst, he might ask whether she really, really wanted her child. Or, he might accuse her of being a "refrigerator" mother. Both questions imply that her child became autistic because she was frigid, thus that she suffered from a lack of *jouissance*. He will then prescribe psychoanalysis for the mother and intense psychoanalysis for the child. Or is it vice versa?

Sophie Robert's film was a micro-budget production. It was distributed on Youtube by a group called *Autism Without Borders*.

For French Lacanians, it would be their Waterloo.

In her film Robert interviewed senior French psychoanalysts. Some were physicians; some were not. Some were true-believing Lacanians; others belonged to the International Psychoanalytic Association. All were thrilled to regale her with their Freudian theory of autism.

One after another, they insisted that autism was an infantile psychosis and that it was laden with unconscious meanings. They explained that they could help these children by bringing unconscious meanings into consciousness.

Obviously, it was difficult to justify using the "talking cure" on children who could not talk, but psychoanalysts were up to the challenge. One of them opined that the children's silences were filled with meaning.

Others suggested that it would be helpful to psychoanalyze the children's mothers. They imagined that if these mothers could access their unconscious desire they would cease passing on their complexes to their children. Presumably, they could help their children by opening themselves to more satisfying decadent experiences.

The analysts interviewed for the film barely mentioned that there might be other ways to treat autism. After all, they were fighting the good cultural war against the Anglosphere. They did not want to corrupt the pure souls of autistic French children by subjecting them to something that had been "Made in America."

Happily, most of them demonstrated very high self-esteem if not supernormality. They evinced the false pride you gain when you believe yourself worthy of the empty encomia you receive from your fellow cult members.

Unfortunately, they showed little concern for the plight of autistic children. Affectless to a fault, they might as well have been talking about potato chips.

In effect, they were so thoroughly infatuated with their grand ideas that they had very little caring left over for the children.

In an effort to offer a more sophisticated theory of autism, and of course, to *épater la bourgeoisie*, one analyst trotted out her version of totemic thinking. She said that the mothers of autistic children were like crocodiles devouring their children. In the best cases, she added, father crocodiles could, if they chose, prevent the infantophagia.

Other analysts explained that mothers of autistic children were consumed with incestuous longings. They believed that these women, barely able to control their depraved desires, alternated between being too hot or too cold, too close or too distant. It was little wonder that their children were crazy.

The analysts' minds were so thoroughly addled by Freudian thinking that they could only see autism as a symptom of degenerate parental desires. They could not imagine that parents might want nothing other than what was best for their children.

Intercut with Sophie Robert's interviews were reports about two autistic children. One child had been treated with American behavioral techniques. The other had suffered the approach that French psychoanalysts preferred.

The difference was striking, even frightening. The child who had received behavioral treatment was attending school, earning good grades and enjoying a limited socialization. He was visibly autistic but he was preparing to become a contributing member of society. Think Temple Grandin.

The other child was withdrawn and dysfunctional. His time in a psychoanalytically correct outpatient program had prepared him for lifelong institutionalization.

Sophie Robert's revelations should not have been news. Several years before she made her film, the Council of Europe had condemned France's approach to autism. And yet, it took a documentary film to bring the truth to a larger public.

The film was rhetorically brilliant. When it first appeared on Youtube it attracted a modest number of viewers. French politicians expressed some interest in the problem and television stations scheduled broadcasts.

As more people saw the film, French media began addressing the issue. Chagrined to see their dark arts exposed to the ultimate disinfectant, sunlight, some French psychoanalysts found that the movie was attenuating their *jouissance*. They knew they had to revolt. That is, they knew they had to do something revolting.

After a short time, the trinity of hard-core Lacanian analysts who appeared in *The Wall* decided that the Empire had to strike back.

They did not call for better treatment for autistic children. They did not accept responsibility for having created a cultural climate that had hindered treatment. They did not call for more research.

They sued.

It was a pungent irony. A group that defined itself as the last line of defense against an American cultural invasion adopted one of America's worst habits: litigiousness.

For the record, all of the analysts had signed releases permitting the filmmaker to use their words and images freely. They had also given her the right to edit their contributions.

But, three of them sued because they did not like the way they looked in the film. They believed that their reputations had suffered grievous harm. Naturally, they did not imagine that they were, in any way at fault.

Unable to accept responsibility, they blamed Sophie Robert. They were happy to show the world that all of those years of psychoanalysis had taught them something valuable: how to shift the blame. It had to have been good for something.

In their lawsuit they declared that the filmmaker had employed nefarious editorial practices to distort their words and damage their public personae. Confusing desire for demand, they demanded roughly $400,000 in monetary compensation, around ten times the cost of the film's production. They asked the court to suppress the film immediately.

More specifically, they wanted to shield themselves from the impression that they were blaming mothers for autism.

Unfortunately, that is exactly what they had done. They were too clever to say so explicitly, but they were suggesting that autism enacted a mother's unanalyzed issues.

Unable to defend themselves against an army of mothers led by the world's most reputable scientists, Lacanian psychoanalysts decided that they had to repress the truth.

Ironically, practitioners of a technique that had promised to free people from censorship wanted to use the power of the state to censor the arts. Count it as another *peripeteia*. And count it as more evidence that Freudian psychoanalysis is the enemy of freedom.

Funnily enough, when Sophie Robert was editing the film, she chose not to use outtakes where one psychoanalyst, a party to the lawsuit, explained that, of course, autism was caused by bad mothering, but that she did not want to say so publicly. The outtakes were later posted on the website of the French magazine, *L'Express*.

Concern for public reputation was a novelty in the world of French psychoanalysis. If these analysts had understood Lacan half as well as they thought they did, they would have known that Lacan wanted his followers to show a saintly insouciance about what others thought of them.

Besides, I have witnessed many public performances by senior French Lacanians. They do not need anyone's help to make fools of themselves.

If I were to speculate I suspect that the three Lacanians were grievously offended that a woman, a Frenchwoman no less, had not succumbed to their seductive wiles!

To those who believe that civilized countries guarantee free creative expression the suit looked frivolous. After all, where would Michael Moore be if he had to worry about the delicate sensibilities of the people who appeared in his films?

But, French law is not American law. In the French civil code, someone who appears in a documentary film has a "moral right" to his image. His right remains inviolate even if he has signed a release.

To the shock of everyone who does not know French civil law, when the case came to trial, a judge in Lille invoked this principle to find in favor of the psychoanalysts.

The court ordered Sophie Robert to pay approximately $40,000 in damages to the aggrieved parties. It further ordered that the film be suppressed immediately, even before the decision was appealed.

Youtube took down the film and French television stations canceled scheduled screenings.

So it went, until January 16, 2014 when an appeals court in Douai overturned the lower court ruling. It decided that the freedom of creative expression was more important than the delicate sensitivities of thin-skinned Lacanians.

In so doing, the court restored a measure of French national pride. The film is currently available on the site, *Dailymotion*.

Even before the appeals court ruled, French psychoanalysts, especially French Lacanians suffered a cultural Waterloo.

The lawsuit produced more negative press than a Youtube posting could ever have. The incident generated so much noise that the international press covered it. The story even made the *New York Times*.

Eventually, the French health ministry took notice. In March, 2012 it removed psychoanalysis from the list of acceptable treatments for autism.

The BBC described the scene in April, 2012:

> *For autism campaigners, it is one of the most serious health scandals of our times.*
>
> *How for decades France turned its back on the latest scientific thinking, and treated autism as a form of psychosis.*
>
> *How, as a result, tens of thousands of children were misdiagnosed – or not diagnosed at all – and consigned to lives of misery.*
>
> *And how, to this day, in its approach to autism, the French medical establishment continues to believe in the powers of psychiatry and psychoanalysis – long after the rest of the world has switched to alternative methods of treatment.*

Now the world knows that in France autistic children are being systematically mistreated. It knows that psychoanalysts are responsible.

In the matter of Sophie Robert's film French psychoanalysts revealed their true face. They showed themselves to be petty tyrants, enemies of science and freedom, caring more for their own ideas than for the well-being of sick children.

They had learned their Freud, a little too well.

The story of French psychoanalysis contains one more *peripeteia*.

One appreciates why Lacan expected that his philosopher-pupils would keep psychoanalytic theory alive as a vibrant intellectual enterprise. Were he surveying the scene today he would be severely disappointed in their work.

I am not going to tax them with misreading texts. Their sin is more serious than that. Obsessed with the letter of the text they have gotten lost. They can't see the forest for the twigs.

Acting more like echo chambers than thinkers, today's Lacanians have transformed a living theory into a collection of dead letters.

Filled with Freudian anxiety, they repeat Lacan's formulas over and over again. They seem terrified that the least deviation will cause Lacan to arise from the depths and smite them.

In the thirty or so years since Lacan died his most devoted followers have produced nothing of real theoretical interest. If Lacan returned today he would not feel that he had missed a thing.

True enough, they have advanced the Freudian cause. They have built a Wholly Freudian Church. Like modern day conquistadors they have colonized vulnerable Latin American cultures.

In this latter regard Argentinians stand out. They know, better than most others that psychoanalysis is not going to cure them. Still they flock to Lacanian psychoanalysts to seek something better than mental health. They do not care about getting well; they want to become French.

As it happens, the most influential Lacanian thinker today is neither a French nor an Argentinian analyst. The man who picked up the theoretical torch that Lacan's cult followers discarded is a lone-wolf Slovenian philosopher named Slavoj Zizek.

A prolific writer and confused thinker, more philosopher-clown than philosopher-king, Zizek has advanced Lacan's theoretical work by deepening the connection between psychoanalysis and Franco-Germanic idealism.

He has unashamedly affirmed the kinship between psychoanalytic theory and radical leftist thought. And he has marketed it brilliantly by obscuring it in a blizzard of references to popular culture.

If Lacan played Jesus to Freud's Moses, Zizek has been Lacan's St. Paul. No one today has done more to proselytize the true Lacanian faith.

Lacan wrote relatively little. He preferred public performance over scribbling. Zizek is an incorrigible graphomaniac.

A natural born entertainer, Zizek is, like Lacan himself, one of a kind, *sui generis*. Like Lacan he is idiosyncratic and eccentric. But, unlike Lacan, he seems to be completely out of control.

A reporter for *New York Magazine* recently described him as possessing:

...a Rasputin beard, a bundle of somatic motor tics and twitches including nose rubbing, mouth rubbing, jeans smoothing, and clutching at the black T-shirt that bears his monogram, Ž...

You might not want to think that Zizek exemplifies Freudian supernormality, but he is certainly unique.

Perfectly shameless, Zizek shows no concern for reputation, decorum, dignity or respectability. He has no interest in being intelligible. For his pains he has garnered a worldwide cult following of disaffected youth.

When it comes to the talking cure, Zizek is all talk and no cure. As might be expected, many of his fervent followers have failed to understand that, not being a psychoanalyst, he disdains clinical matters. Some of them are, not surprisingly, so confused that they ask him for help and advice.

During a recent interview Zizek told a reporter from the *Guardian*:

I especially hate when they come to me with personal problems. My standard line is: "Look at me, look at my tics, don't you see that I'm mad? How can you even think about asking a mad man like me to help you in personal problems, no?"

But, if Zizek is so enamored of Freudian theory, why didn't he try to use psychoanalysis to resolve his "issues?"

As it happens, he did. He was psychoanalyzed by Lacan's son-in-law. Perhaps the experience was intellectually edifying, but it also demonstrated, once again, that psychoanalysis serves no useful clinical purpose. Slavoj Zizek is the end of the clinical line.

Since he does not have to pretend to be a respectable bourgeois professional Zizek has been able to work more seriously on the connections between Freud and radical politics. He has demonstrated that psychoanalysis is more an instrument of cultural transformation and less a clinical practice. He has forthrightly exposed the scandalous intimacy of Freud and Marx.

It did not require a great leap into the theoretical void. Lacan himself took the decisive step when he interpreted some of Freud's ideas in Hegelian terms. If Hegel was the forefather of both Freud and Marx, the two must have been brothers in spirit, that is, *Brüder im Geiste*.

For his part Zizek has declared himself to be an unreconstructed Communist. He qualifies as one of today's leading Neo-Communist thinkers. Surely, he is well qualified to articulate the relationship between psychoanalysis and Communism.

It takes a special warp of mind to remain loyal to Communism today, but Zizek has risen to the challenge. He must believe that Communism's disgraceful failures are a test of his faith.

Why do Zizek and his ilk adhere to failed ideologies? Why are they so enamored of ideas that have, when implemented, produced nothing but misery?

The answer is: they believe that they have no choice. Since they reject free will, they believe they have only two options: riding or being ridden by a great historical wave that, like the curse that the god put on Oedipus, will play itself out, whether they like it or not.

They believe that they must choose between letting themselves be tossed hither and yon by the Other's desire or fighting it and losing.

They foresee the day when the triumph of the Hegelian World Spirit will eventually produce a culture where people can act on their desire without fearing the judgment of others.

Whether a Worker's Paradise or a Lover's Boudoir descends with the New Jerusalem—or the New Babylon—they expect that it will free everyone from shame and responsibility.

Yet, if Francis Fukuyama was right, the World Spirit might find its full realization, not in a culture of shamelessness or in an earthly version of the Heavenly (or Hellish) City, but in the triumph of free market capitalism and Anglo-American values.

If that comes to pass, the world historical joke will be on Zizek and the Freudians.

That would be "the most unkindest cut of all."

About the Author

An internationally recognized authority on psychoanalysis, Stuart Schneiderman has written several books and numerous articles on the subject. His book *Jacques Lacan: The Death of an Intellectual Hero* has been translated into six languages. Currently, he no longer practices psychoanalysis, but consults in New York City and blogs at *Had Enough Therapy?*